The Inverted Bell

D0768323

BATON ROUGE AND LONDON

The Inverted 🐚🐚🐚 Bell

Modernism and the Counterpoetics

of William Carlos Williams

JOSEPH N. RIDDEL

Copyright © 1974, 1991 by Louisiana State University Press
Quotations from all previously unpublished writings of William Carlos
Williams copyright © 1974 by Florence H. Williams
All rights reserved
Manufactured in the United States of America
Designed by Albert Crochet
Library of Congress Catalog Card Number 73-77655
ISBN 0-8071-1697-1 (paper)

Louisiana Paperback Edition, 1991
00 99 98 97 96 95 94 93 92 91   5 4 3 2 1

Quotations from the following works by William Carlos Williams are reprinted
by permission of New Directions Publishing Corporation, MacGibbon &
Kee, Ltd., Laurence Pollinger, Ltd., Carcanet Press Limited, and Florence H.
Williams:
The Autobiography of William Carlos Williams. Copyright 1948, 1949, 1951 by
William Carlos Williams
The Collected Poems of William Carlos Williams, 1909–1939, Vol. I. Copyright
1938 by New Directions Publishing Corporation
The Collected Poems of William Carlos Williams, 1939–1962, Vol. II. Copyright
1944, 1948, 1950, 1963 by William Carlos Williams
Imaginations. Copyright 1920 by The Four Seasons Company; copyright 1923
by William Carlos Williams; © 1970 by Florence H. Williams
In the American Grain. Copyright 1925 by James Laughlin; copyright 1923 by
William Carlos Williams
I Wanted to Write a Poem. Beacon Press, 1958
Many Loves, and Other Plays. Copyright 1936, 1942, 1948 by William Carlos
Williams; © 1961 by Florence H. Williams
Paterson. Copyright 1946, 1948, 1949, 1951, © 1958 by William Carlos
Williams (Book VI, © 1963 by Florence H. Williams)
Pictures from Brueghel. Copyright 1954, 1955, © 1962 by William Carlos
Williams
The Selected Essays of William Carlos Williams. Copyright 1954 by William Car-
los Williams
The Selected Letters of William Carlos Williams. Copyright 1957 by William Car-
los Williams
A Voyage to Pagany. Copyright 1928 by The Macauley Company. Copyright
1938, © 1970 by New Directions Publishing Corporation
MSS. Located in the Beinecke Library of Yale University and the Lockwood
Library of the State University of New York at Buffalo

for

K
VALERIE
VANESSA
I
GINNY

According to Hegel, the ancient Greek was amazed by the natural in nature; he constantly listened to it, questioned the meaning of mountains, springs, forests, storms; without knowing what all these objects were telling him by name, he perceived in the vegetal or cosmic order a tremendous shudder of meaning, to which he gave the name of a god: *Pan*. Subsequently, nature has changed, has become social: everything given to man is already human, down to the forest and the river which we cross when we travel. But confronted with this social nature, which is quite simply culture, structural man is no different from the ancient Greek: he too listens for the natural in culture, and constantly perceives in it not so much stable, finite, "true" meanings as the shudder of an enormous machine which is humanity tirelessly undertaking to create meaning, without which it would no longer be human. And it is because this fabrication of meaning is more important, to its view, than the meanings themselves, it is because the function is extensive with the works, that structuralism constitutes itself as an activity, and refers the exercise of the work and the work itself to a single identity: a serial composition or an analysis by Lévi-Strauss are not objects except insofar as they have been made: their present being *is* their past act: they are *having-been-mades*; the artist, the analyst recreates the course taken by meaning, he need not designate it: his function, to return to Hegel's example, is a *manteia*; like the ancient soothsayer, he speaks the locus of meaning but does not name it. And it is because literature, in particular, is a mantic activity that it is both intelligible and interrogating, speaking and silent, engaged in the world by the course of the meaning which it remakes with the world, but disengaged from the contingent meanings which the world elaborates: an answer to the man who consumes it yet always a question to nature, an answer which questions and a question which answers.

ROLAND BARTHES

Every great poet creates his poetry out of one single poetic statement only. The measure of his greatness is the extent to which he becomes so committed to that singleness that he is able to keep his poetic Saying wholly within it.

The poet's statement remains unspoken. None of his individual poems, nor their totality, says it all. Nonetheless, every poem speaks from the whole of the one single statement, and in each instance says that statement. From the site of the statement there rises a wave that in each instance moves his Saying as poetic saying. But that wave, far from leaving the site behind, in its rise causes all the movement of Saying to flow back to its ever more hidden source.

MARTIN HEIDEGGER

Contents

Preface

This is a study in "poetics," as distinguished from a study of poetry; a study of neither intentions nor forms, but of the problematic of language and of "intention." Such definitions, however, tend to deceive or to be misinterpreted, innocently or deliberately; for they call attention away from the primacy of the poem, from the privileged status of poetic language, from the immediacy of the poem as experience or object, and lure us into a mediated world of reflection, of sweet, sad thought. They call attention to the criticism itself. It is probably necessary, then, to reassert the problematical nature of intentionality, to call attention away from the preconception of intention as cause, as the fallacy of the origin which lies outside the poem. That is, one begins by pointing to, and questioning, the metaphysical presumptions of "intention." But this, of course, leaves us with the Husserlian sense of the "intention," which is no less problematic and no less metaphysical. For even phenomenology implies the presence of the "subject," and ultimately the priority of the subject. "Intention" becomes the presence incarnated *in* the work, a reified point of departure, a thematic.

Let me assert, then, that I assume poetics to be something like a "deep structure" of poetry, something interpretable but not ultimately recoverable from the field of utterance, a poet's works, which it structures. To interpret is not to recover a thing itself, a meaning, but to involve oneself in the context in which the structuring principle is presumed to inhere. It is to take the poetic text as pre-text. In this case, it is not Williams' intentions, but Williams' poetics that summons my discourse. For my argument is that a poet's poetics cannot exist before the poem as a cause of that "object," or

even inhere or be incarnated in the body of any one particular poem
or canon of works. A poet's poetics is his discoveries, his interpretations, which in turn can only be known by interpretation.

A poet's poetics, like his individual poems, can never be complete,
never whole or coherent, never a totalization of his "theories." Thus
a poetics can never be exhausted by interpretation. Like the
discovery of the Modern long poem, the end of poetic discovery leads
to a beginning, to the openness of discovery, to the necessity of
another adventure of interpretation. Just as a poem needs a reader to
complete its circle, a poetics needs an interpreter. Poet, work, and
critic revolve in a hermeneutical circle. There is no interpretation of
a poem which is not in search of a poetics, and none which fully and
completely states a poetics. Poetics, then, assumes the idea of a text,
something whole or complete which conceals within itself a presence
or nondifference, a meaning. But this is only an assumption, the
recognition of a mystery which beckons to the interpreter and
involves him in a violation of the sanctity of the text. This text, call it
the poem, the "work" or object of art, at once asserts its purity of
wholeness and offers its mystery for interpretation. Like the Unicorn
of *Paterson*, Book Five, the poem calls for its own "murder." Poetry
summons the critic to interpretation, to transgression, though the
critic may profess that he comes to worship, to analyze the relation
and integration of the parts in order to prove the presence of a whole,
the presence of *presence*.

For this reason, to assert that one's primary interest is poetics, and
not poetry, almost invariably calls down upon the critic accusations
of insensitivity or of preoccupation with a low order of discourse.
The New Criticism is our modern classical example of scientistic
mysticism. Its assumption that we might describe systematically the
poem as "object," in order to affirm its privileged status as a form of
presence, and thus of immediate value, embraces the notorious
paradox of the inside and the outside which lies at the core of
Western thought (which Martin Heidegger calls onto-theological
metaphysics). The very idea that we can describe exhaustively the
particulars of the poem as system, as style, as a multiple of parts
which cohere into a perfect whole according to certain principles of

linguistic resolution, all the while performing the analysis in order better to listen to the silent purity of the whole, to allow this coherence to overwhelm us and take us up into its peace—this paradox has long since been exposed by critical thought. But as a habit of criticism, and as a rhetorical reflex, it still haunts the teaching of literature and justifies the *study* of poetry as a surrogate form of worship.

My concern with poetics as the inevitable subject of criticism, then, is a concern with the demystification of certain critical habits. But it is no less an interest in the directions of post-Modern poetry, that poetry which has long since confronted and dispatched the rhetorical mysteries of its Modernist predecessors and in the process generated its own "texts." In Williams I find a poet who combines in another degree that post-Romantic crisis of consciousness which is manifest in a self-reflexive poetry, an art involved not simply in the historically inevitable act of interpreting its predecessors or bringing those texts of its immediate ancestors into question, but an art forced to reflect on itself and thus on its own act of reflection. If, to use the term of Jacques Derrida, it "deconstructs" the past, it deconstructs itself in the same time of its unfolding. It is an art, then, which fully reveals the preoccupation of poetry to be poetics. If the Modern, or post-Modern, poem tends to be habitually a poem about poetry, a metapoetry, it is because it has discovered the function of poetry to be discovery. Poetics, in this sense, is the subject of the poem—in the sense, exactly, that Wallace Stevens could write that "Poetry is the subject of the poem." A poetics is the question from which the poem issues, the "difference" of which it is the utterance. A poetics is the initial freedom (or as I will argue later, the "freeplay") in which the poetic act originates. A poetics may be described, then, only as the residue, the sign or trace, of some lost origin. It is the "subject" of the poem, that question of which the poem is a sign, and finally a profound questioning of the "origin" itself.

As Paul Valéry has said, a poetics is not simply the accumulation or exposition of "rules, conventions, or precepts" concerning the composition of poetry, nor is it the logical argument a poet mounts within his canon of discursive utterances. It is not simply apology

(T. S. Eliot, one recalls, said that a poet's criticism was nothing more than an apology for his own poems) or even the plausible explanation of a poet's "world." It is the presence of his desire. That a poetics exists in the matrix of a poet's utterances, as the structure or ground of his "world," is the inescapable assumption of every critic, every reader. It is the "meaning" which if touched will allow immediate communication. It is that which will generate the copresence of author and reader, and manifest in the space of language the fundamental intimacy of two subjects. The critic, on the other hand, is the thinker of difference, whose very act of interpretation exiles him from the structure he studies, yet holds him in interested relation to it. It is for this reason that the New Criticism so resisted its own expulsion from the field of the poem. It could not at the same time study the poem and listen to it. It could not abide the possibility that the poem might be only a fiction of recovered presence.

To put it another way, a poetics thus described would be something like the "deep structure" of utterance sought alike by psychoanalysts and anthropologists in their interpretations of the language of dreams or of myth. This deep structure does not exist outside the matrix of the poet's utterance, nor can it be revealed without an interpreter; and yet, because it ex-ists only in interpretation, any one interpretation can never grasp it purely. It is not an "it"—not a generative idea or origin, not an *archè*. The nature of a "poetics" is that it must always remain somewhat hidden from both its creator and its expositor, like the structure and function of myth of which Claude Lévi-Strauss speaks in his various efforts toward a comprehensive structural methodology, or like the laws of language that function in speech but are never thought by the speaker. Poetics, Valéry has said, "is less concerned with solving problems than with stating them." It is an attempt, and here he echoes Heidegger, at *situating* poetry, locating its *site*. And Valéry himself cites the dangers for the poet of this kind of thinking about *making* (see "Opening Lecture on Poetics," in his *Aesthetics*, Bollingen Series XLV), in the very terms Lévi-Strauss uses to distinguish the speaker from the thinker of the rules of language.

There is, of course, a major complication in comparing poetics and myth. Whereas Lévi-Strauss considers myths to be authorless, or to have no identifiable "subject," we habitually presume, both in our critical strategy and critical rhetoric, that literature has such a "subject" and that indeed we are interested in nothing other than that "subject," as incarnated in the author's objects or structures or speech or forms or whatever. Either that, or we presume an interest solely in the object, or in its affect, and thus in the audience as the affected. When we profess an interest in poetics, we speak of this poet's theory as against that poet's, this poetic "world" as distinguished from that. We speak of intentions and origins, but seldom of the problem of origins. Our generic distinctions, not to say our categories of historical or stylistic or ideological periods, all include the assumption that artistic utterance takes an individual and distinctive form and thus, unlike myth, has an author, be it person or *Zeitgeist*. When the "author" or the "intention" disappears, literature drifts through anonymity toward myth, and the problem of interpretation, at least we say, becomes more problematic. Literature, therefore, has a "history"; myths do not. And the relations of authors, including of course chronological relation, though not exclusively, are a part of that "history." Perhaps our last myth is the myth of the "subject," of the individuality of literature (both in form and content); but at the present there seems to be no getting beyond it—except, of course, in the radical utterances of poetry itself. For there, we may discover with Heidegger, language speaks the subject as surely as he speaks it. In any event, the problem of intentionality remains a problem, even though the rhetoric of our criticism, and even our poetry, acts as if it were not a problem.

My subject in this study is William Carlos Williams, a Modern poet, identifiable by an extensive canon of poems, plays, novels, short stories, prose poems, criticism, discursive fragments, polemic—that is, *his* utterance. Of course, the Williams we speak of as doctor and the one who speaks through the various works are to be considered at one and the same time identical and separate subjects. We speak of Williams and Dr. Paterson (a persona?) synonymously in our examinations of *Paterson*. We know what we mean and therefore maintain a clarity of critical focus, but only by ignoring the problem of repeatedly trying to locate the "subject" we take for granted as a presence (and thus a generative center of the poem *qua* object). This is only one of many examples of the way in which criticism avoids the problematic of language, and particularly the unexamined priority of the subject, in order to achieve its own complementary coherence. In speaking of literature we assume the necessity of form (of coherence, of wholeness, even perfection); but when we of necessity begin to rethink the nature of form (or better, to use Derrida's phrase, when we must begin to think the "structurality of structure"), we reenter the problematic. Modern criticism has repeatedly done this, perhaps most obviously when it has been confronted by poets who have long since anticipated the problem and engaged it. The work of these poets *is* the problematic; the work takes itself as both subject and object and reveals the interpretive nature of all language.

Williams, then, is the "subject" of this study in two senses (at least) of the term. And his texts are, to extend the pun, pretexts for interpretation. Williams is the least philosophical of our poets; of this there is little question, especially if we accept Santayana's definition of the philosophical poet as one whose utterance is pre-formed as well as in-formed by an assumed or received system or vision. But like Wallace Stevens, though perhaps with less panache of phrase, Williams was given occasionally to pseudo-philosophical utterance, and even, like Stevens, to bursts of rhetorical contradiction which postured as philosophical discourse but which revealed a naïveté and lack of rigor that repels systematic thinkers. Williams' "no ideas but in things" is well on its way to becoming a scandal of literary criticism, if for no other reason than that it tempts one to scrutinize it extrapoetically and metaphysically as an objectivist response to subjectivism. Yet, the phrase radiates throughout the Williams canon, and it can no more be treated as an assertion that the object gives rise to the subject than as a refutation of the opposite. It is an attempt, poetically yet rhetorically, to bring into question the field of ordinary logical discourse—something we have always been able to accept of poetry so long as it divorced itself from scientific rigor and made itself the utterance of unreason or emotion or intuition or immediacy.

It is an attempt, characteristic of modern critical thought, to rescue poetry as a privileged language.

To examine Williams' poetics, or any other poet's (subject's?) poetics for that matter, is to take such statements seriously, as a part of the "philosophical" rigor of that poet's total utterance, his "world." But then again, poet's "worlds" overlap and enfold one another. The language of one is the language of the other, at least on one level, and the effort of each to dissolve the common properties into a distinct (hence, original) utterance becomes a part of the poetics. It is an effort doomed, in a very special but essential sense, to failure—the failure, we might say, of the subject to realize itself originally, either in innocence or transcendence. His utterance, after all, must finally depend on another, an Other; and that Other, as the psychoanalyst Jacques Lacan has indicated, is language itself. Criticism is an act of interpretation, and thus, to use Heidegger's terms, an act of violence, of translating, or carrying over. It is a carrying over of language by language into language—an interpretation (the poem) by interpreta-tion (criticism) into interpretation (poetics). There is no unmediated criticism; none that leaves the work as it was, as *itself*; and thus none which is itself a final *word* on the work. No matter the objective or scientific ideals of the critic, what he is after is a poetics (the structure of poetry), though he may desire, anxiously or desperately, to know or possess or worship the "work" (sacred object, art) without transgression. One of the motives, and one of the illusions, of criticism has been that the critic can "know" the work, that criticism can be transparent. And this depends, in turn, on the illusion that there is a *work itself* (like the philosopher's *thing itself*).

My argument is that criticism deceives itself when it thinks it can preserve the sacred, aesthetic object in its purity by assuming a rhetoric of homage, or by affecting its own literary-isms, or by encapsulating the work in a language of description, analysis, or explication which will not do violence to the illusion of wholeness or totality. I have therefore deliberately translated the language of a poet—who claims rightly that the language of abstraction (distancing word from thing) characterizes the ultimate dilemma of modern man—into a philosophical (or at least, abstract) discourse inimical to his concrete poetic language. And I have done this consciously and strategically, in the tradition, perhaps, of Heidegger, a bewilderingly poetic philosopher whose own compacted abstractions (interpretations) serve his purpose to demystify and deconstruct language back to its primordial function—Heidegger, whose own worship of the poets (particularly Hölderlin) never swerved from his recognition of the necessary transgression of interpretation. "Whatever an explanation can or cannot do," he wrote, "this always applies: in order that what has been purely written of in the poem may stand forth a little clearer, the explanatory speech must break up each time both itself and what it has attempted. The final, but at the same time the most difficult step of every exposition consists in vanishing away together with its explanations in the face of the pure existence of the poem." I would only add that this "pure existence" is not the "pure" object of the New Critics, but a silence left for yet another interpretation. It is a radical questioning of the metaphor of the "pure" and of poetry's access to some original, originating undifferentiated center.

Like Heidegger's ideal poet, Williams writes a basically contradictory poem. Rejecting the priority of ideas over things, he nevertheless writes a poetry of homelessness, of the problematic distance between the two. He writes, that is, a poetry about poetry, a poem of history and thus of lost origins. His poetics is inseparable from his poems, and his discursive utterances on poetics need the same kind of exegesis visited on his poetry. Poems become commentaries on other poems, and on the whole. The canon reverberates. Text becomes pre-text for subsequent text, generating a hermeneutical circle that will not close. The function of criticism is to sound this re-verberation, and to allow it to re-sound in another idiom. I have intended the violence, rhetorically and functionally, of my analysis. But in no sense do I believe that my analysis of individual poems or passages gets at or excavates a "meaning" which "inheres" there, any more than it can withdraw from the enticements of that pure undifferentiated center. For the language of poetry and poetics is inseparable from metaphysics, and is contaminated by the lure of the secret, the meaning—what Wallace Stevens calls "The the."

My chapters are thematically interrelated, and occasionally repetitive, in that they of necessity examine common passages from different points of view. The first, taking up the problem of origins (and the problematic of language) which haunts Williams' criticism and permeates his every utterance, examines metaphors of poetic structure which touch on every other chapter. The second deals basically with Williams' theory of language, in relation to problems in Modern linguistics. The third considers the sense of history which informs his poetics, but that sense is not separable from the problem of language and especially the history (largely Gnostic) of the "Word" which is so crucial to our Modernist poetics and so questionable for Williams. The fourth chapter treats Williams' own vision of the creative act as a violence, or his view that creation and destruction are simultaneous, in terms of modern philsophical conceptions of violence and interpretation. And the fifth, focusing intensely on Book Five of *Paterson*, projects a theory of post-Modern poetics, of the poetics of "failure," considered not in terms of aesthetic incompletion or incoherence but of the recognized problematic "play" inherent in poetry itself.

In the process of this "radical" interpretation of Williams' language, I have invoked, sometimes at inordinate length, the arguments of contemporary thinkers on the problem of language and interpretation—Nietzsche and his own more recent heirs and interpreters, Heidegger, Georges Bataille, and Jacques Derrida, along with a number of critics and analysts identified with French structuralist thought. In the case of Derrida especially (whom I have already mentioned twice), I have chosen to test the reader's patience and my own uncertain abilities to abbreviate a complex, subtle, rigorous, and often devious philosophical counterargument, because Derrida and his kind of analysis are not widely known in this country. The texts which are known remain at best question marks to many readers. Unlike Heidegger's writings, only a relatively small portion of Derrida's have been translated: at the time of this writing, only one book and a handful of essays. So, at crucial points I have dared to offer substantially large segments of his writing and to chance summations of a mode of thought that resists summation and simplification. Derrida's thought is difficult not only in content but in method, for what he calls the deconstruction of metaphysics, and its direct application to the problematic of language, has few predecessors in the history of philosophy. There is the further problem of how this kind of thinking can apply to the work of a poet, especially one so apparently innocent of metaphysics as Williams. The only answer can be that it does not, at least in the sense understood by those who want the poet and philosopher to complement each other substantively. What is common between poet and philosopher, I will argue here, does not lie in the history of ideas, but in the "event" (as Derrida calls it) of having to recognize the very medium in which one is conducting his discourse as the problem of the discourse, and therefore having to confront directly the "tradition." For it is the tradition or the history of thought that has managed to repress the question of language, and of the structurality of structure. If this deflection of philosopher against poet seems to burden the poet with unaccustomed or unwarranted abstraction, or to attribute to him a rigor of thinking about language and the theory of poetry not substantiated by the surfaces of his discourse, it is only to suggest that the most recent philosophers have had to turn to a certain "poetic" kind of thinking, to a kind of antilogic, to what is called deconstruction, and therefore to a "play" with language that complements both the poet's "play" and the critic's unsystematic analysis. This deflection of philosophers against poetry, then, is part of a "play" of interpretation, and not an attempt to write footnotes of the history of ideas to the poetry of the end of that history.

Williams' poetics is only the deflected center of several overlapping circles. What I wish to do here is project a theory of post-Modernism, anticipated by Williams but imagined variously in the whole variety of Modernist experimentation—in Imagism, Vorticism, Objectivism, the poetics of H.D. and Pound, Louis Zukofsky, and Charles Olson. But the larger design can only be a projection. Williams remains the locus; *his* poetics, the *subject.* I want to argue the radicality of Williams' poetics: how repetitively original he was, how anxious to destroy, as he said, "the whole of poetry as it has been in the past." How metaphysically anti-metaphysical. How "American"!

Acknowledgments

In a project of this kind, there are always numerous debts, many of which the project-or remains, almost necessarily, unconscious of. Among those I'm very conscious of, however, there are certainly two: the Poetry Collection of the Lockwood Library of the State University of New York at Buffalo; and the Collection of American Literature of the Beinecke Library of Yale University. I owe a special thanks to Mr. Karl Gay, curator of the Lockwood collection, who as a friend and colleague not only made the vast Williams holdings available to me over a long period of time, but made my working conditions both comfortable and convenient. This is all the more remarkable because of the unfortunate physical facilities in which he and his staff have to work. Mr. Donald Gallup of the Yale library performed a similar courtesy, in much more ample circumstances. Mr. James Laughlin, of the New Directions Publishing Corporation, and Mrs. Florence Williams gave their kind permission for me to consult the unpublished materials and manuscripts at the Yale and Buffalo libraries.

I am indebted to the Research Foundation of the State University of New York, and to the Graduate School and the Faculty of Arts and Letters of the State University of New York at Buffalo, for subsidies and research time, including two Summer Research Fellowships. Both Marcus Klein and Joseph Fradin, past and present chairmen of the Department of English at Buffalo, made special provisions of time and assistance during the research, writing, and preparation of the manuscript. I also owe an especial thanks to Mrs. Hilda Ludwig who struggled with my typing and gnarled handwriting, my incessant subtractions and (mostly) additions, while typing

xxi

the manuscript into the somewhat bizarre IBM machine which then
spewed forth its version of a completed manuscript. (I have
occasionally indulged myself with the fantasy of the machine's
combining all the on-going manuscripts of the English department at
Buffalo into one vast palimpsestic "work," but I leave that fantasy to
an ex-colleague, John Barth, who may already have written it—
though some might say that the critical vision realized herein is
indeed the epigone if not the epigenesis of that genre.) And to
Beverly Jarrett of the LSU Press, who has now edited two of my
books, I offer my profound thanks for her clairvoyant eye and
remarkable patience.

My debt to other Williams scholars and critics can never be fully
discharged, no matter how my interpretations strategically diverge in
repeating theirs. I make particular mention of the work of J. Hillis
Miller, Louis Martz, and Roy Harvey Pearce, whose critical tracks I
have often followed, but also the studies of Sherman Paul, James
Guimond, Linda Wagner, Sister M. Bernetta Quinn, James Breslin,
and the recent important book by Mike Weaver, which contains the
kind of contradictory detail every exegete of Williams thrives on! I
owe a special thanks to my former colleague Jerome Mazzaro, whose
own very recent book on Williams has been a critical and scholarly
standard against which I have measured my own divergences. He
was also an invaluable help with sources and cautions. Richard
Macksey of the Johns Hopkins University lent his complex and
discriminating eye to the manuscript, and brought to bear on its late
pre-textual state a rare knowledge both of Williams' writings and the
critical method I was employing. Eugenio Donato, another cherished
former colleague, has served as a kind of mentor for my explorations
of recent continental thought, and has guided me toward a critical
method derived from that body of thought. And lastly, I need
mention a number of other former Buffalo colleagues and friends
who over a number of years engaged me in conversation and
argument about the uses and abuses of criticism, and who remain
always in my thoughts when I think of the precarious adventure of
the "double science," of writing words about words: Ed Dryden,
Fred See, Roy Roussel, Charlie Altieri. And present colleagues:

Richard Lehan of the University of California, Los Angeles, and
Herbert Schneidau of the University of California, Santa Barbara. I
hereby absolve them one and all of responsibility for my "doublings."
References in the text are to the following works:
The Autobiography of William Carlos Williams. New York: Random
House, 1951. (Copyright 1948, 1949, 1951 by William Carlos
Williams)
The Collected Early Poems of William Carlos Williams. New York:
New Directions, 1951. (Copyright 1938 by New Directions
Publishing Corporation)
The Collected Later Poems of William Carlos Williams. Rev. ed., New
York: New Directions, 1963. (Copyright 1944, 1948, 1950, 1963
by William Carlos Williams)
Imaginations [contains *Kora in Hell, Spring and All, The Great
American Novel, The Descent of Winter,* and *A Novelette and Other
Prose*] New York: New Directions, 1970. (Copyright 1920 by
The Four Seasons Company; copyright 1923 by William Carlos
Williams; copyright 1970 by Florence H. Williams)
In the American Grain. New York: New Directions, 1956. (Copy-
right 1925 by James Laughlin; copyright 1933 by William Carlos
Williams)
I Wanted to Write a Poem. Boston: Beacon Press, 1958.
Many Loves, and Other Plays. New York: New Directions, 1965.
(Copyright 1936, 1942, 1948 by William Carlos Williams;
copyright 1961 by Florence H. Williams)
Paterson. New York: New Directions, 1963. (Copyright 1946, 1948,
1949, 1951, and © 1958 by William Carlos Williams; copyright ©
1963 by Florence H. Williams, for Book Six) [Page references
here refer to the later printings, c. 1968, which include revisions
and additions to the original edition as well as a change of format,
typescript, and pagination.]
Pictures from Brueghel, and Other Poems. New York: New Directions, 1962. (Copyright 1954, 1955, 1962 by William Carlos
Williams)
The Selected Essays of William Carlos Williams. New York: Random
House, 1954. (Copyright 1954 by William Carlos Williams)

The Selected Letters of William Carlos Williams. New York: McDowell, Oblensky, 1957. (Copyright 1957 by William Carlos Williams)

A Voyage to Pagany. New York: New Directions, 1970. (Copyright 1928 by The Macauley Company; copyright 1938, 1970 by New Directions Publishing Corporation)

Manuscripts of published and unpublished material deposited in the Poetry Collection of the Lockwood Library, State University of New York at Buffalo.

Manuscripts of published and unpublished material deposited in the Collection of American Literature of the Beinecke Library, Yale University.

List of Abbreviations

A	*The Autobiography of William Carlos Williams*
CEP	*The Collected Early Poems of William Carlos Williams*
CLP	*The Collected Later Poems of William Carlos Williams*
IAG	*In the American Grain*
Imag.	*Imaginations*
IWWP	*I Wanted to Write a Poem*
ML	*Many Loves, and Other Plays*
P	*Paterson*
PB	*Pictures from Brueghel, and Other Poems*
SE	*The Selected Essays of William Carlos Williams*
SL	*The Selected Letters of William Carlos Williams*
VP	*A Voyage to Pagany*

Yale MS and Buffalo MS are used, respectively, to cite the manuscript collections of William Carlos Williams' works at the Beinecke Library of Yale University and at the Lockwood Library of the State University of New York at Buffalo.

The Inverted Bell

What I conceive is writing as an actual creation.
It is the birth of another cycle.

In the past the excellence of literature has
been conceived upon a borrowed basis. In this you
[the new wife] have no existence. I am broken
apart, not so.much with various desire—but with
the inability to conceive desire upon a basis that
is satisfactory to either.

The common resort is to divorce. What is that?
It is for the police.

But to me it has always been that until a new
plane of understanding has been established—or
discovered, all the values which we attempt are
worthless.

This is literature. . . .

You, I, we, cannot you see how in the singleness of these few days marriage and writing have
been fused so that the seriousness of my life and
common objects about me have made up an actuality
of which I am assembling the parts?

(Imag., 293–94)

Introduction

There is an anecdote, reputedly Stephane Mallarmé's as related by Henri de Regnier, that succinctly characterizes the crisis of the Modern. "Poetry," Mallarmé said to his friend Elémir Bourges, "has followed entirely the wrong line since Homer's original error." "And what was there before Homer?" replied Bourges. "Orpheus," said Mallarmé.[1] Orpheus is the myth of poetry, of the poet. Homer is the poet of myth. Homer's "original error" is the error of self-consciousness, of "writing." Orpheus is the figure of unmediated, pure, ecstatic utterance. But the Orphic myth bears within itself a number of contradictions. Orphic song is inevitably the song of loss. It therefore discloses the tragedy of self-reflection, of looking back, of the violence of original mediation. Orpheus' song nostalgically recalls the lost plenitude, and that ecstatic moment must remind a modern audience not only of the initial violence of Eurydice's ravishment, the whoring of the virgin, but of the inevitable failure of man's attempt to recapture a lost presence. Orpheus' ecstasy bears within itself the inevitability of his own sacrifice and dismemberment. It also embodies the nostalgia without which poetry cannot be pure—that is, be purified of the language of history.

1. Quoted in Daniel-Henry Kahnweiler, *Juan Gris, His Life and Work*, trans. Douglas Cooper (New York: H. N. Abrams, 1969), 140.

3

Homer, on the other hand, accepts the loss of plenitude, and thus his distance from the gods. His hero is the wanderer, homeless because of an initial violation. He recognizes the violence which lies in all origins. He accepts his alienation and the common purpose of his adventure. He recognizes that to recover the whored virgin, Helen, cannot mean the return of the old plenitude. In other words, he accepts history because he accepts the initial violation which launched him into time, and he recognizes man's history as desire. The desire to return home, to renew the marriage, to recover not some pure time but man's place—these constitute Homer's original error. Yeats, in "Vacillation," is even more emphatic than Mallarmé: "What theme had Homer but original sin?" For both, Homer represents the error of alienation, self-reflection, and defines the poet from the very beginning as the victim of an original mediation.

"We were the last romantics," Yeats writes in "Coole Parke and Ballylee, 1931." Here is Modernism's apocalyptic sense of an ending. But the context also makes clear that Homer rode in the same "saddle" as these "last romantics": "chose for theme/ Traditional sanctity and loveliness," but lived to sing of man's departure, his homelessness. Was Homer a "romantic"? The question has nothing to do with literary history. Mallarmé's anecdote touches the core of Modernism. Language has fallen into the manifold; Orphic song, which originally rent the veil of Maya, now recalls only the distance of the origin, the lost plenitude of words. The contemporary poet's choice is either to be a "last romantic," and attempt the return to Orpheus (to "purify" the "dialect of the tribe"), to play the vacillating game of Yeatsian antithesis (yoking heart and soul, soul and body, Christian and pagan in an eternal opposition), or to embrace Homer's "unchristian heart" and relive the myth of original error or original sin.

Revealingly, Homer and not Orpheus is Williams' figure of

the poet, the figurative "first" poet. Like Scheherazade, Sappho, and the prehistoric cave painters, also figurative first poets, Homer "follows" Orpheus as inevitably as poetry follows song, action follows vision, or writing follows speech. Orpheus does appear in Williams' early work, in the beginning of *Kora in Hell*, where his eternal hope to recover Eurydice (Imag., 32) forms a complement to the metaphor of the title, the Kore myth in which temporary recovery of presence is guaranteed. Both myths, it is true, contain the idea of an original violence or rape, but whereas the Kore myth certifies the eternal return, the recovery of plenitude, the Orphic myth certifies recovery only in nostalgia or ecstasy. Orphic tragedy has no place in Williams' world. But the problem of the origin is crucial, and Homer, the figurative first poet, is central to Williams' thematic. For Homer, like all first or original poets, like the old cave painters or Paul Klee, stands at the site of poetry, which is somewhere beyond the origin and at a proximate distance from the "place" of plenitude (of the gods). And Williams' first poet resigns himself to original error and repudiates the tragedy of loss. He leaps into the world, and takes his place happily in the site of language's fall. He embraces the paradox of the whored virgin. He writes down (or someone or many with his name) the myth and demythologizes it.

The figurative first poet is for Williams original, because his utterance is not unmediated song. He speaks from the place of language, at the site of an original violation and departure. His language is "immediate" precisely because it does not nostalgically lament a violated purity, or lost origin; for this poet language is originally diacritical. This poet, this Homer, takes as his original theme the violence of man's break with the origin (the original violence itself) and the freedom of his heroic wandering. His themes are violence and wandering, the epic of "pursuit" initiated, as Williams puts it in "Asphodel,

That Greeny Flower," by "Helen's public fault" (PB, 158).
This fault, imaged in the figure of the sea upon which man is
cast, introduces man into time and defines him as time. It
leaves him homeless; it violates marriage and produces divorce;
and it leaves one to dream the paradox of the original dance
and to desire the recovery of the "garden" (PB, 156, 160,
164–65, 166). "Were it not for that [Helen's public fault]/
there would have been/ no poem" (PB, 158). Williams'
figures of Homer's beginning do not conceive the original
error (Helen's) as original sin, but as the mystery of
originating violation. What follows is epic, the action of men
and not the tragedy of the single isolated voice. This fault
breeds a storm that breaks up the garden, but it leads no less to
a flowering, and the engendering of an action. It is, therefore, a
dance which generates a wandering. History is man's search to
recover his loss, to fulfill his need, to return home. It marks
the simultaneous beginning of being and time. It calls forth the
poem: "It is like Homer's/ catalogue of ships:/ it fills up the
time" (PB, 159). It therefore defers the end, the return, that is
the object of its desire.

This is to "speak in figures" of Williams' conception of the
poem, as "Asphodel" clearly recognizes (PB, 159). These
figures, which are like the patterns on the dresses worn by the
wife whom the poet addresses, allow the two to meet. One
only escapes the silence by filling it up, with words, with
conversation, with whatever reduces the distance between two
people and effects a meeting. A poem is a configuration of
words, a flowering of words, a bringing together of words, a
garden in which the manifold of flowers may suggest some
original unity from which they sprang and hold out the dream
of its recovery. It is a "design." Williams' concern, however, is
not with some ideal garden that is the model of gardens, or
with the recovery of some nostalgically remembered place, but
"love," and love is "a garden which expands" (PB, 160). A

poem re-members, gathers together again, recovers the original marriage, as "Asphodel" plays out the "figures." But the original marriage involved an origin violence, a whoring of the virgin.[2] It therefore becomes the "place" of the "imagination" (PB, 177). Its "design" depends on an act which "de-signs," or breaks up old designs. His poems do not lament the lost Orphic source, but celebrate the original place of marriage, the time of lovers' youth, the presence of two interpenetrating opposites standing in the "light" (PB, 181). The figures all revolve around a place of illumination, of flowering, of opening, of the coming to light—the figures of some primordial emergence which supplant some old place. Yet, the place is a "fault." The origin is not some One, but two. The "site" of the poem, as Heidegger calls it, is the place where words bloom, but also where the idea of a pure origin before or behind or outside the place is dispelled.[3] Thus, new texts dis-place old texts, as new places replace old, as interpretation succeeds interpretation. In the beginning was writing, language and not pure song.

The legend of Orpheus, though mythic, conceals the legend of original error, a strangely Western myth of man's tragically lost origins. The Homeric theme, on the other hand, becomes the theme of scattering and gathering, of homelessness and wandering, of desire and curiosity, of the razing of the city (and hence the idea of the ground) and the search for a new ground or home, the original starting point and original marriage. It is the myth of the hermeneutical circle. The original home or marriage is never recoverable in its originality, but only as the fiction of history or poetry. The Homeric theme is the theme of the human adventure, of

2. This is to anticipate the argument of Chapter 5, where the whored virgin motif of *Paterson*, Book Five, is treated at length in relation to Williams' figure of the poem as marriage.

3. Martin Heidegger, *On the Way to Language*, trans. Peter D. Hertz (New York: Harper & Row, 1971), 159–98. (Translation of *Unterwegs zur Sprache*, 1959.)

language itself. And if Williams did not fully articulate this awareness of what his choice of the Homeric model implied, his poetics—even when concerned with style, technique, metric, or form—speaks with a revolutionary rhetoric which in its own deep resonances evokes the seminal adventure of some figurative "first" poet: of "Homer, the blind; Scheherazade, who lived under threat" (Imag., 101).

Take, for example, the famous early utterance of *Paterson*: "Say it, no ideas but in things" (P, 6). Or the later repetition: "No ideas but/ in the facts" (P, 28). They both appear parenthetically, emerging from out of the tapestry or collage of elements to unfold over the entire poem. They ask to be taken as credo, as commentary on the poem of which they are a part. They indicate an exasperation with the figurative evasion of what has immediately preceded them. But criticism has tended to take the statement as proposition, extrapoetic, a kind of metacommentary. It has become the measure of Williams' objectivism, his revolt against the priority of the subject and the reign of the unblooded abstraction. Williams becomes a realist of the imagination, to borrow Marianne Moore's phrase; the priority of the subject is replaced by the priority of the object. In short, Williams' figure, his saying or utterance, becomes one more return to the *other* in the Romantic vacillation between self and world. Williams as realist becomes another of the "last romantics," taking as his point of departure the thing, nature, reality.

Without trying to contest this placement of Williams in the Romantic, or post-Romantic tradition, to which in the history of poetry he surely belongs, I want nevertheless to suggest that "no ideas but in things" is in effect a saying about saying, and is not at all concerned with the priority of thing over idea or thing over word. Following as it does a labyrinthine metaphor of the dream as place or locus of elemental forces, of the dream as a place because it resides and moves in a locus of otherwise chaotic sounds, Dr. Paterson's "Say it" becomes the initial unscrambling and relocating of a field. The utterance does not say that ideas emerge from things, but that there are no ideas unrealized and thus no thing except in the identity and difference of things. This initial saying brings to expression a primordial difference, primordial because it denies priority. It denies unity, the master Idea. It therefore denies or leaps beyond what Heidegger has called the fundamental misinterpretation that governs Western thought, the Socratic and Platonic elevation of the *logos* to a status of priority and origin. Intuitively, this "saying" recalls for the poet a more original, primordial moment, when language is made to speak itself and the poet puts "into language the experience he undergoes with language."[4]

In his subtle, complex analysis of Stefan George's poem "The Word," Heidegger revolves the metapoetic utterance of the poem's last line, "Where word breaks off no thing may be," until it is made to speak primordially of language as the "house of Being" or even the "bourne of Being."[5] Heidegger's theme is the inseparability of poetry and thinking, and hence of saying and being; but his argument runs a devious course to escape the habits of logic which see either of these fundamental differences as prior to the other. Saying, the act of utterance, becomes the reconciling point of these two parallels; saying is the "is" which, by breaking up the stillness of the individual word, ushers it toward its silence, and makes way for a new "is," a new flowering. "Language is the flower of the mouth," so Heidegger repeats Hölderlin.[6] In saying, words and things,

4. *Ibid.*, 59. The most useful exposition of Heidegger's continuing argument against the original misinterpretation which governs Western onto-theological metaphysics is in his *An Introduction to Metaphysics*, trans. Ralph Manheim (New York: Anchor Books, 1961). (Originally published in 1953; translation first published by Yale University Press, 1959.)

5. Heidegger, *On the Way to Language*, 60 ff.

6. *Ibid.*, 99. This entire essay, "The Nature of Language," is concerned with the inseparable parallels of thinking and poetry.

ideas and things (or in Heidegger's restoration of the original
pre-Socratic terms, *logos* and *physis*) arise into being, into a
field of difference. They come to light; they *are* because they
have place, are gathered. *Logos* and *physis*, gathering and
scattering, are reciprocal differences. Ideas do not precede and
give birth to things.

In his line, however, Williams does not say that words give
being to things but that ideas *are* only within things. Heidegger, happily, continues with George's phrase: "The closing
line, 'Where word breaks off no thing may be,' points to the
relation of word and thing in this manner, that the word itself
is the relation, by holding forth into being, and thereby
upholding it." [7] Williams, as I read his saying, discovers the
intricate relation of words and things to be this "relation."
When words are considered factual (representative, mimetic
signs)—and not the nexus of the relations of facts which give
facts being because they have a place—then words drift away
from each other, become abstractions or ideas, assert their own
priority. They generate the illusion of ideas before things. This
sudden saying of it in *Paterson*, then, is the poet's realization in
language of his experience with language. If Paterson, the
modern industrial city, is a place without a poet, Paterson is
not a "place." It has no locus. But if a poet come, then it may
become *Paterson*. That is, it becomes a poem, a field of
language or a house of being, a "measure" of things, a
"relation." The poet cuts a design, dis-covers a trace, brings an
environment to expression, because he penetrates to the site of
language. But to do so, he must declare ("Say it") the break of
language with the old metaphysics and poetics, with the Idea.

Words are not things for Williams, nor is he guilty of
committing himself to the pathetic task of restoring words to
some lost ideal identity with things. On the contrary, his

7. *Ibid.*, 73.

compulsion to restore language to its facticity, to sharpen the edges of images, acknowledged the fundamental difference between the word and the thing as the very thing that defined this relation. Facts become facts in the relation provided them by language. And poetry, original poetry, is the refreshing of the discovery of this relation. It is interpretation. "Experience," says Heidegger, "means . . . to obtain something along the way, to attain something by going on a way. What is it the poet reaches? Not mere knowledge. He obtains entrance into the relation of word and thing. This relation is not, however, a connection between the thing that is on one side and the word that is on the other. The word itself is the relation which in each instance retains the thing within itself in such a manner that it 'is' a thing." [8] If the "word did not have this bearing," he continues later—and by bearing he means precisely the power of bringing forth and holding the relation—"the whole of things, the 'world,' would sink into obscurity, including the 'I' of the poem, him who brings to his country's strand, to the source of names, all the wonders and dreams he encounters." [9]

Williams' insistence on a poetry of the local can, of course, be studied in terms of his use of a geographical region or place. The problem of his Americanness, the influence especially of Whitman and the strange attraction of Poe, has been for most of his critics the point of departure in identifying the special quality of his work. His concern with touch or contact, with divorce and blockage, with the city, with the modern failure of language, with the need of a "new measure"—these are surely American in character, even if they are not altogether of a piece. Yet they are of a piece. The particularity of Williams' experiments can be traced almost exclusively to his insistence on the use of a manifold of local detail, on his employment of the "anti-poetic," to use Wallace Stevens' phrase which so

8. *Ibid.*, 66.
9. *Ibid.*, 73.

antagonized Williams.[10] It was his refusal of selection which
led Charles Olson to attack him for allowing himself to be
rolled under by time, by an excess of detail which could not be
brought to focus in a comprehensive "field." [11] The sustained
apology which runs through his prose and poetry is his
justification for staying home and not, as he says in *Paterson*,
running off "toward the peripheries" in search of "authority,"
"other centers" (P, 36). This "authority" lay in some remote
past, or in tradition, and was manifest in cultural monuments,
enduring works of art, or ideal cultures. It was the authority of
presence, evident only in the fragmentary signs (the ruins) of
contemporary history, signs of a lost plenitude. Williams'
refusal of the center, of the ego- or subject-center and of the
transcendental origin, generates in his poetry what Michel
Foucault has called the "refus du commencement" of Nietzsche, the refusal to believe that one can trace a present thing or
occurrence back to some remote, distant origin.[12] This
"refusal" rejects any nostalgia for an ultimate ground that is
itself undetermined or *not* an interpretation of some previous

10. Stevens' phrase, which also led to his calling Williams' interest in the primacy
of things "sentimentalism," appeared in a preface he contributed to Williams' *Collected
Poems, 1921–1931* (New York: Objectivist Press, 1934), and is reprinted in Stevens'
Opus Posthumous, ed. with introd. Samuel French Morse (New York: Alfred A.
Knopf, 1957), 254–57. Williams' criticism, and even some of his poetry, is filled with
vigorous counterattacks on the implications of this remark (*e.g.*, IWWP, 52). It may
now be said that Williams' refusal of the idea of the anti-poetic is likewise a rejection
of the idea of the poetic, a concept which assumes the onto-theological center of
Western metaphysics in its assumption that certain "things" or a certain kind of
figural language is privileged, the symbolic manifestation of some transcendental order
of ideas, truths, or values. Therefore, one can assume a poetic and an anti-poetic
subject matter. The poetic implies the idea of plenitude and presence; the anti-poetic, a
kind of metaphysical "poverty," to use another of Stevens' terms. Stevens himself
came to understand Williams' irritation and to reject the pejorative implications of the
anti-poetic and the privileged language of the poetic.

11. See Charles Olson, *Selected Writings*, ed. with introd. Robert Creeley (New
York: New Directions, 1966), 82–83. The significance of this distinction is treated at
length in Chapter 3.

12. Michel Foucault, "Nietzsche, Marx et Freud," *Nietzsche*, Cahiers de Royau-
ment, Philosophie VI (Paris: Editions de Minuit, 1967).

metaphor. The "refus du commencement," as Foucault says of Nietzsche, posits a world of interpretation grounded upon interpretation, of text preceded by pretext. The search for authority leads backward from interpretation to previous interpretation, to the bottom, which, as Nietzsche said, can only turn out to be itself an interpretation. Rejecting this search for some lost center, authority, presence, or plenitude, Williams turns to the local as a centerless center, and rediscovers the "joy" of Nietzschean invention.

Williams recognized intuitively that the problem of the "ground" was a problem of interpretation. He sharply distinguished the solid, dark "ground" of mystery on which the natives of Tenochtitlan based their projections of faith, and thus their city (IAG, 33–35), from the illusory ground of the "Traditionalists of Plagiarism" (Imag., 94, 97), as he called those who assumed an absolute ground, whether ontological or theological, at the head of the past or in some transcendent future. Williams' refusal manifests itself in an argument against the conventional function of metaphor and simile. If Nietzschean man is free of God, and thus free of something outside himself that defines him, language also regains its power as it forfeits its subordinate role as reference. Detail calls attention primarily to itself and to its relative position in regard to other detail, thus marking its edges or difference, its otherness rather than nothingness. The authority of the detail asserts itself, proclaiming itself as antipoetic because it does not refer back to an essence or idea which lends it significance and defines it as a shadow. Williams' world flattens out into a chaosmos of random but related particulars. Historical detail, as in *Paterson*, is wrenched out of the historical perspective which lent it meaning. The detail of recorded history is exposed as primarily interpretation related according to an absolute that preceded and subsumed it. As in the case of Mrs. Cumming's death (P, 14–15), the recorded facts are really the facts of an interpretation, made in terms of an unstated but culturally assumed set of moral absolutes. The poem brings the historical interpretation, now collected in a book of objective if anecdotal events, into question by the act of bringing its rhetoric forward out of a context where that rhetoric can plausibly refer to an origin and meaning of the event, in this instance, God's will. Williams deprives detail of the perspective in which it dwells as meaning, and thus brings it to dwell in a new place. The result of this deprivation is to return to detail a sense of its presentness to itself.

It is a mistake, however, to assume that Williams' refusal of the beginning makes him an empiricist. His detail—deprived of the meaning of its previous context, or of what its previous place of interpretation conferred upon it—appears to overwhelm him. He appears to refuse to interpret the interpretation. What it really overwhelms, however, is the illusion of distance which, because it could maintain the fiction of the beginning as past or before or outside, could also allow the fiction of the priority of the subject, of ideas to things. Like Heidegger's "deconstruction of metaphysics," as we shall see, like Homer's catalogues that fill up time, Williams' gathering of local detail does not reveal the priority of things to ideas but, on the contrary, unveils the true ground of ideas as the undetermined relation of things. Williams seeks a "new measure" between things because the old measures have been exposed as interpretations, fictions of the center. What he projects as the new must escape the fate of the old. It must recognize itself as interpretation, as fiction. It therefore must recognize itself as measuring, and not a set measure, as saying and not the said. The first act of new measuring, then, is to bring into question old measures, to create a dissonance.

Williams did not choose or select the detail of his own personal local, for example, of Paterson, New Jersey, in order to exemplify or even reinterpret a local history. Nor did he create the illusion of nonselectivity, of arbitrary choice of detail, of inclusion rather than exclusion, of chaos rather than recognizable form, in order to accentuate either the priority of detail or the disorder of the modern world. His strategy was not mimetic. The difference Olson noted between Pound's authoritative, ego-centered selection, which emphasized the priority of space to time, as against Williams' refusal to select, which led to an aleatory poetry of random detail, has tended to perpetuate the view that Williams forfeited any principle of selectivity at all. Still, criticism cannot admit a formless poetry. Indeed, Williams criticism has been preoccupied with trying to discover his principle of selectivity within the conventional sense of form. Olson's distinction between a poetry of space and a poetry of time cannot finally escape the old, dualistic either-or poetics, no matter his attempt to escape the alternatives of subjectivism-objectivism in *objectism*.[13]

Questions concerning the unity of *Paterson* are posed characteristically in terms of some unifying figure. Admitting the lack of an identifiable subject, a central meditative voice or consciousness which brings the poem to focus, critics nonetheless seek an organizing center, a controlling image, a mythic

13. See Olson, *Selected Writings*, 83. Olson, of course, uses Pound and Williams as respective opposites in contrasting a subjectivist (ego-centered, spatial, synchronic) poetics and objectivist (object-centered, temporal, diachronic) poetics, for which he is seeking a synthesis. Pound's ego-center, however, should not be considered subjectivist in the Romantic sense of an esemplastic power, but in the sense of a centering, focussing, selecting, ordering transcendence of Time. Olson goes on: "Each of the above jobs are HALVES, that is, I take it (1) that the EGO AS BEAK is bent and busted but (2) whatever we have that we can call its replacement (Bill very much a little of it) HAS, SO FAR, not been able to bring any time so abreast of us that we are in this present air, going straight, out of our selves, into it. . . ." Olson is seeking a "correct methodology." Elsewhere, in his essay "Projective Verse," part of which Williams quoted in his *Autobiography*, Olson had coined the term *Objectism* as his alternative to either "subjectivism" or "objectivism," because the latter two had become dialectical and hence inseparable opposites in an epistemological quarrel which Olson thought without end and no longer relevant. Still, Olson's poetics everywhere holds out the possibility of a recaptured beginning that is an origin, a city that is also a presence and not simply a port of departure.

predesign. The river, the cycle of seasons, the quadrilateral structure of four books, the metaphor of the city, the tapestry, the idea of a geographically identifiable place—each in its way has been made to serve the need to affirm the poem's unity as a *concordia discors*. And though each does not exclude the other, there is implicit in the search for a central or controlling image or image cluster the assumption that in any poem some body of detail subsumes or subordinates the rest. In the case of the "local," there is the realist assumption, perfectly mirroring the subjectivist view that the organizing principle stands outside the poem but can be taken inside in the form of a concrete, objective language, a "measured" language that exists within history's accumulated layers of meaning.

The word *literature* bears within itself this assumption of an organizing predesign, of an identifiable or nameable origin which precedes the work and stands outside it. Either the work or object of art is the intention of its creator, or reflects the unity of his emotions, or bears its own *telos* within (is "autotelic"). The word *poem*, with its more or less implicit assumption of internal coherence or wholeness, suggests a totalization of elements that likewise implies the presence of a center, an organizing principle. This principle, whether author, consciousness, intention, or imagination, is fundamentally the principle of *logos*. Is it possible to escape the rhetoric of intentionality and still maintain the idea of the poem? Can literature step outside or beyond itself? can language? As Williams repeatedly warned both his readers and himself, any attempt at the "new" must first appear as a kind of chaos or anarchy. It therefore stands in need of apology. Any new art demands a corollary criticism, and that criticism is often a part of the internal function of the work itself. Still, the question remains whether art can call itself into question, step outside itself, and declare itself new and thus beyond the definitions it uses to deny definition.

E. H. Gombrich has observed of cubism—the techniques of which helped shape Williams' notions of new possibilities for his verbal art[14]—that its methods were radical efforts to call attention to the work as man-made, as artifice, and thus to break the mimetic illusion: "If illusion is due to the interaction of clues and the absence of contradictory evidence, the only way to fight its transforming influence is to make the clues contradict each other and to prevent a coherent image of reality from destroying the pattern of the plane." [15] Cubism, says Gombrich, works by accentuating the contradictory and disharmonious, and by bringing together in the same plane elements normally separated into different relational planes by the mimetic illusion. This not only suspends illusion but suspends the representational ambiguity of the detail, its tendency to mean something, symbolically, that lies outside its new set of relations. Cubism frustrates our attempt to decipher the sign in terms of referential meaning. It frustrates interpretation, if by interpretation we mean the mimetic attempt to relate the spatial design of the work to another more comprehensive world that lies outside it—let us say, the world of reality, or the world of ideas or symbols.

Cubism, Gombrich continues, disallows us the reference point of an ideal meaning. It "scrambles clues" that allow allegorical or mimetic renderings in terms of a received code, and brings us back to the object itself: "The function of representational clues in cubist paintings," Gombrich writes, "is not to inform us about guitars and apples, nor to stimulate our tactile sensations. It is to narrow down the range of

14. See especially Bram Dijkstra, *The Hieroglyphics of a New Speech: Cubism, Stieglitz, and the Early Poetry of William Carlos Williams* (Princeton, N.J.: Princeton University Press, 1969); and Jerome Mazzaro, *William Carlos Williams: The Later Poetry* (Ithaca, N.Y.: Cornell University Press, 1973).

15. E. H. Gombrich, *Art and Illusion: A Study of the Problem of Pictorial Representation*, Bollingen Series XXXV (Princeton, N.J.: Princeton University Press, 1961), 281.

possible interpretations till we are forced to accept the flat pattern with all its tensions." [16] Williams, as we will see in detail later on, made similar observations about cubist collage, and drew explicit analogies between the flat plane of that art and the function of words in poetry. There are at least two important conclusions to draw from his analogy: (1) his own elimination of perspective and breaking up of the expected (representational) syntax of relations (between things, words, values) creates an art which tends to define itself as other than art, since art presumes another kind of coherence (centered); (2) his use of historical detail, like his use of words, tends to strip the detail of any interpretative ambiguity altogether and thus to set going a circle of interpretations which return always to the thing as it is.

The thing as it is, however, is the thing *where* it is, defined in its plane by the set of relations. In its field, the thing defines itself reciprocally. There is no point of departure, nor does the thing as image speak for the thing it images, as Gombrich notes. It is temporarily de-signed. Interpretation may proceed from any of a manifold of things or points. The relationships may be read in several directions. Any one interpretation simultaneously asserts its pertinence and brings itself into question. The detail of Sam Patch's history, Mrs. Cumming's death, the fire in the Paterson Library, the records of Indian tribes which lived along the Passaic, and the innumerable contemporary observations by the poet, including his memory of both personal experience and works of art which have touched him—this plethora of logically unrelated detail is brought into the single plane of a language where one thing exists beside another or after another or echoes an earlier appearance not because of some identifiable meaning and value which precedes its appearance but because it happens to gather

16. *Ibid.*, 286. See also Mazzaro, *William Carlos Williams*, 50–51.

there. Nor does the detail gather to a focus around a central "I," which in interpreting the detail makes the detail phenome- nologically incarnate that "I." If a controlling subject or center (a central imagination) is not operating in the poem, however, a system of measuring and relating is there. And the system appears, or is discovered, in the progressive unwinding of the logically unrelated events.

Obviously there is some principle of selectivity in *Paterson*; otherwise it would be something like the absolute chaos Lévi-Strauss envisions as the product of a totalized history.[17] If the poem does not or cannot include everything Williams knows about his historical place, or remembers in association with it, or even casually relates to it, it assumes a principle of selection. But the principle is deliberately concealed, just as the central subject, the poetic "I," is suppressed or fragmented. Like the cubist strategy described by Gombrich, Williams scrambles the clues which might allow us to fix on a point of departure for interpretation. The excavated signs of local detail, which are so integral to the poem's design, were in themselves interpretations, as Williams clearly recognized. But they were interpretations which assumed a privileged point of departure. If cubism opposed itself to the tyranny of the "eye," or to what Gombrich calls the "shortcomings of one-eyed vision," Williams' strategy is similarly directed against the tyranny of the "I," and visual representation. His dislocations

17. See Claude Lévi-Strauss, *The Savage Mind* (Chicago: University of Chicago Press, 1966), 257. (Translation of *La Pensée sauvage*, 1962; translator unnamed.) "Even history which claims to be universal is still only a juxtaposition of a few local histories within which (and between which) very much more is left out than is put in. . . . In so far as history aspires to meaning, it is doomed to select regions, periods, groups of men and individuals in these groups and to make them stand out, as discontinuous figures, against a continuity barely good enough to be used as a backdrop. A truly total history would cancel itself out—its product would be nought." The received and written history of Paterson, New Jersey, which Williams demystifies, assumes a silent teleological continuity. Williams exposes the illusion of totalization in this recorded history, and deconstructs it in the same way the fire opened the closed language of the Library.

of the old signs return us to the more original experience of original naming, of interpretation itself. But its implications are even more significant, since Williams' medium is words and his experience is the experience of a poet with words. If one dimension of his poetry is to disclose the distortions and perversions of language in its historical destiny, another directs itself at an experience which demands that we forfeit all the securities of point of view and the unproblematic relation of word to thing. It demands that we confront the possibility of the "ground" of being as the principle of the game (*jeu*), and not another logocentrism.

Williams' poetry is a sustained assault on the familiar habits of interpretation and teleological history. His attacks on the erudition of some Modern poets, especially Eliot, often take the form of a parody which tempts the reader to a similar hunt for sources in which the meaning of the allusion, image, fact, or whatever is grounded. The source of Williams' facts are hardly more difficult to locate than Eliot's or Pound's, even without footnotes. But the source is invariably a red herring, not because the fact doesn't retain some of its earlier meaning, but because it is so used in the fabric of other detail as to open up the possibility of a nearly infinite polyvalency. Far from being explanations, the facts characteristically offer a point of departure for two or more directions of interpretation, and in turn point backward to other associations, and so on. The circle of interpretation always leads back to the place of the detail itself. Thus in *Paterson* the murder of a man by the name of Van Winkle refers to a particular historical incident that connects with other acts of violence which reach back to the city's earliest times. But the name also echoes a name in American literature, an archetypical dreamer and escapist who, through his association with his dog, can be related to the wanderer Odysseus and his dog. Furthermore, he can be made to recall a recurrent theme in Williams' own work, "turning inland," in search of the ground. The interpretations radiate from the detail, but come to rest at no point. If one follows the clues from point to point he does not arrive at a place outside the poem. He comes to the recognition of design, of the poem as a text interwoven with a number of previous texts, themselves interpenetrating with pre-texts. What the interpreter experiences is the experience of interpretation itself, the experience of words as relations which is the poet's experience. At the bottom one uncovers not a meaning, but an elemental design which can be described in terms of a number of mythic patterns, that is, only in terms of other metaphors.

A poem like *Paterson* is a kind of palimpsest or helix, layers upon layers of interpretations. The same holds true for those poems, like "Locust Tree in Flower," which have nothing at all to do with specific local detail, but which, on the contrary, appear at first to be representations of a generalized kind. Such poems, however, represent nature neither by description nor by evoking a visual image, but by demystifying the romance of the organic. The poems present themselves as an unfolding sequence of words, each word occupying a place in relation to another which defines it, not semantically or even grammatically but, in the fundamental sense, syntactically. The nouns may name parts of a tree, but the prepositions give equal substance to the place where these parts, like different words, are contiguous, where articulation occurs. The identifiable laws of grammar which govern the language, and give certain words a recognizable place and function, are not thrown out, but through the introduction of spacing, line, disconnection of words from phrase, measured silences, and the like, the priority of meaning is brought into question. The possibility of the game is introduced, as in nature the normal laws of growth are often suspended by a mysterious transformation or mutation which forces us to recognize the true nature of the law, that it is a conceptualization and not a description. The "form/ of

motion" (CEP, 68) taken by words so projected subscribes to
both the analogy of the "machine" and organic form. It is only
because the metaphor of the organic has come to imply the
systematic interconnection of the parts, all held as one in the
unity of some supernatural or genetic origin, that we tend to
forget that a system depends on the difference of the parts.
Indeed, this difference introduces the possibility of a near
infinity of combinations when different parts are substituted or
additions and subtractions take place. In other words, the
machine is like the finite field of language which because of a
fundamental lack of a center allows for free substitution. The
poem's relation of words is a homologue of nature's relation of
discrete parts, but no less an analogue of the relation and
difference between man-made things (culture) and natural
things (nature).

Williams' insistence on a poetry of the "local" must be
understood as something considerably more significant than
mirroring the details of a particular geography, or as an
apology for his staying home while other Americans went to
Paris. His concern, he said, was to bring an "environment to
expression" (SL, 286), to reveal its social nexus. The social
involves relation, communication, and thus place. As early as
In the American Grain he called Poe the genuine poet of the
American "local"—Poe whose landscapes are preeminently
unlocatable outside the story and whose points of reference
seem most bewilderingly subjective and metaphysical. But Poe
is local precisely because he avoids " 'colonial imitation' " or
any kind of representation of place, and therefore *locates* his art
in a true center (IAG, 219). Poe recognizes that the "New
World" means a *"new locality"*: "it is America, the first great
burst through to expression of a re-awakened genius of *place"*
(IAG, 216). Poe's " 'preeminently mathematical' " intellect
penetrates the surface, including the mimetic structure of
American life and literature, to a "juvenescent *local* literature"

which is a literature of the *"beginning"* (IAG, 216–17). Williams' recurrent adjective for Poe is "original." It was Poe's desire for the origin which drove him to aggressive attacks on sentiment and to seek pure form, form being a term also implying *forma* or the originating principle itself. Williams' chapter on Poe is the culmination of the argument of *In the American Grain*, the title of which takes the figure of a gestalt or pattern that is the dwelling place (*Gestellen*) of a revelation. But the origin Poe discovered was not some essential subject or soul, nor even an absence. It was the original violence of beginnings, as in the shattering of the center and the falling away into being in *Eureka*, though admittedly Poe did retain the metaphor of the undifferentiated center, the One.

"What he wanted was connected with no particular place; therefore it *must* be where he *was*" (IAG, 220)—thus Williams on Poe as the exemplar of the local. It is a discrimination Williams makes repeatedly and emphatically, in his poems and fiction as well as in his criticism. And it is perhaps the most ignored position he takes. The famous assertion which appears late in Book Five of *Paterson* that "Anywhere is everywhere" (P, 235), is no sudden whim by which the poet leaps out of the engulfing detail of his local. It is the discovery of measuring, of taking detail into a new place, of framing and relating it, of separating it out from the "things" it supposedly represents or meanings which have accrued to it. In Poe it is the "algebra," the "sense of play," which first separates out things from the sentimental (representational) order that subsumes them in order to reform the field (the place) where they might lie together because of their own relations and differences: for example, the deductive leap of Dupin's logic to a simplification of commonsense relations of contiguous things.

The local, the sense of place, the new measure for a New

World, even the city—these central terms of Williams' poetics resonate into something beyond an empirical or geographical interest in "things." And though Williams' search for a "new measure" includes the primary search for a metric (the "variable foot") which might escape the tyrannies, not to say the unnaturalness, of conventional prosody, his sense of "measure" must be read in an even more original sense. All of these concerns are central to the fundamental question of language, man's and therefore the poet's place of dwelling. Williams' emphasis on the priority of touch, of contact, can likewise be interpreted as an analogy for language. For touch is not only the elimination of the distance created by other senses, especially seeing; it defines being as the proximity of a difference. Where people or things touch, there is a place. That place is defined by the sameness, the "like," that marks the difference—that is, by the design of a relation. A city is such a place; so is a poem. It is a place not because it is a space into which a number of things have been summoned, a space which preceded the gathering of things there. It is a place because it is a dwelling, where things or people come to dwell. It is created by their coming, and being there.

The local for Williams is place *qua* locus, the "acme point of white penetration" where discrete lines converge and connect scattered and remote points, as in the "geometric principle" (Imag., 309). From the first, Williams distinguished a poetry of the local from "local color." His local is that which is defined as a "field" arising in the vectograph of converging planes; place is the locus of differences. The "point of white penetration," however, is not some center or presence which synthesizes and holds the manifold upon the point of some ideal identity. Williams' city is not a city of God, but the place of the mythic gathering of the scattered. It is a city of differences, manifold. A city is a city only if the differences belong together; only if they are proximate and therefore measured. Williams' motif of divorce accentuates the failure of measure, both in human relations and in communication. Touch resolves divorce not simply by closing distance, but by measuring difference. A city, therefore, fails when "language/ fails" (P, 11), when words lose their edges and therefore the measure of their difference. When difference and measure are dissolved, all things collapse into a "torrent" of confusion or are scattered from the proximity which gives them identity. A city must have a poet, then, for only the poet stands in the proximity of the locus (mythically, in the proximity of the gods), and gives measure to the difference, of words and things, which defines place.

Touch, Williams' famous *"tactus eruditus"* (CEP, 63), is an original measure.[18] At its most intimate, in sex, it is a kind of interpenetration which defines most acutely the two partners and binds them to a future. It is social, historical. Marriage is Williams' ideal metaphor for this relationship. In marriage, as

18. In his seminal essay on Williams in *Poets of Reality* (Cambridge, Mass.: Harvard University Press, 1965), J. Hillis Miller explores the phenomenology of Williams' language of the distinct senses, but he does not isolate touch as the metaphorical primary sense, as Williams seems to do in his criticism. Thus Miller sees touch as a way of closing distance, but also as a way of breaking down edges (interpenetrating) of a difference and allowing one thing to flow into another. This function of "internalization," as Miller calls it, does lead, in Williams' thematic, to the sense of the poem as motion, of the flowing together of self and world (p. 317), though it conflicts with Williams' opposite emphasis on the necessary edges (distinctness, difference) of things, images, and the like. In his more recent book, *Thomas Hardy: Distance and Desire* (Cambridge, Mass.: Harvard University Press, 1970), Miller writes of Hardy's fear of "touch" as a fear of being brought from his role of detached spectator into physical relation with others. Miller calls touch the experience of incarnation—of consciousness manifest not simply as consciousness-of, but consciousness-of realized as the object of another subject-consciousness. In other words, Miller is amplifying the Hegelian thematic of desire, of Man as Desire. This sense of "touch" must also be recognized in Williams. Even the illusion of interpenetration, of internalization of the other in touch, cannot for Williams end in the annihilation of difference, lest it annihilate the self. Note that his motif of lesbianism in *Paterson*, Book Four, deals with this appetite of devouring desire as the obverse and complement of divorce, the mirror images of two kinds of annihilation. There is a thematic of distance and desire in Williams' poetics, a poetics which depends on the contiguity of differences, on touch as marriage which heightens the individuality of each partner.

in the dance, the two partners do not become one, as in some
ideal union, but they join in their separateness and therefore
incorporate a third. They confirm society; a new relation
exists. Thus Williams identifies marriage with writing, as Dev
Evans of *A Voyage to Pagany* makes "a wife of his writing"
(VP, 108). In speaking of Marianne Moore's poetry, Williams
isolated "two essential elements": the "hard and unaffected
concept" of the singular object itself, the object "as an idea,"
and "then its edge-to-edge contact with the things which
surround it" (Imag., 315). To have edges, a thing, image or
idea must not only be sharply defined, but sharply related.
Things must be put in touch, "without connectives," for
poetry itself is the "inevitable connective" (Imag., 315). A
poem is not an "object," but a "machine" or a "field" (CLP,
4). Things, detail, facts—like isolated phonemes, they have no
being when they have no relation. Until they are brought to
being in the field of the poem, which is the tapestry or web of
their relations or intersections, they do not exist. Thus the
self—until it achieves a marriage, or brings itself to touch—is
not, has no existence. Marriage, says Williams, was for
Marianne Moore one of the "legitimate object(s) for art." It is
the form of original measuring.[19]

Poetry is like a city, and a city is like poetry, not because of

19. Williams was preoccupied with the figure of language as marriage. In some
notes prepared for *Paterson*, Book Three (MS now in the Beinecke Library of Yale
University, New Haven, Conn.), he contemplated the following: "To marriage: no
ideas but in things. Metaphor is a marriage—right and free." In the manuscript
collection at the Lockwood Library of the State University of New York at Buffalo,
Env. 36, Williams sketched in the theme of "divorce" in relation to the "University,"
the two being opposites of "marriage." Subsequent citations in this chapter will refer
only to the Yale MS and Buffalo MS. (See also, Chapter 5 of this study, and especially
note 42.) Divorce, in the early sketches for *Paterson*, Book One, was related explicitly
to the mind-body split: "Sew the mind and the body, Dr. Axel"; "Knowledge is in
marriage." "The world is a city with a university, perhaps attached to a church, trying
to convert the natives out of themselves to—a litany." He called this the "usury of
knowledge" (Buffalo MS). And again from the Yale MS, the following lines, later
canceled, intended for *Paterson*:

any metaphorical transference—like that which takes place between the city of God and man's secular city—but because the two are "intersection of loci" where "multiplicity may become revelatory" (Imag., 314). They are both *places* of a gathering, that is, structures. A poem, then, may scramble the received syntax of detail, in order to reveal some core or "luminous background" that exists only in the relation of detail. But the detail exists for the revelation and not for itself, as in Marianne Moore's poetry the "interstices" allow the light to show through while the "interstitial web of the thought," or the meaning of the particular detail, is of no real concern (Imag., 315). Marriage can be an object (and metaphor) for poetry because it is an instance of bringing to touch or bringing to place opposites which in their juncture allow the light of original relation to shine through. Poetry, Williams noted in a daring analogy, is the compromise between leaving the page white—thus providing no grid of edged objects through which some light might shine—and making it all black—like prose, which fills in everything with the solidity of continuity, narrative, and the like (Imag., 316). The analogy is all the more remarkable for its inexactness. But it tells us something about Williams' sense of the poem as a gathering of objects which do not singularly mean, but are because they are edged upon others, composing a weave of disparate loci through which there may shine a light. Otherwise, there is no

---

Knowledge is in marriage: Difficult
                    We are
starved for the knowledge of words, the words
fallen from the profitless tree lie under them
the earth like the bottom of an old belly—waiting
for a poetry that never comes to inform them
with new sap—never comes—while
history and erudition father them
into bonfires to burn brilliantly—with pregnant
smoke—
                    or they rot and go
back to the ground
                    subtly deformed . . .

light. In this space, we are witness to the coming into being, or coming to light, of being—which Williams calls revelation, or in other contexts, invention. Marriage is the form of renewal: "For our wedding, too,/ the light was wakened/ and shone. The light!/ the light stood before us/ waiting" (PB, 181), he recalls in "Asphodel."

Touch, then, is inseparable from marriage, marriage from his definition of the local, the local from a geometry of place. By bringing the received history of a place into question, Williams takes us into the moment of history's *événement*, as beginning. His poems take us into the place of illumination, or flowering, a place characterized by the manifold of proximate things. The poem is in this sense a measure. It breaks down the representational surface to the elemental. To be originary it must discover a new measure, quite simply "new" in that to repeat any old measure is to fall into the mimetic fallacy. And the mimetic fallacy for Williams is the fallacy of isolating the object in its meaning; it is the fallacy of content, which is the fallacy of the thing as idea or as symbol. It is the fallacy of repetition as teleological myth; for Williams evolution was as surely a theory of imitation as was Plato's. The bringing of things into contact, edge to edge, on the other hand, is originary, in that it is a repetition of what Heidegger calls the act of "inaugural naming." The poet's naming repeats originally the act of interpretation and the original violence of creation. To do so is to deconstruct the received syntax conferred by the old names.

Beyond its implications for prosody, a subject which tempted Williams throughout his life, his preoccupation with the new measure strikes to the very core of poetics. It is Heidegger, of course, who has spoken most profoundly of the nature of poetry as a "measuring." In one of his several essays on Hölderlin, he dwells upon the poet's vision of man as "dwelling" on earth, dwelling "poetically." [20] To dwell means to build, take ground, establish a place, cultivate, make. And therefore it means to take the measure of one's place. In Hölderlin's poem, "In lovely blueness," the measure man takes is "the measure of man," man's dwelling being the measure of his distance from God, the unknown:

> As long as Kindness,
> The Pure, still stays with his heart, man
> Not unhappily measures himself
> Against the godhead. Is God unknown?
> Is he manifest like the sky? I'd sooner
> Believe the latter. It's the measure of man.
> Full of merit, yet poetically, man
> Dwells on this earth.

Heidegger's reading of this passage is a classic of his kind of hermeneutics, since its own violent deconstruction of the poem's rather conventional language performs an act very like that which the poem itself performs. Heidegger's rendering of Hölderlin's "logic" is remarkably simple. God is unknown; yet He is the measure of man. But how can the unknown be a measure, since we assume that a point of reference is locatable? If God is locatable, He is known, and thus cannot be man's measure. In this case, the manifestness of God, the unknown, is the trace of the mysterious. The unknown is the "measure of man," but only because the poet can take the sky's manifestness as a trace of the otherwise unknown. Unlike Melville's Bartleby, Hölderlin prefers to believe, and takes as his measure the recognized mediation of the sky. But here is Heidegger's rendering:

> What is the measure for human measuring? God? No. The sky? No. The manifestness of the sky? No. The measure consists in the

20. See ". . . poetically man dwells . . . ," Martin Heidegger, *Poetry, Thought, Language*, trans. and introd. Albert Hofstadter (New York: Harper & Row, 1971), 213–29.

way in which the god who remains unknown, is revealed *as* such
by the sky. God's appearance through the sky consists in a
disclosing that lets us see what conceals itself, but lets us see it not
by seeking to wrest what is concealed out of its concealedness, but
only by guarding the concealed in its self-concealment. Thus the
unknown god appears as the unknown by way of the sky's
manifestness. This appearance is the measure against which man
measures himself.[21]

The measure, Heidegger continues, is crucial precisely
because it is a mediation of the unknown; the sky, the sign, is a
trace that marks a break with the problematic origin. It is the
measure of man as earthbound, as "on" and "beneath," two
pre-positions that span and define the human dwelling. Man
measures himself against the unknown by relating himself to a
place that is familiar to him and alien to God, and placing
himself on the earth and beneath the sky. Williams is a poet at
some remove from the mad visionary Hölderlin; yet because he
is a poet who thinks the place of the poet, he is obsessed with
measure. Williams has described his earliest gesture of resigning himself to reality, and thus giving up the idea of God or a
transcendental measure, as the crucial early decision that gives
impetus to his poetic project. (This resignation will be
explored in detail later.) God is not concealed but is dead, and
with Him goes the mediating manifestation of the sky. But the
mysterious unknown, the ground within the ground, remains,
and thus the problem of man's measure remains. In Williams
as in Hölderlin, if we can follow Heidegger's interpretation,
the pre-positions remain. The (re)source of "light" is encased
in the darkness of the earth, like a primal energy, and revealed or
discovered only as the alien of the dark, like a radium within
the pitchblende in the Curies' laboratory. Williams' urgent
need for a new measure is without question the need
inaugurated by the Nietzschean decree; for if God is dead,

21. *Ibid.*, 223–24.

then so is Man. That is, man as the measure, as what Emerson called the "central man," is no more. Man exists only within a measure, an object (not a subject) in a field of objects.

As surely as Hölderlin's, Williams' poetry seeks to take man's measure as on or beneath. But the sky defines him as beneath a system of planetary objects in motion, and moving in remote relation to them. Man is an object subject to the indeterminacy principle of all acts of measuring. On the other hand, the earth "on" which he stands contains its own mystery, and therefore appears as the mediation of the unknown energy which plays within it, an unknown which shines like an "indifference" through the interstices of adequately measured things. It is only the massive prose of reality, undifferentiated and thus unmeasured, that shuts out the possibility of light, that casts a solid surface (like matter) over the ground and refuses man his measure. It refuses him measure precisely because it denies him access to the unknown as unknown, just as materialist theories of the real absorb man into the common origin (undifferentiated mass) and deny him measure because they deny his difference. Thus Williams' theme of "descent," whether to the ground of "desire" (IAG, 136) or in search of the ground of some new place (P, 78), is integral to the act of measuring, of opening new places, of renewal. Descent, as in the Kore myth, follows an initial loss, a violence, and is the measure of the search for renewal. It is also itself a violence, a penetration of surfaces, a questioning of the ground.

"The measure intervenes, to measure is all we know" (P, 239)—thus the beginning of the end of *Paterson*, Book Five. Measure is an intervention, a coming between. Even edges, sharpened by touch, are the margin of a difference. Charles Olson defined the skin, "the meeting edge of man and external reality," as the place where "all that matters does happen. . . .

The meeting edge of man and the world is also his cutting edge," [22] where the transaction of experience takes place. This edge prevents the reification of subject or object, joining the two in an intimate, reciprocal, transactional difference. Louis Zukofsky's use of optics to explain the Object as that point of the lens where the rays of an object are brought to a focus offers a parallel example.[23] For Williams, touch objectifies in that it creates an authentic relation of differences. Touch is more than merely sensation. Touch is being in touch. It is a closing of distance, a bringing into place. Touch, then, is a form of measuring, a kind of dance. For as it brings man to lie with the bride whom he has whored, it measures their discovery against the "forbidden wealth of the Unknown" (IAG, 131) that drives Williams' man of desire to his wandering.

Language is Williams' measure of man. Man lives in the house of language, and carries out his transactions there. And language is the perfect instance of touch as measure. Through language man touches the world of things. He does not take possession of the world but takes his place in it, not as subject but as object. The self or subject becomes object in language, which Williams calls the "embodiment" and "emplacement" of knowledge. It is appropriate that both marriage and the city are at once figures for and manifestations of this kind of knowledge, of relation, and that each is a supplementary figure for the poem. But the modern city and the modern marriage are not such figures. On the contrary, they are manifestations of the failure of language, of its loss of measure, of its historical diaspora: evident in the divorce that characterizes the contemporary relationship of man and woman, in the unbridgeable distance between culture and nature, and most crucially in man's "blockage" from

22. Olson, *Selected Writings*, 60, 62.
23. Louis Zukofsky, *Prepositions* (New York: Horizon Press, 1967), 20.

others, or from the "other," and thus from the relation called "marriage."[24]

24. In part two of *Paterson*, Book Four, Williams explores the theme of discovery as dissonance, or as a violence which breaks up the mass of undifferentiated matter to disclose the luminous origin of matter itself. That is, he explores the problem of the discovery or invention, as a form of interpretation. He takes Madame Curie's discovery of radium as his central example of discovery through violence or dissonance, but no less as the example of discovery as curiosity, as a kind of innocence, in contrast to discovery based on a pre-planned method of experience or rational deduction. At one crucial place in the sequence he includes the following rather cryptic lines: "Love, the sledge that smashes the atom? No, No! antagonistic cooperation is the key, says Levy" (P, 177). (See Chapter 4, in which the theme of deconstructive interpretation is explored in detail.)

The Levy to whom it refers is H. Levy whose *A Philosophy for Modern Man* (New York: Alfred A. Knopf, 1938), projected a Socialist theory of revolution upon the new science of probability theory. Levy argued that language manifested man's attempt to achieve stability and thus to deny the governing entity of change which is central to the nature of the universe. In Levy's theory, any idea of the "static" is an error, and the "inertia of speech" manifests that idea most universally (p. 17). Levy, therefore, rejects all dualistic theories of reality (all mind against matter theory) for the "primary factor of activity" (p. 25). He also rejects all teleological theories as inertial. And he argues that man's ordinary habits of measure, his arbitrary isolation of something in order to establish a standard of measure, was representative of the old teleological theories of presence: "Motion . . . is not formed out of these two measures, length and time, but these are derived from it . . . Motion is primary" (p. 71).

All systems of measuring are arbitrary, then, except the one which assumes the centrality of systematic motion. Levy advocates the scientific method because it is *"a precise plan for practising systematic interference"* (p. 106). That is, man does not change nature but only assists in the nature of her changes. Scientific discovery is systematic interference. History consists of periodic transformations in generalization, in the language which describes the laws of change, just as there is a constant change of phase in nature. Levy uses as example the discovery of the Periodic Law in chemistry (Mendelief table, as Williams calls it in *Paterson*, Book Four) which led to a "study of radio-active substances and then . . . to attempts at formulating the Quantum Theory that brings us to a new level of understanding of the constitution of matter" (pp. 118–19). This transformation (battle) of ideas (generalizations) he depicts as the "struggle between content and form, the attempt to retain the old form of statement in the face of a too vigorously growing content of fact" (p. 123). He even calls the University (or any large institution) the manifestation of this inertia of form. Einstein and then Heisenberg become his heroes in the struggle of the modern—Werner Heisenberg, especially, because of his contribution to the inevitable place of man in the measure (or in the role of experimenter who cannot be detached from his experiment).

Levy then continues on to adopt the new science of probability and indeterminacy to economic capitalism and political fascism, both of which are the inertial systems of legislated restraints against natural change. "Uniformity in the presence of diversity is, in fact, the keynote of this whole chapter of history" (p. 259). And Levy ends by

Homer and not Orpheus is the model for original writing,
then; for if the Modern (or in Williams' case, as I shall argue,
post-Modern) poet is blocked from his origins he no longer
conceives himself, as did Mallarmé in his Orphic desire, as
forever dispatched from home. On the contrary, like Homer,
and like the Homeric wanderer, Williams saw the American
poet as blocked from his origins by the authority of history, the
tradition. Language had become knowledge, had accumulated
a semantic destiny which separated writing from its origin.
Symbolism was only the most recent instance of this rupture of
words and things. The search for some new measure meant
having to overthrow the authority of history, and of the
literary tradition, which placed the center of measure in an
origin somewhere in the receding depth of the past. But it also
meant having to recover the original sense of measure itself.
This means recovering the "knowledge" of the original poet:

> If, as writers, we are stuck somewhere, along with others, we
> must go back to the place, if we can, where a blockage may have
> occurred. We must go back in established writing, as far as
> necessary, searching out the elements that occur there. We must
> go to the bottom.
>
> If we suspect that, in past writing, archaic forms give the
> significance a false cast we are under an obligation to go back to
> that place where the falsity clings and whence it works. We must
> unravel it to the last shred; nothing is more important. . . . We
> have to dig. For by repeating an early misconception it gains

predicting a new era, a change of phase in the human structure, a breakoff from the
old. Truth, for him, cannot be defined in regard to a teleological structure, but is the
"Unity of Theory and Practice," and thus is inseparable from the process of measuring
or interpretation in the "now" (pp. 298–308 passim).

Levy's popularization of the new science and critical philosophy, particularly his
shift of theory from science to society, no doubt satisfied Williams' need to make the
same analogy. But it is the implications of this need, particularly to understand the
origin as change (or as I will call it later, drawing upon the more rigorous thought of
Jacques Derrida, the origin as freeplay), that I take to be the crucial problem of
post-Modern poetics. It is the problem which brings into question the onto-theological
nature of Western poetics in general, and perhaps the one thing which might restore
to criticism the dignity of a necessary "human" enterprise.

acceptance and may be found running through many, or even all, later work. It has to be rooted out at the site of its first occurrence. (SE, 202)

The essays which follow are explorations of Williams' venture in searching out the original elements of writing, of going back to the place of blockage, of his attack on the mimetic tradition which has distanced us from the source of some original writing. But one must recognize at the outset that this adventure is never completed, because the "site" Williams seeks is the site of an original misconception. Writing is about writing in search of the origin of writing. It is not to be paralyzed by the loss. Indeed, the loss of the origin launches the adventure, and the origin is lost from the start. It is this freedom of inaugural naming which the post-Modern writer seeks—a freedom not only from the authority of the tradition, but the knowledge that man's measure is his knowledge that he has "a choice among the measures" (P, 278). A true knowledge is grounded in play, the dance. *Paterson*, Book Five, that consummate metapoem in Williams' canon, concludes with the figure of the dance, the "satyric dance" made to a contrapuntal "measure," that is transformed at the poem's final word into "the tragic foot" (P, 239). Earlier in the poem, the dance of the satyrs was called "pre-tragic" (P, 221). The measure Williams' poems repeatedly seek is the measure which takes place on this original site, where pre-tragic steps into the tragic, where the primordial dance of form and power, or word and thing, broke off. It is the point of departure of man into history, the place of blockage. In *A Voyage to Pagany*, the writer Dev calls it the "place of my birth . . . the place where the word begins." (VP, 116).

Williams' descent becomes a process of deconstruction, an attempt to get back through writing to the "place where the word begins," to "shoot a clarity through the oppressing, obsessing murk of the world" (VP, 116). Like Heidegger's

realm of the concealed, or place of the gods, Williams' figures
for this place harbor all the preconceptions of the philosophy of
presence that characterizes Western (onto-theological) metaphysics. Yet, like Heidegger—especially the Heidegger found
in the analyses of Jacques Derrida—Williams' concern with
the "point of departure," with the "place where the word
begins," with "radiance," ambiguously maneuvers a language
of presence into a questioning of presence, a deferring of the
concept of unity at the origin. Heidegger's *site* of poetry, like
his ontological argument, turns the language of metaphysics
upon itself, until the *site* becomes a proximity to a source that
must forever remain concealed if anything is to be unconcealed. This leads to a deconstruction of all the metaphors of
presence, of the language of unbroken immediacy, or the
nostalgic language that promises a possible reclaiming of the
unbroken. At the center of Heideggerian analysis, both of
philosophy and poetry, is the problem of the center, and the
question of the privileged or valorized language of the poet.
The poet's language is already contaminated with the metaphysics of presence, and thus condemned to a dualism which it
can overcome only by forgetting. This language assumes a
unified origin, an original unity, and implies the inevitable
closure of all systems that emanate from this generative source.
It promises the redemption of the fall into language. Words
like *history* incorporate this opening and closing, this *archè* and
telos, and man cannot think history without thinking its
ultimate suppression of difference. The same presumption is
contained in the idea of *poetry,* whether one thinks of the poem
as an autotelic form or as an imitation or representation of
some ideal form, some model of order; or even as an organic or
generative product of some "primary imagination."

Derrida's brilliant analyses of Heidegger's "deconstruction
of metaphysics," along with his own deconstructions of
Heidegger and others, have pointed up the ambiguity with

which even Heidegger confronts the priority of *presence,* or logocentrism, in his attempts to redefine the *logos,* to catch the original misinterpretation of Socratic and Platonic thinking.[25] He also points up how inescapable is the language of that kind of thinking to one who is bringing it into question. Heidegger's own thinking, therefore, cannot escape the language of logocentrism in its efforts to resituate the "subject"; he cannot get beyond metaphysics. (We will return to this again, and again.) As we have seen, his analyses of Hölderlin and other continental poets maintain the traces of a metaphysical language that they also bring into question. Heidegger explores the problem of the poet's adventure, his linguistic

25. Jacques Derrida's works include *De la grammatologie* (Paris: Minuit, 1967) and *L'écriture et la différence* (Paris: Seuil, 1967); the former, a sustained exploration of Rousseau's theory of language as the culmination of logocentric thinking, in which the priority of speech (*parole*) to writing (*écriture*) signifies the metaphysics of presence; the latter, a collection of essays on the writings of Michel Foucault, Antonin Artaud, Freud, Georges Bataille, Husserl, Heidegger, and Lévi-Strauss, among others, pursuing a similar line of deconstruction of metaphysical or logocentric thinking as evidenced in philosophical attempts to think beyond metaphysics. The concluding essay of *L'écriture*, "La structure, le signe et le jeu dans le discourse des sciences humaines," has been translated into English and published in Richard Macksey and Eugenio Donato (eds.), *The Languages of Criticism and the Sciences of Man: The Structuralist Controversy* (Baltimore: The Johns Hopkins University Press, 1970), under the title "Structure, Sign, and Play in the Discourse of the Human Sciences." It is a discourse on the methodology of Lévi-Strauss and also a broad statement on the difficulty of carrying interpretation beyond metaphysics, of deconstructing metaphysics, when the only language one has is the language of metaphysics. The long essay "Violence et métaphysique," appearing in *L'écriture*, is an indispensable text for understanding Derrida's analysis of philosophical texts and his view of the problem of interpretation. It is also a crucial statement of his debt to and difference from Heidegger, and his approach to studying the place of *logos* in Heidegger's thought.

More recently, Derrida has published *La dissémination* (Paris: Seuil, 1972), another collection of essays, including "La double séance," the long two-part "La pharmacie de Platon," and the title essay, which suggests the ramifications of Derrida's attempts to think away the center. "La différance," which first appeared in the *Bulletin de la Société Francaise de Philosophie,* LXII (1968), was reprinted in *Theorie d'ensemble* (Paris: Seuil, 1968), and has been translated and included as an addition to Jacques Derrida, *Speech and Phenomena: And Other Essays on Husserl's Theory of Signs,* ed. and trans. David B. Allison (Evanston, Ill.: Northwestern University Press, 1973). *Speech and Phenomena* is a translation of Derrida's *La voix et le phénomène* (Paris: Presses Universitaires de France, 1967).

adventure into the proximity of an origin, the place of the
gods, that can never be unconcealed. The origin must be
named to be questioned, and can be questioned only in terms
of the possibility that there is an authentic language. The poet's
adventure is to uncover this language of proximity. Is the poem
Heidegger describes, therefore, symbolic or representative of
the concealed it can never unconceal? Is this concealed a truly
generative source, a presence that emanates into the form of
the unconcealed, into the word where being comes to be?
There is no easy answer, beyond the kind of detailed
deconstructions which Derrida has performed on Heideggerian language.

On the other hand, a poet like Williams—by rejecting the
transcendental place of the gods that Hölderlin names and
Heidegger takes as the starting point and problem for placing
the poet—seems to offer the critic a clearer, less ambiguous
problem. Does he not simply substitute immanence for
transcendence, things for ideas, and therefore one concept of
the *ground* for another? If so, isn't his search for the point of
blockage an attempt to penetrate the mediate to the immediate,
like the "dark ground" of the natives of Tenochtitlan described
in *In the American Grain* which stands in contrast to the
Puritans' God? It would seem so, especially when one
considers the recurrent figures for poetry and the ground
which occur in Williams' canon: *Kora in Hell* and her implied
return; Dev Evans' search for the "point of his departure";
Madame Curie's for the "radiant gist"; the poet's search
through the "variable foot" for a constant, like Einstein's
"light" within a relative universe; even the poet's concern for
the "Beautiful Thing" which always has a "busted nose."
These are trace metaphors of a very common kind in poetry,
figures for a ground or origin, a plenitude or presence, that was
once possessed and now is lost, like the Word scattered among
words.

Still, these figures occur, as we shall see, with the same ambiguity in Williams as does the *logos* in Heideggerian thinking. They become not the center but the central problematic of his poems. They resonate with an initial contradiction. They are not the figures of either an origin or an end, but of a beginning, a breaking off; and they are associated with violence, with dissonance. Thus the "dance" lies at both beginning and end, a "satyric" dance which, unlike Yeats's Image, does not pose a question (itself unanswerable) of how we can know One in two, or the two within the One, but asserts the priority of an initial dualism. Even the "radiant gist," which can easily be associated with nineteenth-century versions of *energeia,* and therefore with the metaphysics of presence—even the figure of "radiance" and the "dissonance" which is its first sign—becomes under the pressure of a deconstructive analysis something contrary to *presence:* not a concept of the origin at all, but the name of a "beginning" that is arbitrary and diacritical. If, as Dev Evans says, man wants to discover the "place where the word begins," what he discovers is the place of "birth" that is a place of violence—pagan, mysterious, and volatile. It is also the place where he discovers the beginning of writing. In fact, that book is an exploration into the origins of a writer and a discovery that his writing launches him into a voyage of exploration which can only lead back to a new beginning, the beginning of an American writer who must also invent the ground of his writing, rather than appeal to some traditional ground. Like all of Williams' figures that seem to belong to the tradition of a poetry of presence— even his arguments in *Spring and All* for the separate and privileged origin of poetry in contrast to prose, and his insistence that the language of poetry is hidden within the language of everyday—the figure of "radiance" tends to accentuate its own problematic the more it is accentuated. It becomes the name of a starting point, a beginning that is not

valorized as an immutable and present presence, another form
of the "beautiful illusion," but something that precedes the
concept of presence. It has no name. It precedes the word. It is
primordial. It is not a unity, but a dissonance. And it is
therefore an opening, a violent and inaugural beginning of the
word which the word can never name. It therefore precludes
the idea of closure, of its being recaptured in the language
which took birth from it. One must begin again, as Williams
repeatedly warned, to think the beginning. It is a problem for
criticism as well as poetry.

1

The only human value of anything, writing
included, is intense vision of the facts, add
to that by saying the truth and action upon
them—clear into the machine of absurdity to
a core that is covered.
   God—Sure if it means sense. "God" is
poetic for the unobtainable. Sense is hard to
get but it can be got. Certainly that destroys
"God," it destroys everything that interferes
with simple clarity of apprehension.
                                        (Imag., 259)

The concept of the beginning of a river is of
course a symbol of all beginnings
                                        (IWWP, 74)

The Ek-stasy of Beginnings

I

"I am a beginner," says the narrator of *The Great American Novel*, "I am an American. A United Stateser" (Imag., 175). The sentiments recall Whitman, but the bravado protests too much. Adam has grown testy. Williams is certainly in the "Adamic" tradition of American poetry, as one of our major critics has called it; but he stands at the near end, the doubly self-conscious end, of that tradition. He writes in and of a time when, in Wallace Stevens' words, the old gods have been "annihilated," leaving us "feeling dispossessed and alone in a solitude, like children without parents." [1] Stevens' figures are a measure of the passage of the Adamic poet beyond "Hegelian formulas," as Whitman once called his poems; they are the language of the poet who has doubly fallen. [2] "A great poem is no finish to a man or woman but rather a beginning"—thus the

1. Wallace Stevens, *Opus Posthumous*, ed. with introd. Samuel French Morse (New York: Alfred A. Knopf, 1957), 206–207.
2. I am using *fallen* here not simply in the theological sense of Adam's or man's fall, and certainly not to invoke the paradox of *felix culpa*, but in the sense of Heidegger who defines existence, or "factical existence," as a "falling *from* primordial, authentic temporality." See Martin Heidegger, *Being and Time*, trans. John Macquarrie and Edward Robinson (New York: Harper & Row, 1962), 486 and *passim*. The Heideggerian concept is also extended to language which comes into being as the disclosure, and therefore the "house," of being; being comes to stand in *place* in language, is inflected, thus falls or declines (*enklisis* or *declinatio*) into its temporality. Also see Heidegger's *An Introduction to Metaphysics*, trans. Ralph Manheim (New York: Anchor Books, 1961), 48–49.

43

bard of the 1855 edition of *Leaves of Grass*, who recognized like Charles Olson's Melville, though with less shock, that "We are the last 'first' people." [3]

It would be possible to write a "history" of American poetics in terms of "beginnings," or better, in terms of the changing sense of beginning. For as Williams concluded, *American* is synonymous with *beginner*, and a beginner is one who, if he is not to be condemned to repeat the past, is bound to reinterpret it and thus to create his own time. He is not Whitman's "literatus." [4] The American poet, Williams suggests, is any poet committed to the endless search for his own origins. He is committed, that is, to the paradoxical role of depriving himself of all his myths in his effort to discover a primary myth—an idea coincident with things, where his new beginning will not be repetition. He is committed, therefore, to doing violence to the very thing he loves, the romance of his

3. Charles Olson, *Call Me Ishmael* (San Francisco: City Lights Books, 1947), 14. "Beginner—and interested in beginnings"—this is the way Olson describes Melville's original Americanness. "Melville had a way of reaching back through time until he got pushed back so far he turned time into space"; "Melville went back, to discover us, to come forward." Melville's quest is for the point where origins and beginnings are one, where time is space. Also see Edward Dahlberg, *The Sorrows of Priapus* (Norfolk, Conn.: New Directions, 1957), 59: "All men hunger for Alpha. . . . The first shall be last and the last shall be first is geologic scripture." The passage is from a section of the book dedicated to Williams.

4. I by no means wish to deny the significance of Whitman for Williams, or deny that Williams can be studied in the Whitman tradition. James Breslin's *William Carlos Williams: An American Artist* (New York: Oxford University Press, 1970), is only one of several important studies of Williams as a Modern Whitman. On the other hand, Williams' relation to Poe has been largely ignored if not completely dismissed, perhaps because of Poe's renown as the inspiration behind *Symbolisme* and as a poet whose work reflects nothing of his native ground. But Williams, especially in *In the American Grain*, viewed Poe otherwise, as a poet of the local and a seeker after originality; he claimed that the French misinterpreted Poe. My concern here is to define Williams' Americanness in this figurative sense of a seeker after origins, the ground of creation. Therefore, I will tend to emphasize Poe as a principal reference for Williams' poetics. See also James Guimond, *The Art of William Carlos Williams* (Urbana: University of Illinois Press, 1968), and Sherman Paul, *The Music of Survival* (Urbana: University of Illinois Press, 1968), for important studies of Williams' Americanness.

native history, in order to reveal the ground of his own historicity. For he is aware, ironically, that his every effort to recover his innocence, to speak the primary myth, which is the act of Adamic naming, is an act of mediation (of interpretation) which throws him once more into history. He must repeat a beginning that is already broken with the origin.

Williams' "United Stateser" is different from Whitman's "literatus," to put it another way, as the idea of play is different from the idea of presence and absence.[5] For Williams, the poet must be a beginner because he can no longer accept the myth of presence, of meaning given from outside one's "place." American poetry and American history have been misinterpreted, Williams argues, because of the poets' and historians' embrace of tradition, their perpetuation of the myth of the Idea, whether it is the myth of Western history, of Christianity, or of Literature. Every attempt to escape the myth of presence, even Whitman's radical democratization, only reconfirmed it. The beginnings Whitman speaks of, then, disguise the myth of the Idea in the metaphors of process and continue the dominant Platonic tradition which bears within itself a self-evident plenitude of meaning. This plenitude fills language, permeates all utterance, and words become at once things themselves and a transparence of Spirit.

The continuity of American poetry, to employ Roy Harvey Pearce's appropriate metaphor, is characterized by a series of radical discontinuities. Our Adamic poets have, at every turn, had to try to begin again, to supply and resupply a succession of privileged centers as old ones were demystified and

5. As Jacques Derrida has shown, the one identifying characteristic of Western onto-theological thought is the idea of presence or of the center, or the idea of structure or system the center of which exists at the same time outside and inside the system. See especially his essay, "Structure, Sign, and Play in the Discourse of the Human Sciences," in Richard Macksey and Eugenio Donato (eds.), *The Languages of Criticism and the Sciences of Man: The Structuralist Controversy* (Baltimore: The Johns Hopkins University Press, 1970), 247–49. This will be explored in some detail in Chapters 3, 4, and 5.

disappeared: the Puritans' wrathful God for the Anglican Word; the Deist's Reason for the Puritan God; the Transcendental Spirit for Deity; Self for Spirit; self for Self. Finally, as Wallace Stevens says, the dominant Idea became the idea of deprivation and dispossession, and the poets found themselves in the last believable center. The creative self, the "literatus," the imagination became the latest myth of the subject as presence, and when it in turn was questioned for its immanence, it proved to be "unreal": "When the time came for them to go, it was a time when their aesthetic had become invalid in the presence not of a greater aesthetic of the same kind, but of a different aesthetic." [6] This is the moment of double self-consciousness which marks the Modern poet's Adamism from the Transcendental Adamism of Emerson or Whitman. It envisions a world with an *absence* rather than a *presence* at its center, and thus a world, or more precisely, an "aesthetic," that is different from the old. It would be something of an oversimplification to distinguish the two aesthetics as a difference between a privileged consciousness and a dislocated self-consciousness; indeed, Stevens' insistence on naming the new time an aesthetic reveals the sameness (or *like*) implied in any talk of *difference*. Absence (Stevens' "unreal" imagination) ties itself to presence (the real of reality). Stevens' poetics remains uneasily within presence/absence metaphysics.

The continuity of Adamism in American poetics is certainly the continuity of successive (not progressive) new beginnings, of having to provide a new aesthetic, to reinvent the subjective and thus to reinvent history and language *as if* at their origins. And this is true whether the poet is intent on recovering some original Word, like Hart Crane, or, like Stevens, on providing a new aesthetic which "from the point of view of greatness was

6. Stevens, *Opus Posthumous*, 212.

that of an intenser humanity." [7] But the most radical invention, Williams discovered, was provoked by the metaphysical deprivation that ultimately brought even the finite self into question, as Nietzsche's death of God pronounced the end of man. For that not only emptied the house of being, it dispersed the locus of history. It made the "point of departure" a fiction. In Stevens' words, this forces the "American" poet to accept the possibility that our primordial "parents" were not human after all and that the dream of an "intenser humanity" was simply the last great "fiction," the "passion for yes." It also forces him to confront the violence of origins, the terrifyingly inhuman power of the origin which we name in order to pacify.

Stevens, it is true, had played with that very possibility as inherent within his new aesthetic. The annihilation of the gods was, for him, a freeing of the self from the "old nostalgias," or beliefs, which tied the self to a parent before or beyond the world. It was at once a deprivation and a dislocation of the self, an emptying of the self to the point of nothingness. But even at that point of utter "poverty"—when as Crispin experienced it the "whole/Shebang," including man's "mythology of self," exited—absence itself had to be imagined: "The absence of the imagination had/ Itself to be imagined." [8] Stevens clung to the late Cartesian fiction, of an "increasingly human self," the fiction of the center in man, even when he admitted it was problematic: the moonlight and Aquinas "spoke,/ Kept speaking, of God. I changed the word to man." [9] Stevens' humanism, however, presumes that we "believe without belief, beyond belief": "the nicer knowledge of/ Belief, that what it believes in is not true." [10] And though his "imagination"

7. *Ibid.*, 212–13.
8. *The Collected Poems of Wallace Stevens* (New York: Alfred A. Knopf, 1954), 37, 28, 503.
9. *Ibid.*, 245.
10. *Ibid.*, 336, 332. One might also compare the adage in *Opus Posthumous* (p. 163): "The final belief is to believe in a fiction, which you know to be a fiction, there

retains vestiges of Romantic "nostalgia," the idea of a "shaping spirit," he is just as likely to place the center elsewhere, in reality, and more important, in the ultimate belief-beyond-belief in the possible marriage of idea and thing. In other words, Stevens employs every doubt except a doubt of the fictional necessity of presence. He can thus maintain a belief in the "source of perfection." The source of perfection lay in the self's capacity to think beyond itself, to be other in the presence of the Other. This allows man to live in discontinuous and successive acts of the mind (those incarnations of the self in words) and thus to perpetuate a fiction of a continuous self. The imagination could project the "giant on the horizon," the "giant of parental magnitude," as an image of man the seeker after a perfection he could never possess. In that projection, man could give himself the fiction of futurity. He could cast an image of himself, paradoxically, as potentially the "centre on the horizon." [11] In the end, Stevens is a Modernist poet on the verge of a new beginning. He never quite escapes the ultimate Cartesian cleavage: "Adam/ In Eden was the father of Descartes," [12] and the "supreme" must therefore always be a fiction, that presence which is unimaginable except that its absence cannot be imagined. The later Stevens marks the impasse of a sophisticated Adamism, for his Adam is the father of Western history, of consciousness. His poet or "central man" is the figurative father of the problematic of language.

In that notoriously contentious prologue to *Kora in Hell*, Williams first recorded his clash with Stevens over the place,

---

being nothing else." And his remarks, in the same volume (p. 202) on the consequences of Max Planck's investigations in quantum theory on Planck's will to believe: "It is unexpected to have to recognize even in Planck the presence of the poet. It is as if in the study of modern man we predicted the greatness of poetry as the final measure of his stature, as if his willingness to believe beyond belief was what had made him modern and was always certain to keep him so."

11. *The Collected Poems of Wallace Stevens*, 443.
12. *Ibid.*, 383.

or centrality, of imagination. Responding to a letter from Stevens, in which Stevens had remarked on the unnecessarily miscellaneous character of the poems in *Al Que Quiere*, Williams rejected what he called the "apparition" of a "finality" in nature, comparing the fiction of that belief to a belief in literature as a sacred order of its own (Imag., 13–16). The argument, very briefly, turned on Stevens' insistence that a "book" should have a center, or be centered around a "fixed point of view." To "fidget with points of view," Stevens had written, "leads always to new beginnings and incessant new beginnings lead to sterility." Stevens' insistence on the idea of a "book," and hence on the superior order of poetry with its privileged and stable center (of imagination locating itself in the world) is clear enough evidence of an early romanticism about which his later work would vacillate. Williams, on the other hand, had recognized his own affinities with Imagism, and responded that his apparent randomness was in fact his belated version of " 'Vortex' after the fashion of London, 1913." Stevens' insistence on the central imagination, says Williams, creates a poetry of "associational or sentimental value" which is, indeed, "lack of imagination." The imagination, he goes on, must not subsume the "object" and compose things by an "easy lateral sliding," that is, relate things metaphorically by resemblances.[13] On the contrary, it must

13. Stevens, indeed, could never resolve the problem of the center and until the end held to the fiction of presence even if one had to recognize it as a fiction. In "The Effects of Analogy" and "Three Academic Pieces," both included in *The Necessary Angel* (New York: Alfred A. Knopf, 1951), he emphasizes the centrality of metaphor to his poetics, even though it is a horizontal rather than a vertical conception of metaphor: "Resemblance between things . . . [is] one of the significant components of the structure of reality" (p. 72); "Poetry is a satisfying of the desire for resemblance" (p. 77). As for the problem of the center this concept of horizontal resemblances generates, Stevens could only respond with his idea of the necessary fiction: "It is easy for us to propose a center of poetry, a *vis* or *noeud vital,* to which, in the absence of definition, all the variations of definition are peripheral"; "If there was, or if we believed that there was, a center, it would be absurd to fear or to avoid its discovery" (pp. 44–45). In late Stevens, the search for the center displaces the preoccupation with its actuality, and the search becomes "never-ending."

bring things into "one plane," and allow for the "flexible, jagged resort. It is to loosen the attention, my attention since I occupy part of the field." The argument between Stevens and Williams comes down to something like the distinction Roman Jakobson has made between metaphor and metonymy, and thus between two reciprocal functions of language that in turn imply two very different origins.[14] The field of metonymic art, characterized by contiguity and successivity, and by difference, reveals a center which is everywhere and nowhere, in which imagination is a force and not a focus.

It could very well be argued here that the germ of Williams' poetics is contained in this debate, but at this point it is necessary only to stress the "field" or single "plane" on which self and objects mutually coexist in an imaginative category. The self and nature are different, but they occupy the same field, and are not defined hierarchically. Indeed, self and thing are identical only in the relation of their reciprocal difference. In the imaginative category, each is a center or locus of intersecting forces. The field admits no fixed or locatable center, and thus no a priori subject. This is, in effect, Williams' new aesthetic which, as Stevens foresaw, would demand incessant new beginnings, Williams' very antidote to the sterility of literature. For literature, as he admonished Hilda Doolittle (H.D.) in that same prologue, had assumed a

---

14. See Roman Jakobson and M. Halle, *Fundamentals of Language* (The Hague: Mouton, 1956), particularly the last sections of Jakobson's "Two Aspects of Language and Two Types of Aphasic Disturbances," where he draws broad generalizations between poetry as metaphoric and prose as metonymic, but does suggest that the "sign systems" of certain arts, particularly the "language" of cubism and the montage techniques of film are fundamentally metonymic as opposed to metaphoric. Most important, however, is Jakobson's observation that the two opposites cannot exist in isolation, but are binary, and that if a style tends toward one of the poles it must inevitably return toward the other. Williams' interest in the cubist techniques as an analogy with his poetic experiments, as we have seen and will again see, suggests that he is trying to move poetry from the primary metaphorical language it is toward a more primary metonymic language, a primordial language as Heidegger calls it.

sacredness by arriving at a "point of arrest where stabilization has gone on past the time"—or, to put it simply, literature had come to repeat itself in its search for a perfect order. Literature had valorized itself, or become institutionalized, as our new fiction of presence. "There is nothing sacred about literature, it is damned from one end to the other. There is nothing in literature but change and change is mockery" (Imag., 13)— thus Williams commits himself to an imagination which will "make its way by compass and follow no path." It will follow no prescriptions of truth and beauty. It will not metaphorize or anthropomorphize nature. Modern poetry must take the way of the "wanderer," the self moving amid things on the plane of things, in a field of incessantly changing relations and hence of "incessant new beginnings." Only then will it be like ancient poetry, or better, like original poetry. But if one has memory, how can one escape history? How can one avoid the knowledge of his distance from origins, the pathos of his repeated beginnings?

II

At one of the crucial points in *Paterson*, Book Three (a poem of acute reversals) where apocalypse and revelation, beginning and end, meet and entwine in a complex of styles and thematic evocations, Dr. Paterson confronts the problematic of his utterance:

> How to begin to find a shape—to begin to begin again,
> turning the inside out : to find one phrase that will
> lie married beside another for delight . ?
> —seems beyond attainment .   (P, 140)

In its larger context, the passage becomes an "American" style, a glimpse of what Williams means by beginnings. In three full pages preceding this quotation, Dr. Paterson has offered: an example of "broken" style, including a surrealistic exercise in

typographical violence; a "letter" from Pound offering him a
reading list which includes myth, history, and anthropology as
correlative studies; and a page devoted entirely to the measure
of Paterson's geological substrata, as recorded at an artesian
well near the Passaic Rolling Mill, a careful reminder that
one's pursuit of water to the source involves a precise, scientific
measure of the ground one lives on. Immediately preceding the
passage cited above, Dr. Paterson repeats a phrase from
Thomas Gray's churchyard "Elegy" (in the parodic visual
form of an inverted pyramid, or drill) in order to suggest,
possibly, the implications of a probing descent to the elemental
ground, to the darkness where ends and beginnings intersect.
The "Elegy" reference is followed by a broken prose stanza on
the effects of the Paterson flood of 1902, from out of the
"detritus" of which there appears the "attractive brokenness"
of a few recovered "stones" (like the other ubiquitous "rocks"
of the poem) which the poet envisions for future "garden uses."
Thus Williams counters Pound's "Rock Drill."

Immediately following the question of how to find a new
"shape," Dr. Paterson records George Barker's remark that
*"American poetry is a very easy subject to discuss for the/ simple
reason that it does not exist."* The context, however, doubles
Barker's irony and defines "American" poetry with a proper
tautology—it is literally the poetry of ex-istence, of coming to
be or standing forth, and is to be identified only in its
primordial qualities as a language which always precedes
reflection. Like the attractive brokenness of the stones emerging from the "granular stench" of the flood; like the fragmentation of the surrealist montage; like the original madness of
Pound, conflating Frobenius' Paideuma and Ovid's *Metamorphoses* as a primordial "Everyman" library of beginnings; like
the layer-on-layer of sandstone (water rock) which lines the
artesian well at Paterson—like all these, American poetry performs an unlayering (a de-structuration) or descent toward the

primordial, hence a quest for the elemental "shape." Williams would later figure this fetal "shape" as the old man on the bridge in "The Desert Music," just as earlier he had tentatively defined the "great American novel" (see Imag., 158–227) as the emerging new form itself, altogether different from the aesthetic of the traditional (English) novel form. An "American" novel must literally precede definition. But in this same sense, of course, its consciousness of its own newness becomes a discourse on its own primordiality—a metapoetry.

"To begin to begin again"—that is "American" poetry. And thus if one insists on looking at it as "literature," as a precious object with a revealed presence and traditional value, he will see the very opposite of the traditional "work" of art, the formal product of a creative imagination. For beginning implies beginning "to find," and thus a "broken composition," as Williams called it in the prologue to *Kora in Hell*. In poetry, this implies a launching out without prescribed rules, with a compass but no marked path; in history, it is the urge to explore, to go beyond the boundaries of the named and known, a desire to know the original point where water and rock were one, where time and place were married—to know, as he puts it in *Paterson*, "the myth/ that holds up the rock," the "inspiring terror" concealed in the "cavern" where the "profound cleft" first took place (P, 39). These are figures of a primordial time of emergence, the moment of that "profound cleft," and the voice of the "father of all/ speech." The beginning, for the American poet, is his beginning of his search for a new language, and thus for the origins of language itself. His beginning, therefore, is never at the source, but somewhere downstream from the source, or outside the cavern whence he came and where the "father" of his cleaved (historical) thought remains shrouded.

The American poet begins in a history, and thus as the recipient of a language, which he must deny or destroy or,

more exactly, turn inside out if he is to "begin again." "Now I
am not what I was when the word was forming to say what I
am," proclaims the narrator of *The Great American Novel*. His
beginning is preoccupied with the problematic of beginnings.
"If there is progress then there is a novel," he begins.
"Without progress there is nothing. Everything exists from
the beginning. I was a slobbering infant" (Imag., 158).
Ex-istence is a fall into a language which carries the "I" farther
and farther from that beginning, an experience which brings
the teleological idea of "progress" into doubt even as it creates
the "I." The "I" does not create but is created with the fiction
of progress, the fiction of the cause as Nietzsche called it.[15] *The
Great American Novel* progresses by turning the idea of
progress inside out—progress away from the beginning toward
an ideal end, the teleological view of progress, becomes
progress inward toward origins: "Words progress into the
ground" (Imag., 158); "A novel must progress toward a
word," but not toward "*the* word" (Imag., 165); and progress
is a "game," the game of liberation, of moving "with the

15. One might compare this with Pound's remarks: "In the 'search for oneself,' in
the search for 'sincere self-expression,' one gropes, one finds some seeming verity.
One says 'I am' this, that, or the other, and with the words scarcely uttered one ceases
to be that thing." Ezra Pound, *Gaudier-Brzeska, A Memoir* (New York: New
Directions, 1970), 85. The urgency to escape subjectivity had inevitably to produce a
discourse on the ontological nature of the subject which, as Nietzsche had
demonstrated, could only disclose the fiction of the subject: " 'Everything is
subjective,' you say; but even this is interpretation. The 'subject' is not something
given, it is something added and invented and projected behind what there
is.—Finally, is it necessary to posit an interpreter behind the interpretation? Even this
is invention, hypothesis. . . . Through thought the ego is posited; but hitherto one
believed as ordinary people do, that in 'I think' there was something of immediate
certainty, and that this 'I' was the given *cause* of thought, from which by analogy we
understand all other causal relationships. However habitual and indispensable this
fiction may have become by now—that in itself proves nothing against its imaginary
origin: a belief can be a condition of life and nonetheless be false." Friedrich
Nietzsche, *The Will to Power*, trans. Walter Kaufmann and R. J. Hollingdale (New
York: Vintage Books, 1968), 267–68. See also *The Will to Power*, 294–95, and
Friedrich Nietzsche, *Beyond Good and Evil*, trans. Marianne Cowan (Chicago: Henry
Regnery, 1955), Section Four.

words" to the point where the words are broken free "from the world," or received knowledge; and the self is there with them, as in a "church" which is also the "Wife," everything co-existing in the "dreams of his babyhood" (Imag., 166–67). Progress is backward and inward, the "movement" of words or of "writing" (Imag., 173) which breaks up the novel's "fixed form" in its pursuit of what the Dadaist's called *rien*, the place of the origin of things. But each step of this progress, this deconstruction of successive ideas of the center, only produces another figure for origins, each pointing further back to the point of birth, that original violence.[16] The novel progresses by violence, the play of interpretations over other interpretations.

"So this is the beginning" (VP, 256). Thus the end of *A Voyage to Pagany* announces the novel's journey, and also the novel, as a pretext. The new beginning follows Dr. Evans' return from a search for the "point of his departure, the place of his birth" (VP, 116). The place is Rome, where pagan and Christian history converge. Rome is the origin of the myth of history, the city which barely suppresses the pagan roots which would bring into question the teleological myth of the West.[17] Rome also is imitation Greece, but it has suppressed the pagan vitality of classicism. (VP, 101). Evans' trip to Vienna, where he studies pediatrics but more significantly strikes up an affair with some mysterious dark lady and begins to write, provides the clue to the meaning of the voyage. There, he discovers himself to be an obstetrician of the "word." The most obvious implication of his brief affair, and his studies in this Freudian

16. Cf. Nietzsche, *The Will to Power*, 70: "Faith is *'progress'*—in the lower spheres of intelligence it appears as an ascending life; but this is self-deception; in the higher spheres of intelligence as descending life."

17. See also, Sister M. Bernetta Quinn, "*Paterson*: Landscape and Dream," *Journal of Modern Literature*, I (May, 1971), 530, for the derivation of "pagany" from *pagus*, as explained by editor Richard Johns of the "little magazine" *Pagany. Pagus*: "any sort of collection of peoples from the smallest district or village to the country as an inclusive whole." One cannot, however, avoid the implications of the pre-Christian, and even prehistorical, in Williams' search for a "point of departure."

center, is its release of his own suppressed energy, the beginning of his birth as a writer-discoverer that leads inevitably toward the novel's end and his beginning. What Evans seeks to recover at his "place of birth" is the buried "gods." The "death of the gods," and therefore the beginning of Western history, has impoverished Europe he discovers: the Europeans "starve, not because there is no food but because there is no one to give it to them any more" (VP, 8). His search for his sources, for the old dead gods, is the manifestation of his desire for a "burning presence under the veneer of to-day" (VP, 109). In his feverish writing, "he had penetrated too far the veil of dust the gods had thrown up about their secrets to protect them," and therefore, "Panting with desire to possess" the secret, "he feels it slipping away nevertheless and calls it, strives to call it by a name, strives to fasten it in his sight—real among its everyday disguises" (VP, 109). Writing pursues a "secret" endlessly, and possesses only what slips away or what it destroys: he "liked the unknown best . . . a presence nearer than the nearest day he had ever known" (VP, 104).

In *An Introduction to Metaphysics*, Martin Heidegger records the history of what he calls the original misinterpretation in metaphysics, the cleavage which took place in the Socratic interpretation of the pre-Socratics, the original error of separating words from things, meaning from being, or, in the original Greek terms, *logos* from *physis*. It is a sophisticated and complex argument, but the gist of it can be summarized as follows: that the history of philosophy is the history of thought separating itself from being, so that we can no longer stand in the presence of being as that which is disclosed or unconcealed. Therefore, we no longer understand the reciprocal difference between *logos* and *physis*, thinking and being, as it existed, for example, at the beginning of philosophical thinking, figuratively in the pre-Socratics. For *logos* and *physis*, he argues, were originally words which incorporated in themselves "being," in the sense of that which comes into being—is disclosed, or unconcealed (*aletheia*)—in the sense of opening out from some hypothetical origin. In the rational breaking apart of the two words, the original sense of this emerging power was lost to both, *physis* being reduced to something like physics or nature and *logos*, to idea or reason. The cleavage of rational thinking has led to an obscuring of the reciprocal difference of *physis* and *logos*. The inextricability of being as that which emerges or breaks out or stands up (*physis*) and of being as that which is gathered together or collected (*logos*) changes into the priority of *logos* or reason to *physis* or things. It must be the effort of original thinking, says Heidegger, to return to original thinking, and thus to repeat itself. But this does not mean to take received thoughts and apply them to the world. To repeat original thinking is to return, in the act of thought, to the original unfolding, or unconcealment, to the experience of "origin as emergence." This thinking reveals to us not that "thinking and being are the same," as the Parmenidean maxim has historically been interpreted (subordinating being to the a priori of the *logos*) but that thinking *and* being are reciprocally interrelated as primordial opposites, and thus the irreducible pairs of all beginnings.[18]

Heidegger demands a new beginning to our thinking man's historical adventure: "But we do not repeat a beginning by reducing it to something past and now known, which need merely be imitated; no, the beginning must be begun again, more radically, with all the strangeness, darkness, insecurity that attend a true beginning." [19] Man's power is language; man is the creature who realizes his humanness by being projected

18. Heidegger, *An Introduction to Metaphysics*, 110–11, and 98–165 *passim*.
19. *Ibid.*, 32: "Repetition as we understand it is anything but an improved continuation with the old methods of what has been up to now." Cf. Williams' preoccupation with repetition as "plagiarism" in *Spring and All*, and the need to begin again.

into the *place* of his speech. Thus poetry is, for Heidegger, language involved in its original work—the disclosure of being. But it is always involved in the crisis of beginnings. "Unconcealment," the original coming into being, is a beginning which man is repeatedly losing:

> Since it is a beginning, the beginning must in a sense leave itself behind. (Thus it necessarily conceals itself, but this self-concealment is not nothing.) A beginning can never directly preserve its full momentum; the only possible way to preserve its force is to repeat, to draw once again . . . more deeply than ever from its source. And it is only by repetitive thinking . . . that we can deal appropriately with the beginning and the breakdown of truth. The need (Not) of being and the greatness of its beginning are no object of a merely historical observation, explanation, and evaluation. This does not preclude but rather requires that the historical course of this collapse be as far as possible elucidated.[20]

Thus we return to "unconcealment" through "work"—"the work of the word in poetry, the work of stone in temple and statue, the work of word in thought." [21] Poetry and philosophy become original poetry and philosophy not by extending received truths but by repeating the original act of unconcealment, which involves a breaking up (deconstruction) of the already unconcealed, those received historical forms.

Heidegger offers a number of entrances into Williams' poetics. For as Heidegger knew, the search of the philosopher (especially the modern philosopher of "deconstruction") and of the naïve poet is a common search, though they occupy, in the phrase of Hölderlin held so dear by Heidegger, dwellings on the "peaks of time" which are "near to one another,/ Tired on mountains farthest apart." [22] Williams' intuition that, at the

20. *Ibid.*, 160.
21. *Ibid.*
22. Quoted in Martin Heidegger, *Existence and Being*, trans. Douglas Scott (Chicago: Gateway edition, 1967), 256. From "Patmos, Dem Langrafen von Homburg," the relevant lines go as follows: "Drum, da gehauft sind rings/ Die Gipfel der Zeit,/ Und die Liebsten nahe wohnen, ermattend auf/ Getrenntesten Bergen"

origin, there are "no ideas but in things," his sense of modern man "blocked" from his sources, his awareness that the "language has failed" man by divorcing him from the power of his beginnings—these reveal the common *ground* the post-Modern poet and the "deconstructive" philosopher must seek. The poet is aware that he "begins" historically somewhere apart from his sources, and thus within the received language and values of history, so that his beginning is a search for beginnings. Yet, it is a beginning which like all beginnings launches him out from the unknown into the unknown. It is an act which involves him in "all the strangeness, darkness, insecurity that attend a true beginning."

If beginnings are necessarily concealed, left behind, they are, as Heidegger says, "not nothing," since they are everything that being is "Not." The seeker after beginnings is a seeker after his necessarily concealed sources who, like the poet breaking down language in search of its concealed primordiality, acts out his role at a point nearer the source than other men. Thus Heidegger's figure of the *site* of poetry. The poet acts in a "place" (*topos*) that is neither a total unity (the place of the gods) nor totally within history (like the place of the common man, who is spoken by his language, that "idle talk" which constitutes the "they").[23] The poet *places* himself at the point of e-mergence, of disclosure, of the coming to light of being. He is an in-between man. The significance of

and are translated by Michael Hamburger, in *Hölderlin, Selected Verse* (London: Penguin Poets, 1961), 194, as follows: "Therefore, since all around the summits of Time are heaped, and the most loved live near, growing faint on most separate mountains. . . ." The poem begins (in Scott's rendering), "Near and/ Hard to grasp is the god. . . ."

23. See Heidegger, *Being and Time*, 211, 213. "Idle talk" (*Gerede*) is not a "disparaging" term, says Heidegger, but signifies everyday "understanding and interpreting," the "possibility of understanding everything without previously making the thing one's own." Williams' "roar" of the "great beast" in *Paterson*, the latter term borrowed from Alexander Hamilton who did use it disparagingly, corresponds to Heidegger's term in that it stands for a language which fails of the authentic.

Williams' poetics lies in the rediscovery of the poet's *place* in history—not as an individual talent who stands at the present point some distance from the source of his continuous tradition, but as one standing in the proximity of his source, and thus in the proximity of history's beginning.[24] Williams' poetics echoes Heidegger's in insisting that the role of the poet is to participate in the act of "inaugural naming"; therefore, his *place* is the place where language breaks out, where we are brought into the presence of its first appearing, its beginning to take "shape," its flowering.[25]

Williams' first significant poem, "The Wanderer" (CEP, 3), is an adventure of the poet taking his "place," of his ADVENT. The young "novitiate" of "The Wanderer" has his advent in a question put to him by his muse-crone, an old woman in the form of a "young crow" who compels him to seek a new place and role: "How shall I be a mirror to this modernity?" The question is accompanied by her own natural metamorphoses, her final form being that of a "great sea-gull" who vanishes with a "wild cry": and "in my mind all the persons of godhead/ Followed after." The vanishing of the "godhead"

24. For Heidegger's treatment of the "place" of the poet, his proximity to the "source," see his essays on Hölderlin in *Existence and Being*, and especially the essay "Language in the Poem," in Martin Heidegger, *On the Way to Language*, trans. Peter D. Hertz (New York: Harper & Row, 1971).

25. In *Spring and All* Williams concluded: "Sometimes I speak of imagination as a force, an electricity or a medium, a *place*" (Imag., 150). In his contribution to the MANIFESTO for the little magazine *Pagany*, he wrote: "the word, a meaning hardly distinguishable from that of place." And in a review of Kay Boyle as an artist, which is really an apology for American expatriation or alienation from place: "I speak of a work of art as a *place* where action has occurred as it occurs nowhere else" (Imag., 341—my italics). As I suggested in the Introduction, Williams' "place" has much in common with Heidegger's place of "gathering," or "*logos* as gathering and togetherness" in contrast with the idea of place as things unified by a common center or One: "never a mere driving-together and heaping up. It maintains in a common bond the conflicting and that which tends apart. It does not let them fall into haphazard dispersion. . . . It does not let what it holds in its power dissolve into an empty freedom from opposition, but by uniting the opposites maintains the full sharpness of their tension" (Heidegger, *An Introduction to Metaphysics*, 113). Compare Williams' figure of the city and the poem as a "*gathering up*" (P, 2).

leaves him alone, at one with her in "whom age in age is united," attendant upon the "first day of wonders." He comes to occupy, with her, a place of original difference, "out of sequence." It is a place without perspective, without past or future, with one "face." The young poet is brought into the presence of "the first day," a day of the primordial "Taking shape" of a "high wanderer." He becomes a part of, not apart from, nature as change.

Awkward and tentative though it is, "The Wanderer" struggles to articulate the perspectiveless moment of human beginnings, the simultaneous beautiful terror of life emerging from the immediacy of a "gutter," of life coming to definition as culture out of nature, or language out of the simultaneity of things and forms. He pleads to be "lifted still, up and out of terror,/ Up from before the death living before me." His initiation, then, is an introduction to the necessity of taking his place as wanderer, in the midst of the river's "rottenness." The river is a place of simultaneous ends and beginnings, where a chaos of potential forms broils about him, without "sequence." His "ecstasy" (literally, his ek-stasy) ended, his "life" begins. It is a "new wandering." His leap into the "filthy Passaic" is a baptism, a sinking in, a resignation to nature, a return to the "crystal beginning of its days." But at that place, the river "rebound[s]" and leaps forward. The melting of sense and sense, of subject and object, is a point of "rebound," the renewal of the eternal movement "backward and forward," a reversal. It is also an e-mergence, the beginning of the new difference of subject and object. He has moved from place to act (ecstasy—ek-stasy). Poet and river are not married in a primal unity, or stasis, but in terms of a primordial or original opposition. The poet, the subject, is born a wanderer: not an essential or pure self, detached from the world, or a soul with transcendent origins; nor, especially, is he a subject lost in the primacy of the other. The wanderer takes his identity, as poet, only in his immediate and reciprocal relation with the river. He is situated. The relation is the essential opposition and reciprocity of thinking and being. The "wanderer" is the language of the river, admonished by the old woman to "Be mostly silent." Time is "washed finally under," and a new time begins in the river's "rebound." [26] The "new wandering" of the young poet is (to be) the on-going speech of the place, which is "mostly silent." It is a new speech emerging from the reversal of the old, a turning of the inside out. Wandering, quite simply, is the condition of original cleavage. The wanderer is original man. He is historical man, a Cain figure, an ecstatic condemned to repeated new beginnings.

In his *Novelette*, Williams' narrator speaks of the beginning of life in terms very similar to the young wanderer's beginning, not as a "progress upward" but a "progress downward to the beast. To the actual. To the devil with silks. But there cannot be an objection to an intelligent cutting away of obscurity that is not a return to an old cesspool. Violent nonsense" (Imag., 300–301). This progress, like that of *The*

26. This baptism in the stench of an alien but elemental and primordial other (both earth and water) is only the first of Williams' many figurative descents (a motif treated elsewhere and at length), to be repeated almost endlessly in his poetry from *Kora in Hell* to "Desert Music." For one thing, it is an act of resigning the privilege of the subject, and of escaping the alienating distance from the world of which the subject is simply one part, like a thing. For another, it constitutes the act, the dynamic, which is not a dialectical condition implying some future resolution or ultimate synthesis. It is, therefore, another of the metaphors of beginning, and in its way a repetition of the timeless beginning of history.

As Heidegger notes, in a commentary on one of Georg Trakl's poems, this descent into a beginning is intricately related to wandering: "Day goes through evening into a decline that is not an end but simply an inclination to make ready that descent by which the stranger goes under into the beginning of his wandering. Thus change conceals a departure from the traditional order of days and seasons." In Chapter 3 I discuss the "seasonal" structure of *Paterson* in much these same terms. It should be noted now, however, that this is an attempt by the philosopher, which Williams himself confronted, to entertain the idea of beginning which would escape from repetition, and thus from copying or plagiarizing nature. Also, as Heidegger notes of Trakl's "persona," the descent recalls that of Nietzsche's Zarathustra, who begins his journey with a descent toward his primeval childhood in order to recover the power of his departure. Heidegger, *On the Way to Language*, 172, 174.

Great American Novel and *Kora in Hell,* involves a violence and a sinking of sense into sense, a descent into "nonsense." It enacts the necessary closing of Cartesian distance that Hillis Miller finds to be the starting point of Williams' poetics.[27]

Years afterward, Williams described the experience which motivated "The Wanderer" as his "resignation to existence," a "sort of nameless religious experience" which wiped out the distancing, sequential order of time and reconciled him with his present world and thus with the "first day of wonders": it was "a despair which made everything a unit and at the same time a part of myself. . . . Where shall one go? What shall one do? Things have no names for me and places no significance. As a reward for this anonymity I feel as much a part of things as trees and stones. Heaven seems frankly impossible. I am damned as I succeed. I have no particular hope save to repair, to rescue, to complete" (SL, 147). His confession illuminates the condition of "new wandering," for the wanderer is one deprived of all hope of self-transcendence, or even of an identity apart from place, of a self apart from the field it walks, and takes intimate measure of, or designs. But the wanderer is not merely an object among objects; he is a language, a completer or rescuer. Williams' "resignation to existence," like the young poet's leap into the "filthy Passaic," is in two senses a "nameless religious experience": it is the assumption of anonymity and a reciprocal placing of the subject in the field of a mutually defined and defining other. It is literally a re-sign-ation, or the beginning of a new act of naming. "To repair, to rescue, to complete"—the poet as namer does complete by re-signing his place, and his new naming is intrinsic to the simultaneous coming into being of himself and his place. It is a place not so much defined as in process of definition, of being named.

27. J. Hillis Miller, *Poets of Reality* (Cambridge, Mass.: Harvard University Press, 1965), 287.

The artist, Edward Dahlberg once reminded Williams in a
letter which is included in Book One of *Paterson* (P, 29), is
an Ishmael whose wandering incorporates the "affliction" of
restlessness, of desire. But the name of the original wanderer is
Cain, the exiled and violent "son"—the son of the original
namer. The archetypal wanderer exists in the land of Nod (of
dream), a murderer and man marked for murder. He is a man
resigned to existence, and thus man who willfully murders the
unobtainable "God" for the obtainable "sense," the "simple
clarity of apprehension," as Williams calls it. He is a man
unwilling to accept the old names of his father, one hungry to
pursue sense to the concealed "core" of being. He is a man
whose freedom is reciprocal with his mortality, who exists in
"action." [28] The wanderer is one who takes his place somewhere beyond the concealed and silent origin of history but
refuses to be dominated by history. He is not quite at
"home"—and thus, like Cain, wanders in the land of dream—
but neither is he entirely of the people. He is restless for some
new ground, some city.[29] The wanderer is a builder of cities, as
we will see.

28. Heidegger, *Existence and Being*, 283–84. The "field of action of poetry," says
Heidegger, "is language. Hence the essence of poetry must be understood through the
essence of language. Afterwards it became clear that poetry is the inaugural naming of
being and of the essence of all things—not just any speech, but that particular kind
which for the first time brings into the open all that which we then discuss and deal
with in everyday language. Hence poetry never takes language as a raw material ready
at hand, rather it is poetry which first makes language possible. Poetry is the primitive
language of a historical people."

29. The enduring historical role of the poet (and the image of man) as wanderer
in the labyrinth of time has been recently studied by Angus Fletcher, in his *The
Prophetic Moment: An Essay on Spenser* (Chicago: University of Chicago Press, 1971).
Fletcher's opposing categories of temple and labyrinth, of closed and open space,
paradise and fallen world, are as he says not confined to a medieval and Renaissance
mythology or history of ideas or to a pre-modern visionary and prophetic literature,
but are the enduring polarities of man in his struggle to interpret his historicity. See
Williams' *Autobiography*, p. 60, for his account of an early Keatsian and Spenserian
poem of wandering (which preceded "The Wanderer"), the story of a young prince
lost in a "foreign" country "whose language was barbarous," seeking his way "home."

The poet, as Heidegger says in his remarkable essays on Hölderlin, stands somewhere between the gods and the people, and thus is an outcast, an in-between man who stands closest to the unnameable, mysterious power of origins. It is only through him—his naming of the gods or mediation of their otherwise silent signs and the common voice (idle talk) of the people—that we can come to understand the true nature of man as the coming into being of language. For in the end, Williams gives a role to the poet, outcast and anonymous, that recalls Heidegger's paradoxical view of the poet whose original utterance is also a poetry about poetry:

> Hölderlin writes poetry about the essence of poetry—but not in the sense of a timelessly valid concept. This essence of poetry belongs to a determined time. But not in such a way that it conforms to this time, as to one which is already in existence. It is that Hölderlin, in the act of establishing the essence of poetry, first determines a new time. It is the time of the gods that have fled *and* of the god that is coming. It is the time of *need*, because it lies under a double lack and a double Not: the No-more of the gods that have fled and the Not-yet of the god that is coming.[30]

III

In one of the improvisations of *Kora in Hell*, Williams muses on the fate of the old gods and the situation (the site) of the Modern poem:

> Giants in the dirt. The gods, the Greek gods, smothered in filth and ignorance. The race is scattered over the world. Where is its home? Find it if you've the genius. Here Hebe with a sick jaw and a cruel husband,—her mother left no place for a brain to grow.

Later, in *Paterson*, he would reinvent the city-labyrinth of which Fletcher writes, but a city which lacks, though it needs and the poet desires, a poem-temple.

30. Heidegger, *Existence and Being*, 289. Heidegger's essay forcefully dismisses the common charge against Modern poetry, that it fails of energy because it is so much about itself. It is not, he says, an "exaggerated narcissism due to inadequate richness of vision," but an indication of the poet's recognition of his place and of the "time" from which he speaks.

Herakles rowing boats on Berry's Creek! Zeus is a country doctor
without a taste for coin jingling. Supper is of a bastard nectar on
rare nights for they will come—the rare nights! The ground lifts
and out sally the heroes of Sophokles, of Æschylus. They go
seeping down into our hearts, they rain upon us and in the bog
they sink again down through the white roots, down. . . . It's all
of the gods, there's nothing else worth writing of. They are the
same men they always were—but fallen. Do they dance now,
they that danced beside Helicon? They dance much as they did
then, only, few have an eye for it, through the dirt and fumes.
                                                              (Imag., 60–61)

If all writing is of the gods, it is not of the old departed gods
but of their eternal power to return. The gods anticipated by
the Modern poet are "fallen gods," or gods scattered through
the single plane of the earth. That is, the present gods, which
all writing is about, are not transcendent; and because they are
not, writing emerges from a different place—any "local."
Imaginative writing may be an attempt to recover presence;
but self-consciousness, its own historicity, leads it to question
its own constitutive act. It becomes in turn a questioning of the
ground. The traditional place of art is turned inside out, or is
brought to the "ground." The presence of the modern gods is
not locatable in some transcendent site; their power is suffused
throughout the earth. They are fallen in the sense of scattered,
like the languages of Babel.

In the prose of *Spring and All*, Williams explores this "fall"
in terms of the new imaginative plane of cubist art. Modern
art, he says, takes "familiar, simple things" and, while
maintaining their independent reality (difference), arranges
them contiguously to compose a new space. The individual
things are distinct, mimetic of the "real," but the new relation
is imaginative, as in a painting by Juan Gris in which things as
logically unrelated as a "shutter, a bunch of grapes, a sheet of
music, a picture of sea and mountains" are related in a "unity"
of "admirable simplicity and excellent design" (Imag., 110–

11). It is a picture (even a picture within the picture) which calls attention to itself as art, as imaginative. Or as dream. This assertion of its "detached" plane, says Williams, was "not necessary where the subject of art was not 'reality' but related to the 'gods'—by force or otherwise. There was no need of the 'illusion' in such a case since there was none possible where a picture or a work represented simply the imaginative reality which existed in the mind of the onlooker. No special effort was necessary to cleave where the cleavage already existed" (Imag., 111).

Classical art recognized the cleavage of ideal and real in taking the gods for its subject and denying the illusion of realistic space, but the new art "cleaves" and asserts its cleavage. Classical art could assume the presence of the gods, and could represent their reality as an Idea. Thus it represented the constitutive power of the Idea. "The only realism in art is of the imagination," Williams asserts, not because art uses real things but because it "detaches" things from the ordinary and de-signs them on a new plane. The realism of cubist synthetic art is classical realism turned inside out, undoing the "beautiful illusion" of perspectivism. Juxtaposition, not perspective, is the order of relation; particularity and difference, not an expected syntax of relations—this defines the "field" lifted out of the ordinary. Modern art must retain the illusion of the ordinary and thus the presence of the cleavage, whereas the old art assumed the cleavage between the world and the ideal, with their respectively ambiguous and pure centers. The old art, in a sense, was at "home" in the ideal; it was a symbolic art, yet mimetic. The new reveals the artist as wanderer, in that plane between the gods and the ordinary, where "age in age is united" and "out of sequence." The old art could re-present (in Williams' terms, copy) the idea of the gods and thus was metaphorical; the new must present (in Williams' terms, imitate) the flowering of the new gods, and thus be metonymical. The "new" therefore brings the idea of Art into question.

The new presents, however, what Heidegger calls the "new time," of the "double-Not." This new time is the time of e-mergence and, consequently, of the creative moment itself. It is a "double lack" because it reveals neither the classical decorums of hierarchical forms nor the undifferentiated chaos of immediate sensations. This "time" becomes a field of distinct yet logically unrelated but contiguous things. It is decentered. As Heidegger said of Hölderlin, this kind of poet writes a "poetry about the essence of poetry," not in the sense of a paradigm to be repeated but in the sense of what Williams calls a "force moving" (Imag., 120). Thus the poetry exists at the place of cleavage, including, as *Spring and All* demonstrates, the cleavage between prose and poetry: the "jump from prose to the process of imagination is the next great leap of the intelligence" (Imag., 133–34). Writing "separates" words from their referent (Imag., 120). Inevitably, this cut demands an art that is self-reflexive. This art becomes an incessant commentary on itself, calling attention to its process of removing itself inwardly (plane by plane) from the ordinary: "The study of human activity is the delineation of the cresence and ebb of this force, shifting from class to class and location to location—rhythm: the wave rhythm of Shakespeare watching clowns and kings sliding into nothing" (Imag., 135). The imaginative process accentuates its artifices, the removal of things from their expected, perspectival, symbolic place.

To participate in this force, then, the poet must necessarily write a poetry that is at once doubly self-conscious and naïve, sophisticated and primitive.[31] He willfully attacks the old forms

31. Paul Klee's remarks on the primitivism of Modern art are relevant: "If my works sometimes produce a primitive impression, this 'primitiveness' is explained by my discipline, which consists in reducing everything to a few steps. It is no more than

and celebrates the primordial emergence of some new, embryonic ones which were spectrally there all along. Therefore, he must be his own critic, as the poet of *Spring and All* recognized: "whatever of dull you find among my work, put it down to criticism, not to poetry. You will not be mistaken— Who am I but my own critic? Surely in isolation one becomes a god—At least one becomes something of everything, which is not wholly godlike, yet a little so—in many things" (Imag., 111–12). This leads to a poetry not simply of self-exploration or prophecy, but to a poetry of self-questioning. It breaks up the illusions of perspectivism by a persistent questioning of the surface, by penetrating to the creative force "at work" in the *work*. It reveals that the force of "great works of the imagination . . . stand[s] between man and nature as saints once stood between men and sky" (Imag., 112). The poet of *Paterson*, both implicitly and explicitly, recognizes the poet's double lack, his desire which places him somewhere between the silence of the gods and the roar of the everyday language.

Paterson, in fact, begins with the death of the old gods, and the double negation of desire and fall. In an early manuscript version of Book One, Williams experimented with a dialogue between the split halves of the poetic self. He called the two voices Willie and Doc, the first a patient of the second. The Doc drinks to excess, and thinks Willie "reads too much." The Doc is obsessed with the history of the place and reads to Willie out of his numerous volumes of local New Jersey history.[32] But Willie hardly ever reads, because he is an

economy; that is, the ultimate professional awareness. Which is to say, the opposite of real primitivism." Felix Klee (ed.), *The Diaries of Paul Klee* (Berkeley: University of California Press, 1964), 237.

32. The books, of course, are the texts which Williams drew upon for much of the local historical detail of *Paterson*, two of the most important of which are J. W. Barber and Henry Howe, *Historical Collections of New Jersey* (Newark: n.p., 1853), and William Nelson and Charles A. Shriner, *History of Paterson and Its Environs: The Silk City* (3 vols.; New York: n.p., 1920).

"agent" of the "word," the "eternal word." Before it was abandoned, the dialogue went through several alternative versions. What Williams apparently was trying to relate was the place of the poet, the site of his dream, the poet being an agent of the word and thus a deliverer of the word into history. Willie (and the colloquial name may very well intend a pun on *Wille*) has no interest in the Doc's texts, for he is an agent of the vanished origins of those texts. The Doc drinks to escape the question those texts pose, or the answers they will not disclose. The language of Willie and the Doc is the language, respectively, of poetry and prose, of the gods and of man. And the poet must uncover the ground that connects the two, like poetry and prose so apparently irreconcilable—the ground of the double-Not.

The experimental dialogue reveals Williams' concern with the Modern poet's radical self-consciousness, and discloses that his willed dream of recovering a lost presence is the result of a need to fill a lack or an absence. Later, he will discover the meaning of silence as the place of the gods. Whether to be agent of the eternal word, and thus a son of the gods, or the anonymous physician, resigned to his existence and thus no more than a rescuer or completer[33]—this is the divided self, the self as desire, or lack, who is left to contemplate the other as his negative. This self becomes, in the poem's finished version, the figure of the poet as Dr. Paterson, who speaks and is the language of his place. But he speaks simultaneously two languages, like the poet of *Kora in Hell* who distinguishes

33. See *Spring and All*: "men feel an enlargement before great or good work, an expansion but this is not, as so many believe today a 'lie,' a stupefaction, a kind of mesmerism, a thing to block out 'life,' bitter to the individual, by a 'vision of beauty.' It is a work of the imagination. It gives the feeling of completion by revealing the oneness of experience" (Imag., 107). To complete, however, does not mean to resolve into the one, into an in-difference. Thus, marriage is a form of completion; the woman, as I will show later, is his figure of the completer. The argument in *Spring and All* is directed at Anatole France's charge that art is a lie, the fiction of the perfect, the "beautiful illusion."

between the traditional and the contemporary poet in terms of
the latter's need to conceal his artifice:

> *That which is heard from the lips of those to whom we are talking
> in our day's-affairs mingles with what we see in the streets and
> everywhere about us as it mingles also with our imaginations. By this
> chemistry is fabricated a language of the day which shifts and reveals
> its meaning as clouds shift and turn in the sky and sometimes send
> down rain or snow or hail. This is the language to which few ears are
> tuned so that it is said by poets that few men are ever in their full
> senses since they have no way to use their imaginations. Thus to say
> that a man has no imagination is to say nearly that he is blind or deaf.
> But of old poets would translate this hidden language into a kind of
> replica of the speech of the world with certain distinctions of rhyme
> and meter to show that it was not really that speech. Nowadays the
> elements of that language are set down as heard and the imagination
> of the listener and of the poet are left free to mingle in the dance.*
>
> (Imag., 59)

The talk of "our day's-affairs" (in *Paterson*, the "roar" of the
"great beast") is language divorced from its origins, the
language not of the "full senses" but of one limited separate
sense. It is idle talk. The "hidden language" is a language of
"full" sense. It is the language of emerging forms, of
shape-shifting, of which everyday language is a sterile, secondary mediation, the residue of exhausted names. The poet's
role, clearly enough, is to restore to man the sense of vital
mediations, to define man as agent of the eternal word or, in
other words, as the interpreter. The traditional poet moved to
accommodate the world, yet sustain the illusion of poetry as a
mirror not of "our day's affairs" but a transparency of some
more sacred power. But the Modern poet is concerned with
the reality of relations and with the elemental structures which
define man at the point of his beginning, as he departs from the
gods into history. The Modern poet, then, reveals the original
discontinuity of this departure, of his interpretation. The
"dance," a figure which I will return to often in subsequent

chapters, is the field of man's originally free relations. It is the figure of his ritual departure from nature, yet his ritual participation (and reciprocal involvement in) primary being. The Modern poet is a "wanderer," whose "place" is where nature and culture are revealed in their original interdependence and discontinuity. His "place" is language, the site of utterance, where is disclosed the original discontinuity between the gods (our names for which are only the signs of their power we no longer possess) and man. It is the place of new naming, and hence of violence or the primal murder.[34]

The poet as wanderer, then, participates in the experience of original dislocation which Geoffrey Hartman has brilliantly described as the Romantic resistance to self-consciousness and its need to return to mythic thinking.[35] For as Hartman says, the Romantic "journey," the primary Romantic myth, involves the fall into self-consciousness (thus solipsism) and the resulting effort (the creative act) to effect a transition from self-consciousness to imagination; the state of imagination, Hartman goes on, is in effect a return to (or desire for) the original innocence of the state of nature. It is a desire which bears within itself the impossibility of being satisfied. The source of power is inaccessible, except as this source is evoked in the sacred space (a mediation) of art, in which consciousness and nature are sustained in a timeless discontinuity. The return is possible, that is, only in the doubly stressed artifice of art. The Romantic journey repeatedly calls attention to itself as

34. The prose of *Spring and All* is preoccupied with the urgency of discovering "new forms," which are nothing but "new names for experience" (Imag., 117). Naming is bringing to existence (ek-sistence): "When we name it, life exists" (Imag., 115). And it exists because it is brought to stand in a place (language) and thus is "identified with ourselves" (Imag., 115). In the author's note to *In the American Grain*, Williams claims to have "recognized new contours suggested by old words so that new names were constituted." He therefore discovered the "strange phosphorus of the life, nameless under an old appellation." He named and brought to light.

35. See Geoffrey Hartman, *Beyond Formalism* (New Haven, Conn.: Yale University Press, 1970), 3–23, 287–310, and 311–36.

prelude or pre-text, asserts its separateness, as Williams says, or becomes a poetry about poetry. As indicated earlier, Hartman likens the Romantic myth with the myth of Orpheus, the poet doomed to failure in his desire to retrieve the sources of his own power. This myth is a significant contrast to the myth of Persephone, the myth of the cyclic continuity of nature and culture.[36] Orpheus' legend is the legend of discontinuity, of poetry as mediation. But the post-Romantic poem—that is, the post-Modern poem—returns to both to demythologize its desire for an origin that art itself has fabricated.

The poet as wanderer incorporates both the experience of discontinuity and the dream of continuity. Descent and ascent replace either the dream of the "eternal return" (Persephone) or the tragedy of loss (Orpheus). And though Williams plays repeated variations on the Kore legend (as in *Kora in Hell*), he emphasizes the rhythm between two irreconcilable poles rather than the eternal return. Descent and ascent become endless and reciprocal acts of the poet, which generate in their reciprocity a "dance" of "contending forces," a "picture of perfect rest" like the image of the vortex (Imag., 32–33). The picture is the poem which aspires to reveal itself not as perfection, or totalization, but as the "stability" of "contending forces." It is a structure of necessary opposites which denies the possibility of a superintending or transcendent source. But it is a "picture" of "perfect rest," calling attention to itself as fictional, imaginary—as art rather than nature. This distinction is crucial for Williams, because it saves him (or his poet) from the ultimate Orphic tragedy—the exhaustion of imaginative energy in the failed quest to restore or renew itself at the source, the dilemma, for example, of Hart Crane.[37] The poet

36. *Ibid.,* 16.
37. See Joseph Riddel, "Hart Crane's Poetics of Failure," *Journal of English Literary History,* XXXIII (December, 1966), 473–96.

who has "resigned" himself can escape the ultimate tragedy of
Orphic loss, of inevitably looking back at his own inevitable
loss of presence. The self-consciousness of the Romantic poet
is doubled, and therefore transformed into a resistance.

It is, perhaps, in the spirit of this recognition that Williams
began an early draft of *Paterson*, Book One, with an excursus
on the nature of the modern gods. "The gods should be
without morals," he wrote in some early tentative lines for
"The Delineaments of the Giants," because "for them there's
no one upstairs. . . . They have no one else to talk to but us,
gives them a sense of humor." [38] And elsewhere he speculated
on the consequence of their immorality (that is, lack of
limitation): "This makes them unreal to us and dangerous. We
have no counterparts to their absolutes." But it was a false start.
The old gods are dead; the new ones, fallen. When Williams
begins Book One of *Paterson* with "The Delineaments of the
Giants," he begins with the fragments of the history of place,
the exhausted *topoi* of a "time" which has lost its gods, and to
which new gods have not come, because "no poet has come"
(P, 79). He must take a "common language" and "unravel" its
complex. He cannot proceed, however, as one who speaks with
the absolute authority of the gods, but only as one speaking
from his own tenuous place of mediation, his desire. When the
poet of *Paterson*, Book Five, declares, at the beginning of
March and the reawakening of his memory, that his poem is
"Not prophecy! NOT prophecy!/but the thing itself!" (P,
242), he repeats the condition under which the entire poem
functions—that the poet can no longer speak the word pure, or
reveal what is outside of speech through speech. He can
neither speak of what precedes speech, nor reveal a future
outside the concreteness of his immediate utterance. He
cannot, that is, speak symbolically or metaphorically.

38. MS in the Lockwood Library of the State University of New York at Buffalo,
Env. 37. (Works in this collection will hereinafter be cited as Buffalo MS.)

The thing itself, he reveals, can only be the primary myth of original mediation itself. This myth, like the various marriage ceremonies appealed to in Book Five of *Paterson*, maintains the paradox of the sacred or pure which is necessarily violated in its fall into being. The legend of the virgin and the whore, which is the thematic center of Book Five, is the figure of the poet's act of naming. Williams' "thing itself" is not the philosopher's abstraction for essence or substance, what Nietzsche calls man's "will to power," any more than it is the cry of positivism or of the empirical object. It is his word for the poem as dance or as city, as the space of a gathering which has no origin outside itself and no fixed center within. The poem speaks the "myth/ that holds up the rock" (P, 39), and thus speaks of what can never be unconcealed, the "secret" of the origin. The poem is an image of the "profound cleft" of the rock, where the "shrouded" figure of "Earth, the chatterer, father of all/ speech" (P, 39) stands. The thing itself, therefore, is the form of the myth of myths, of the disclosure of *presence* as a fiction. It is at once the secretion (the trace) of presence and a questioning of the "secret." The poem, like thought, is the trace of a lost origin, an image of original cleavage.

In *Paterson*, however, it is the "giants," not the gods, who are delineated, or who come to stand in the place of the old *topoi*,[39] the giants who are the traditional mythic enemies of the

39. I am using *topos* in the sense of Heidegger, *e.g.*, in *An Introduction to Metaphysics*, 54–56, as the place of gathering, a space defined by what is collected there. In this case, it is the city, the labyrinth of human collectivity which (as Angus Fletcher has shown in *The Prophetic Moment*, 11–34 *passim*) is the classical opposite of the temple in the poet's mythological landscape. The city-labyrinth is the place of the wanderer's invention (Cain, Romulus, Dedalus), a maze which constitutes the secular laws of man exiled from the undifferentiated space of the temple. The city mythologically was founded to protect man against the giants and other outlaws. As C. Kerényi has shown, the city is the content of the act of grounding (*Gründing*) or founding, and hence man's attempt to recover his original lost ground, the ground abandoned or lost in his initial act of violence (Cain's repetition of his father's violation). C. Kerényi and C. G. Jung, *Essays on a Science of Mythology*, trans. R. F.

gods, figures of rebellion loosed by man's original fall. The giants are figures of man's desire, challenging the gods; but in the same sense they are figural marks of the discontinuity between man and the gods. The giants of *Paterson*, Book One, embody the paradox of man's Modern (post-Romantic, and thus self-self-conscious) adventure in history. The giants can be delineated, since they are the shapes of man's emergence; that is, they are the origin and end of man, rebels against the origin, and thus the origin and end of language:

> We sit and talk and the
> silence speaks of the giants
> who have died in the past and have
> returned to those scenes unsatisfied
> and who is not unsatisfied, the
> silent, Singac the rock-shoulder
> emerging from the rocks—and the giants
> live again in your silence and
> unacknowledged desire—   (P, 25)

Here, midway in the poem's first book, the poet "places" himself, and historical man, in the paradoxical condition of his desire—as one who suffers from the problematic of language and therefore endures Paterson's history. Yet, he is committed to renewing himself and thus to renewing the language. He is both Willie and the Doc of the abortive dialogue, both agent and echo of the word. The passage quoted above locates the problem at the level of language, which turns out to be the ground of being, of man's historicity. The giants of *Paterson* are man and woman, city and park, divided by the river and therefore no longer sustained by the source:

> A man like a city and a woman like a flower
> —who are in love. Two women. Three women.
> Innumerable women, each like a flower.   (P, 7)

C. Hull, Bollingen Series (New York: Harper Torchbooks, 1963), 14. In *Paterson*, first the death of the gods and then the theme of the divided and silenced giants express the thematic of a lost "ground." Thus, the motif of the giants, who can only be heard again in the silences of "talk," reveals the inseparable nature of the poem and the city as a grounding. The new "ground" will be a new language.

"But/ only one man—like a city" (P, 7). That is, man is place (or *topos*), a gathering; woman is flowering or emerging, the form of original energy. Woman is nature and man, culture. And language is both—the language of everyday, and the language which is "hidden." The "divorce" of Paterson is the divorce of the two, a cleavage which conceals the original reciprocal marriage of opposites: of ideas and things; man and woman; culture and nature; form and power. The first book of *Paterson* is engaged in no less a primordial adventure than Heidegger's visionary poet, Hölderlin, who provides the philosopher with his paradigmatic line: "Much man has learnt./ Many of the heavenly ones he has named,/ *Since we have been a conversation/* And have been able to hear from one another." [40] (Italics mine.)

As Heidegger makes emphatic, these lines define man not simply as the creation of language, but as the fallen self that is but half of any conversation; and, more important, its past tense records his historical departure from his origins. *Since* we have been a conversation, the gods have been given names, have become fixed as the center or presence which defines our being as a negation. But the pastness of the tense records our own departure from that inaugural act of naming, and we come to exist in a conversation that conceals the original relation. *Paterson*'s "talk" of the "giants" records the poet's awareness that, for man at the end of history, conversation must be renewed, as if at the beginning. Every poem is a renewal of the conversation, a talk which brings a "we" to-gather over the silence of their "desire." The giants, the primordial emerging rebellious energy itself, live only in the talk that marries opposites into a "we," the implied sameness and difference of coexistence. Quite simply, the giants live again only in the "thing itself" of the poem, as supplements of

40. Heidegger, *Existence and Being*, 277. The line which I italicized has sometimes been translated as "Since we have been a discourse."

the origin, the silence or space of original opposition. The remarkable series of passages which surround this central naming in *Paterson*, Book One, indicates luminously that the "silence" in which the giants "live" again is the zero-degree of speech itself. The "talk" is like "air lying over water" which "lifts" (a favorite Williams word for bringing to expression or making to stand up) "the ripples, brother/ to brother, touching as the mind touches,/ counter-current" (P, 25). It marries the classical oppositions of subject and object, power and form, into a structurally reciprocal opposition: "one that whirls/ backward at the brink and curls invisibly/ upward," the forces which make us think "separate/ worlds," or of culture as superior and separate from nature. In their "counter-current," the opposing worlds affirm "desire" as the name of man and thus as the name of language that must be at once transitive (and hence mediational) and stable (structural). The poet is forced to name language as the essentially mediatory power, and thus to name his own discontinuity with the gods. Yet he must reclaim the vitality of the giants as the name of his own desire.[41]

Paterson, then, begins both in dream and in divorce—and the language of Paterson, whether of the place or the poet of the place, is the language of history, "forked by preconception" (P, 6). That is, it is either the language of fixed and recorded events which nostalgically recalls a lost and undiscoverable origin, or the nightmarish "roar" or "thunder/ of the waters," a torrent of undifferentiated fluxing detail that confounds the certainty (and the silence) of its source. Divorced from the source, the people of the place are divorced from themselves

41. Dr. Paterson's "thoughts soared/ to the magnificence of imagined delights / where he would probe// as into the pupil of an eye/ as through a hoople of fire, and emerge/ sheathed in a robe// steaming with light" (P, 31). His thoughts are thinking, acts of original luminosity, of bringing to light, naming. Yet, he must ask: "What heroic/ dawn of desire/ is denied to his thoughts?"—what lost origin, where desire is born, can never be recovered?

(mind and body) and from each other; and since Paterson's language is simultaneously the prose of everyday and the primordial "hidden language" of poetry, it reveals the paradox of man's historicity, of his desire for and his distance from his origins:

Immortal he neither moves nor rouses and is seldom
seen, though he breathes and the subtleties of his machinations
drawing their substance from the noise of the pouring river
animate a thousand automatons. Who because they
neither know their sources nor the sills of their
disappointments walk outside their bodies aimlessly for the most part,
locked and forgot in their desires—unroused.   (P, 6)

Dr. Paterson is "immortal" because he is language and incarnates its problematic: he "lies" at the base of "spent" water (the "Falls," in fact), and thus at the point of maximum energy turning into exhaustion (fallen, divorced, separated out from the origin). His breath is the mystery of water itself, the primal and the renewing element, language. His machinations are embodied in "the noise of the pouring river," at first as the indiscriminate fluction of vague shapes. What is happening here is the happening of language, the original coming into being of being, an original fall or inflection. It is a fall not from the source into separateness, however, but from its originating power into the state of auto-mata, stability. The "automatons" of Paterson are "locked" in their "desires" and do not realize themselves in their fallenness as dependent on their "conversation"—or, on the other, on language. Having fallen into history, they have failed to realize their true historicity: they are the language, the "common language," indifferent. They are "locked" in their separate "desires" (plural), or their nonidentity, and thus cannot act (are "blocked") in terms of their true historicity. Or as Williams put it in a later poem:

Innocence! Innocence is the condition of heaven.
Only in that which we do not yet know shall we

be fêted, fed. That is to say, with ceremony. The
unknown is our refuge toward which we hurtle
. . . .
                                              Flight
means only desire and desire the end of flight
stabbing there with the barbed tongue which *succeeds!*
                                        (CLP, 122)

The ceremony, the poem, is an act which feeds the lack; it is
the action between source and success, between beginning and
end, the language of becoming (desire) as emerging into
being, and the action of language (itself a lack) seeking its
return to the source. Ceremony is conversation—but it is a
relation recognized at the level of ritual as a fiction. The
barbed tongue does succeed, for it is speech which breaks up
the ceremony of innocence and launches the action (the
succession of words in speech) toward the end of desire. It was
not a naïve poet, seeking a way out of language into innocence,
who insisted in the Author's Introduction to the *The Wedge*
(the title itself being a concealed pun on the "barbed tongue"
of lang-wedge[42]) that frustration, action, and poetry were
indivisible:

42. In the manuscript of "Preliminary Arrangement" for *The Wedge*, now in the
Buffalo MS, Env. 15, Williams proposed a title page for the book:
                     The (lang) W   E   D   G   E
                                        A
                              New Summary
In another arrangement he was going to call it simply "The Language," and include a
number of short stories as "prose poems." The manuscript includes the following
unpublished poem, called "The (lang)Wedge":
                     With the tip of my tongue
                     I wedge you open
                     My tongue
                     The wedge of my tongue
                     between those lips parted
                     to inflame you.
    The Freudian innuendo is obvious enough, but as always in Williams the phallus is
related to the signifier, and thus to the word and the violence of inaugural naming, as
opening or bringing to light. Cf. Dahlberg, *The Sorrows of Priapus*, 26: "It is difficult
to know whether the tongue or the phallus is more harmful to man."

It is an error attributable to the Freudian concept of the thing, that the arts are a resort from frustration, a misconception still entertained in many minds.

They speak as though action itself in all its phases were not compatible with frustration. All action the same. . . . Who isn't frustrated and does not prove it by his actions—if you want to say so?

But through art the psychologically maimed may become the most distinguished man of his age. Take Freud for instance.

The making of poetry is no more an evidence of frustration than is the work of Henry Kaiser or Timoshenko. It's the war, the driving forward of desire to a complex end.[43]

(CLP, 3)

There are two kinds of action recorded in Book One of *Paterson*, and both are the result of desire: the action of history as violence, which leads either to a destruction of the other (of nature by civilization or natural man, the Indian, by civilized man) or of the self by itself (Sarah Cumming's swoon and fall, or Sam Patch's erratic drive, both presented as failures of communication which lead to the actors' deaths and return to a silent union with nature). Patch, of course, is the embodiment of Paterson as language, not only because his acting name is Noah Faitoute Paterson (with all the multiple implications of the biblical Noah and the American language maker), but because his act, of bridging chasms by the precarious walk on a tightrope (of overcoming the discontinuity of origin and

43. Cf. Nietzsche, *The Will to Power*, 370–71: "It is *not* the satisfaction of the will that causes pleasure . . . but rather will's forward thrust and again and again becoming master over that which stands in its way. The feeling of pleasure lies precisely in the dissatisfaction of the will, in the fact that the will is never satisfied unless it has opponents and resistance"; "The normal dissatisfaction of our drives, e.g., hunger, the sexual drive, the drive to motion, contains in it absolutely nothing depressing; it works rather as an agitation of the feeling of life, as every rhythm of small, painful stimuli strengthens it. . . . This dissatisfaction, instead of making one disgusted with life, is the great stimulus to life." The "game of resistance and victory arouses most strongly that general feeling of superabundant, excessive power that constitutes the essence of pleasure."

being) confronts in its every gesture the fundamental tensions between motion and form. The arc of his first leap reveals the wonder of man's being-toward-death, his authentic launching out. That Patch's last walk takes place over the Genesee Falls under the conditions of a staged performance, an artifice which pretends to be a "wonder" (P, 17, 10), reveals the condition of language separated from action. And that action is itself a departure. The attempt to rebridge clarifies original cleavage.

Patch's last act is no longer original interpretation. It is divorced from the original need of his original launching out. It therefore denies the primordial madness of his first leap, his thrust into the mystery of his futurity. His last leap is only a staged repetition. He has turned life into art and death. Idea precedes action. In Patch's first leap, "he spoke as he jumped"; in his last, speech preceded act. "What could he say that he must leap so desperately to complete it?" (P, 17). The first is a spontaneous leap that fulfills man's need to begin again. This leap becomes Patch's "starting point" as a performer, the great Jersey "patriot," Noah Paterson. His final leap, ironically, is an exploitation of a culture's hunger for wonder, or revelation, and leads to a "great silence." The first act is an act of original interpretation (P, 16) and reveals the wonder of the original fall-leap itself. It reveals death to be intrinsic to man's desire for wholeness, the doubling of his original fall. The repetitions, made for profit and not in the search for genesis, falsely reveal death as a silence outside the act, the illusory origin. Thus, his last speech reverses his act and returns him to nature, to the state of indifference.

In the case of Mrs. Cumming, her fall (leap? swoon?) is the ironic consequence of her husband's insistence that the two "set our face homeward" (P, 14). Home is the place of wholeness, a marriage, a place named only as that from which they have departed. Their failure of communication (sexual, social, religious) provides them no distance from the mysterious center of their lives; their lack of interpenetration (of facing each other) cannot sustain the needed relationship of "talk," in which the unstated mystery of the center is contained. That mystery is the original difference of man and woman, the fecund difference of marriage. Her vertigo, then, is a historical instance of the ironic *dédoublement* of language, of the reversal of the fall into time. The history of Paterson, New Jersey, those texts which haunt the Doc in the early version and provide detail like the story of Patch and Mrs. Cumming, suggests a mysterious and inviolable origin, like the whirlpool beneath the falls, that simultaneously beckons and resists. This origin is only remembered, like a trace that ambiguously signifies a lost power:

> A history that has, by its den in the
> rocks, bole and fangs, its own cane-brake
> whence, half hid, canes and stripes
> blending, it grins . . .   (P, 22)

The language of history speaks the silence of a primordial mystery, the enigmatic "grin" that is a sign of the unconcealed, not a symbol for it. It therefore marks the discontinuity between culture and nature, the blank of the interface which can only be recalled by "talk." A poet must come not to disclose the mystery or speak purely the language of the unconcealed, but to retrieve the trace of the origin from the debris of historical signs, the "complex" that is language and history.

IV

This "history" conceals a "first wife/ and a first beauty, complex, ovate" (like a seed), a complex which is "innate// a flower within a flower whose history/ . . . laughs at the names/ by which they think to trap it" (P, 22). History tantalizes us with its concealed *presence*. If the rhetoric of Mr.

Cumming's theology ignores the problematic of language, his
fate, the loss of his wife, bespeaks the consequences of his
blindness. The fate of the Cummings is the metaphysical
divorce of language from its source. The Cummings embody
history as divorce; and their story, recorded in the history of
Paterson, is the rhetoric of presence become an absence. That
story, perpetuated in newspapers and in books, is a misinterpretation which hides from itself its presumption of meaning.
The theme of the "first wife," concealed within the "complex"
of a "history" which is doubly concealed, suggests something
of the problem Williams confronted in writing a poem of the
local. For the "first wife" theme brings into question the very
"beautiful illusion" of *presence* upon which the idea of history
centers.

Early in *Paterson*, Book One, in a passage of poetry set
revealingly between two prose units of local history, Dr.
Paterson "remember(s)" a "picture" from the (*National*)
"*Geographic*" [44] of "9 women/ of some African chief semi-
naked/ astraddle a log, an official log to/ be presumed, heads
left" (P, 13). The nine women range from the virginal young
to the aged "last, the first wife,/ present! supporting all the rest
growing/ from her" (P, 13). From old to young, all time is
present upon the continuum of the official log. It is, as any
number of critics have observed, a phallic log. But it is a phallus
not simply in the orthodox Freudian sense meant by these
critics. Rather, it is phallic more in the sense of Freud's current
interpreter, Jacques Lacan, for whom the phallus functions as a
signifier in a linguistic chain. [45] The phallus is a sign, the

44. According to Mike Weaver, *William Carlos Williams: The American
Background* (Cambridge, England: Cambridge University Press, 1971), 202, the
"picture" refers to one in the *National Geographic Magazine*, XLIX (June, 1926),
715–16, which Weaver reproduces in his book (Plate 8). The reproduction shows six
women and, most significantly, no log.

45. See Jacques Lacan, *The Language of the Self: The Function of Language in
Psychoanalysis*, trans., with notes and commentary, Anthony Wilden (Baltimore: The

"signifier of desire," says Lacan, and thus an imaginary symbol. Without overextending the complex and abstruse maneuvering of this symbol in Williams, or claiming for him anything like the Lacanian analysis, it is possible to see in Williams' use of the "picture" a similar recognition of the language of desire. For Lacan, as for Lévi-Strauss, the phallus functions as the missing term in a system of relations and exchanges (for Lévi-Strauss, the exchanges of marriage), and thus is essential in both the familial and the linguistic order. For Williams, the log of this picture (which, by the way, Williams seems to have added) manifests a set of relations and a system of exchanges which are missing from the historical events of Paterson. Thus, the chieftain's marriage stands in contrast to the Cummings'. The poetry stands in contrast to the prose. A primitive system of horizontal yet continuous relation stands in contrast with a historical system which is discontinuous because it has lost the vertical signifier, the God-Father which it once assumed.[46]

For the natural order of the picture, the log signifies that things are "all of a piece" (P, 19, 21, 22). Along the continuum of the log, the nine wives are "packed tight up/ in a descending scale of freshness," the first wife or last wife "present! supporting all the rest growing/ up from her" (P, 13). It is an image of marriage as meaning which contrasts with all the "divorce" and the failures of communication in

Johns Hopkins University Press, 1968), 41–42, 126. Also see Wilden's comment on this distinction of Symbolic, Imaginary, and Real fathers, and the function of the phallus as signifier in a linguistic chain, *ibid.*, 186–87, 270–72, 294–97, and 304–305.

46. For a most remarkable use of the father-phallus motif in contemporary American literature, see Hilda Doolittle, *Tribute to Freud* (New York: Pantheon, 1956). Also see my commentary on it, in "H.D. and the Poetics of 'Spiritual Realism'," *Contemporary Literature*, X (Autumn, 1969), 447–73. In the same issue, Norman N. Holland offers an extensive psychoanalytical critique of this important book ("H.D. and the 'Blameless Physician'," 474–506), though his approach does not suggest the Lacanian dimensions or put nearly so much stress on the linguistic implications of H.D.'s search for the "father." See the opening of Chapter 2, wherein H.D.'s theory of language is treated in greater detail.

Paterson, and thus an image of an order in which the meaning
is driven through time, tying beginning to end along a line of
meaningful relationships and temporal differences. Placed as it
is between the prose passage concerning the Indian wars and
the creation of Jackson's Whites as an initial act of slave
trading, and the passage concerning Sarah Cumming's fall, the
contrast of relationships is self-evident: the history of this place
has been a history of progressive cleavage between the "wild
and cultured life [which] grew up together in the Ramapos"
(P, 12). The war against the Indians and the introduction of
slavery mark the violent beginning of a history which forfeits
the meaningful exchanges of a nature-culture continuum. The
phallus of desire is suppressed and with it the signifier which
allows for meaningful exchange. The culture of historical
Paterson lacks the signifier which allows exchange; and each
person, like Mr. and Mrs. Cumming, is locked in his desire.
Lacking the phallus, it lacks *logos*. It is a history that preserves
presence only through an empty rhetoric. That rhetoric
suppresses difference as it suppresses sex.

When Williams returns to the first wife theme in the
second section of Book One, he associates the wife's "giraffish
awkwardness" with the "mottled branch" that hangs at the
edge of the falls (P, 21). The picture of the first wife is "the
mottled branch/ that sings," a green rather than a burning
bush. And the first wife grips the "log" tightly with her thighs,
the log "that,/ all of a piece, holds up the others." The phrase
"all of a piece" occurs three times in the section: once as a
remark on the "theme/ as it may prove: asleep, unrecognized"
(P, 19) which runs concealed beneath the disparate and
contradictory particulars, the "pouring waters" of the poem's
language; then in the first wife passage; and for the last time in
relation to the poet's identification of his isolated self,
"swaying, all of a piece," with the mottled branch and thus
with the first wife (P, 22). In the last instance, Dr. Paterson

has picked up the theme of breath, the stale breath which was associated with death a few lines earlier (P, 20). "I draw my breath," he says, "swaying, all of a piece." It is the beginning of his speech in the face of "Divorce," the stutter of language which has left him isolated and alone. The speech leads to the "talk" between the man and woman (the "We") in which the giants come to "live" again. The concealed theme, "all of a piece," is the poet's substitute for the chief's log, the assumption of a phallus or signifier which sustains the symbolic chain of his random, disparate, and chaotic detail. His "breath" is the "lack" implied in any measure.

The "theme" of *Paterson*, Book One, is, indeed, the theme of language, of the secreted and perhaps lost law which inheres in a symbolic chain. Thus the poem comments on its own silent "dream":

> . . . a mass of detail
> to interrelate on a new ground, difficultly;
> an assonance, a homologue
> triple piled
> pulling the disparate together to clarify
> and compress (P, 20)

Or, to return to a previous figure, the theme of the poem is to drive a meaning through the diverse, to discover the new ground where the repressed law may be recognized to inhere in the mass of detail. And this in turn is related to the paternal metaphor of the title, where, as if to anticipate the Lacanian figure, the symbolic father gives way to the son, who assumes the role of the phallus-signifier, the redeemer of language. The log of the African chieftain is, therefore, a model for the language which Paterson (the place) has lost or repressed.

V

Whatever the fate of its language, the poet who awakens to the "dream" of his place knows, because he is its poet, that a law inheres there—a "myth" to hold up the "rock," a "father of all/ speech." The poet exists in that place; for he is the language of place, sensing at once that he is dispersed like the chaos of its idle thoughts and yet is "all of a piece," the one who will bring the place to expression once again. The poet is a phallus, a son. One might argue that the prose and poetry of *Paterson* embody respectively the two languages, the everyday and the hidden, that *is* Dr. Paterson's total utterance. But that would be oversimplification, if not altogether wrong. Better to say, for the moment, that the poetry is the "breath" or measure of Dr. Paterson's speech, the "homologue" which reveals, like the "triple piled" layers of a palimpsest, its emergent shape— the shrouded shape of the father of all speech. The shape, however, testifies only to the presence of a father who is absent, a center never completely graspable, an origin that is, in itself, unspeakable.

Paterson, as critics have long acknowledged, is a place name which bears within itself the dominant metaphorical relation of the poem—of father to son. It is a metaphor, however, as complex as it appears fortuitous. And when combined with the name of the speaker, the Doctor, and with his given name, Noah,[47] the son who is surrogate father of us all, another Adam, not to say, the father (Noah Webster) of an American idiom which is in turn the son of a historically given language, the Latin *pater*—when combined with these, the reverberations are nearly endless. The role of the Father in *Paterson* is no less monumental or problematic than it is in any modern discourse on discourse. It is a problem, quite simply, of the shrouded law

47. Whatever the symbolic ramifications, Williams evidently assumed the name Noah in conjunction with Faitoute as the "poetic" names respectively of himself and David J. Lyle, a kind of systems engineer who had come to live near Paterson in the late 1930s. Williams and Lyle carried on an extensive correspondence and personal exchange of ideas. At one time apparently, Williams had thought of condensing the correspondence into an exchange between poet and scientist, creating a montage that was the combined reflections of Noah and Faitoute for inclusion in *Paterson* (see Weaver, *William Carlos Williams,* 122–27).

which can neither be rejected nor comprehended, and of the homeless son, who can be neither original nor mimetic. The poet, to recall an earlier figure, is a wanderer, and thus a son, who desires to be original. And he wanders in the "time" of the "double Not."

"The best thing a man can do for his son, when he is born, is to die" (P, 171), Dr. Paterson quotes Norman Douglas as telling him, early in the second section of Book Four. He has taken his son to the "Solarium/ topping the hospital," to hear a lecture on "atomic fission." The particulars of the event, interwoven with several others, reengage the problem of "invention," or "discovery," and illuminate the problematic of the poet's desire to roll "up the sum" (P, 3) or discover the law which will make the poem whole. For only in such a "sum" is the "radiant gist" revealed, the place where all differences are centered and from which all meaning originates. The Solarium is an apt place to hear a lecture on atomic structure and the discovery of radium; it is a place of gathering, of people and of solar light, and presumably a place of radiance or illumination. The language, as the section indicates, puns incurably on the myth of radiance, and the modern discovery of the god Ra. But the section deals also with discovery by violence, by "fission" or breaking apart, and with the necessary and simultaneous displacement of one center by another. Man's desire to possess the "sum," to know his world whole or possess it by scientific knowledge, has led to the tyranny of the father, of experience or history and its symbolic authority. Dr. Paterson for the moment associates himself with "those pigs," the other doctors, who reproach his son with "experience, that drug,/ sitting erect to their talk:/ valences" (P, 202). Their "valences" are derived from a world already known; they lack curiosity, unlike the young "nurse girl," Madame Curie. Yet he desires to "Smash the world, wide!" and open its "fetid womb," that "sump" which belies the true "sum." Dr. Paterson, that is, bears within himself the contrary impulses of closing and opening, of pater and son, of the law and the *logos*. The son, like the "ignorant sun" of the Preface, which is "rising in the slot of/ hollow suns risen" (P, 12), is the emerging word, coming to replace the father, to bring into question the rigid law and received grammar of the father's world.[48] He represents, therefore, the sacrifice of the father; he displaces the fiction of original unity; like the namesake of the

48. Cf. Jacques Derrida's reading (deconstruction) of the Platonic *logos*, in "La pharmacie de Platon," *La dissémination* (Paris: Seuil, 1972), 84–95. Assuming to explore not simply Plato but that Platonism which buttresses the whole conceptual scheme of Western metaphysics, he proceeds to analyze Plato's "pharmakos" and its function in regard to the *logos:* "l'origine du *logos* est *son père*. On dirait par anachronie que le 'sujet parlant' est *le père* de sa parole. On aura tôt fait de s'apercevoir qu'il n'y a là nulle métaphore, si du moins l'on entend ainsi l'effet courant et conventionnel d'une rhétorique. Le *logos* est un fils, donc, et qui se détruirait sans la *présence*, sans l'*assistance* présente de son père. De son père qui repond. Pour lui and de lui. Sans son père, il n'est plus, précisément, qu'une écriture. C'est du moins ce que dit celui qui dit, c'est la thèse du père. La spécificité de l'écriture se rapporterait donc à l'absence du père. Une telle absence peut encore se modaliser de diverses manières, distinctement ou confusément, successivement ou simultanément: avoir perdu son père, de mort naturelle ou violente, par violence quelconque ou par parricide; puis solliciter l'assistance, possible ou impossible, de la présence paternelle, la solliciter directement ou en prétendant s'en passer, etc." This very important essay is one of Derrida's most exacting deconstructions of logocentrism, treating mythic figures or "sons" like the alphabet god Thoth as a form of the "supplement." In an interview with editors of the French periodical review, *Promesse*, which has been translated and published in the American periodical, *Diacritics*, II (Winter, 1972) and III (Spring, 1973), Derrida reviews his relation to Heideggerian thought and re-explores a number of his favorite terms, like *différance*, the *supplément*, the *pharmakon*, *hymen*, *trace*, etc. He resists calling them concepts; he denies that they have "meaning," or can be defined—that is, that they can function within the horizon of what we ordinarily think of as signs. *Dissémination*, for instance, he relates to language through what he calls "*playing* . . . upon the fortuitous resemblance, upon the purely simulative kinship between *seme* and semen. They are no way interconnected by meaning. And yet in this skidding and this purely external collusion, the accident does produce a sort of semantic mirage, its reflective effect (*effet-reflet*) in writing sets a process in motion" (Winter, 1972, p. 37). One must heed this commentary about the *play* of Derrida's method; otherwise his punning analyses will be only so much nonsense, which in a punning way they are intended to be. His play upon the role of "son" as *logos* depends upon this strategy of deconstructing the intermediary role of the son in a number of myths about writing or language, the relation of son to father, or limited god to the god. In dissemination, there is no return to the father. It is the mark of an absolute break with the origin, and thus the mark of a differ*ance* with an "a"—of writing.

"wanderer," the son lives his own separation. Dr. Paterson bears within himself the linguistic model of place, the anachronistic pater giving way to the emergence of a new son (or *logos*) which is a new place. In other words, he incorporates repetition. But the problem of Paterson (the place) is that the anachronism remains; the law of an imaginary father (a received history and language) dominates, and man is divided from his sources. The people are divorced because they dream of a lost original unity. The poet must give his *"reply to Greek and Latin with the bare hands"* (P, 2).[49] And when he has dispossessed the false father (the historical language, one might say), he can redeem the symbolic father, the shrouded figure of the "father of all/ speech" who embodies the mystery of origins, who stands at the point where the phallus of significance is passed to the son—where, as Jacques Derrida says, the mystery of lost origins gives way to the active *logos*, to an inaugural dissonance. It is a point where history, as difference, begins, where a "nine months' wonder, the city" comes "rolling up out of chaos" (P, 3). The e-mergent reality appears as interpenetrating opposites: "obverse, reverse;/ the drunk the sober; the illustrious/ the gross; one" (P, 4). The "one" incorporates difference; it is the "place" of the city with its multiple of particulars, a structure without an identifiable center or a verifiable transcendent origin. The poem, like the city, is a "rolling up," a sum, a gathering up which is realized in its incessant emergence, its openness.

The paternal metaphor gives way to the horizontally

49. The reference to Eliot and a learned poetry is obvious, as it was in the "Descent" chapter of *In the American Grain*: "It is imperative that we *sink*. But from a low position it is impossible to answer those who know all the Latin and some of the Sanskrit names, much French and perhaps one or two other literatures. Their riposte is: Knownothingism. But we cannot climb every tree in that world of birds. But where foreign values are held to be a desideratum, he who is buried and speaks thickly—is lost" (IAG, 214). This is consistent with Williams' distrust of the tyranny of a history which is closed, history as the authority of an imposed law in contrast with the openness of literature which seeks the "law" within the present ground.

tenuous relationship of marriage, the origin as difference. But the problematic of the father remains, in the repeated violence of the son rebelling against the existing law or in the necessary declarations of independence made in the name of the son. There is, of course, the death of Patch, after he has become the "Jersey Patriot," if in name only; or Phyllis' alienation from her father; and especially the letters from Allen Ginsberg in which he declares himself a son of Paterson who must succeed rather than imitate the father. But the most intricate maneuvering of the paternal metaphor lies in the concluding pages of Book Four, where the murder of Van Winkle by John Johnson leads in turn to the hanging of Johnson in a local historical event which barely conceals the "complex" of a mythical pattern. It is the peculiarly ambiguous role of violence in this sequence which reveals most clearly the function of the father in *Paterson*, particularly its linguistic and literary relevance.

Dr. Paterson's concluding dream (section three of Book Four) begins with the poet's being reminded that he has forgotten his "virgin purpose, the language" (P, 187). It quickly turns to an old "ash-tray" (related both to the ashes of the destructive-creative fire of Book Three and the chemical declensions, or dissonance, which conceals the curative x-rays in the contaminant "ash" of Madame Curie's "retort" (P, 178). The "ash-tray," given to the poet by a friend, is inscribed with the "legend, *La Vertue/ est toute dans l'effort*" (P, 189). It is a "Venerian scallop . for/ ashes, fit repository/ for legend." Legend is precisely that story which appeals to an unverifiable historical origin; it is also an inscription which bears an overload of meaning, a polyvalence. Just as virtue lies in the effort and thus in an act toward satisfying desire, the "legend" in the end comes to ashes. It is the residue of history, the script that reveals only the trace of the original story. Like the scallop shell or, more precisely, like a helix, virtue exists

only in "convoluted forms, takes/ time! A sea-shell" (P, 189).
A legend contains yet conceals its own origins. That is, virtue
is "legend," the sign of an original transgression. Its origins,
like those of language, are signified by a lack, and "Virtue,/
my kitten, is a complex reward in all/ languages, achieved
slowly" (P, 188). It is this virtue, and its mysterious origins,
which the poem has attempted to bring to expression, which all
languages at once reveal and conceal. Legend, that is, defers,
and brings into question, the original story of stories that gave
it birth. It is the sign that something was originally missing: a
meaning, a presence, virtue.

Creative acts, efforts toward virtue, become in themselves
the only virtue. The effort of language, the effort to renew
language, is a mark of both the beginning and end of history.
Creative acts are a violence, the original violence of breaking
out or dissemination:

> Here's to the baby,
> may it thrive!
> Here's to the labia
> that rive
>
> To give it place
> in a stubborn world
> And here's to the peak
> from which the seed was hurled!
>
> (P, 193)

This passage occurs in the midst of Paterson's final dream, near
the end of the poem, at the point where the time (or history)
of the place is enwrapped upon itself, like a Moebius strip or a
sea-shell. It forewarns of the violence within history by
naming the original violence that history endlessly repeats.
The phallus "rive[s]" the "labia" and scatters the seed
("words" or labials, as it were) of a beginning. In the
beginning was the violation. After that, virtue could only be a
dream of purity recovered.

The passage introduces the extended lyrical recounting of Paterson's local history, a pastoral recounting, as it were, interrupted twice by prose interludes: a letter from Ginsberg to Dr. Paterson recounting his settling in Newark where he spends his free time exploring the working class areas at the mouth of the river; and an account of Fred Goodell's murder of his infant daughter because her crying annoyed him. It ends with Dr. Paterson's recalling the once pure water that flowed from the source over the "Falls" and is punctuated by the prose account of the murder of the Van Winkles by John Johnson, whose "object was doubtless money" (P, 199). From that point to the end, the poem counterpoints war and murder with the poet's "dream" of the "whole poem." The cascade of the river toward the sea is simultaneously celebrated and resisted. And the poem ends with the hanging of John Johnson for the Van Winkle murders, a hanging which takes place before a mob of indifferent men who fail to see, as Dr. Paterson does not, the final hurling or dispersing of the seed. The legend of the hanged man becomes the revelation of beginning again.

At the very end of Book Four, the poet, like the Van Winkle of American legend awakening from his dream, turns back from the sea, then plucks

> some beach plums from a low bush and
> sampled one of them, spitting the seed out,
> then headed inland, followed by the dog
> (P, 203)

In other contexts, Williams has indicated that the turning inland is a reversal that redirects the poet back upon his immediate imaginative heritage, a turning toward Whitman's Camden.[50] The motif of turning inland, of course, recalls both

50. See Williams' *Autobiography*, 392: "the man rises from the sea where the river seems to have lost its identity and . . . turns inland toward Camden where Walt Whitman, much traduced, lived the latter years of his life and died." Here is the death

DeSoto and Poe of *In the American Grain*: DeSoto, whose burial was like a "solitary sperm" entering the American ground (IAG, 58); Poe, who "turned his back and faced inland, to originality, with the identical gesture of a Boone" (IAG, 226). The return, like Odysseus',[51] is to his beginning, not the end; and it gathers together the American myth of the poet as original namer, maker of a new language. Thus the hanging of John Johnson, the last note of violence in an originally designed four-part poem, anticipates the spiral of a new beginning. And the hanged man's last erection blasts or disseminates new word-seeds.[52]

Book Four ends by calling attention to its problematic wholeness, to an end which, rather than declaring itself as a text containing a revelation, anticipates its own dissolution into the beginning of some newly emerging, primordial shape. The hanging of John Johnson is the poem's final gaze after "wonder," and the "blast" of some embryonic formation. "Blast," indeed, contains a whole range of suggestion, from destruction to flowering, and includes the ambiguous violent

of another poet-father. The turning back from the sea, which Williams in notes for *Paterson* variously called the "sea of indifferent *men*" (Buffalo MS, Notebook) and the sea of all knowledge, as well as the "sea of blood," is opposed to the "active ocean" (Buffalo MS). In an early draft of *Paterson*, Book Four, MS in the Beinecke Library of Yale University, New Haven, Conn. (works in this collection will hereinafter be cited as Yale MS), Williams contrasted the "profundity of knowledge" embodied as the sea with "knowledge in the form of a woman," and wrote that, confronting her, "we have devoted ourselves, to a lesser service." The passage continues to name Whitehead, Marx, Engels, Cervantes, Cavalcanti, Pope, and Donne, those figures of authority to whom we have turned as the embodiment of tradition, as opposed to Whitman and, I think more significantly, to the father who willingly gives way to the son.

51. In a publisher's release, "News from New Directions" (May 3, 1951), Williams remarks on the poem's lack of an ending: "Odysseus swims in as man must always do, he doesn't drown, he is too able, but, accompanied by his dog, strikes inland (toward Camden) to begin again." The release is reprinted by James Thirlwall, in "William Carlos Williams' 'Paterson'," *New Directions* 17 (Norfolk, Conn.: New Directions, 1961), 262–65.

52. Thus another of Williams' answers to Eliot, and another reminder, like that near the end of Book Two, part two, that the poet of Paterson had also read *The Golden Bough* (P, 74).

purification implied in Pound's and Wyndham Lewis' title for their Vorticist magazine. But it is not literary allusion which characterizes the end of *Paterson*. Rather, we are brought into the presence of a wondrous reversal, a radical alternation of motion, a shift in the controlling signifier which the poem has tried so heroically to illuminate. Approaching its end, Book Four of *Paterson* longs for the "nostalgic sea" of "wholeness," for a meaning or sum which it can speak:

> Oh that the rocks of the Areopagus had
> kept their sounds, the voices of the law!
> Or that the great theatre of Dionysius
> could be aroused by some modern magic
>   to release
> what is bound in it, stones!
> that music might be wakened from them to
> meet our ears   .   (P, 201)

But the "voices of the law" no longer resonate in the space between man and the gods, nor is there a Dionysian "theatre." There is only the poet's recall of dancing Mary, in the park, or the god Priapus suggested by Eisenstein's lost film, both in Book Two. The cry, indeed, is a cry for what is absent, for the absence revealed in the "murder" which is beginning again. It is the violence in particular of present history: of "October 10, 1950," the date of the Red Chinese invasion of Korea, the beginning again of international conflict (P, 200). But that date, of course, is only the latest rupture in the "history" of Paterson, one more beginning to the sequence of violence that has attended this "place" from the beginning. For the pastoral recollection of Paterson's remote past, in Book Four, has begun with the riving of the labia and the hurling of the seed, and has proved to be only another "beautiful illusion," concealing its violence (the routing of the native Indian, the introduction of slaves, the repeated murders) and the blood letting of history itself.

The dream from which Dr. Paterson awakens, "this dream of/ the whole poem" (P, 200), is not simply the pastoral dream of Paterson shattered by modern history, of a chaotic present set against an ideal past. It is the dream of history itself. In the final pages of *Paterson*, Book Four, the myth of original violence displaces the myth of the eternal return, of continuity. The final passages compound the myth of place (one present place, but any place) as the primal myth. In the end we are witness not only to the awakening of Van Winkle from his dream, and thus the murder of Van Winkle or the American dream, but are presented with the paradigm of the American myth: of turning inland or the reversal of an ending. But this, of course, is the myth of the wanderer—not only of Boone and DeSoto, Whitman and Poe and Melville, or even Van Winkle, but the myth of Odysseus both seeking and resisting the indirection of the "sea," eager to maintain his voyaging yet resisting his role as prisoner of his voyage.[53]

But *Paterson*, Book Four, does more than pile one vegetation myth upon another. The final murder and concluding involution do interweave the strands of several apocalyptic myths of renewal: of Osiris murdered by Typhon, the indifferent sea, and scattered throughout the earth; of the Hanged God, both Attis and Christ, slain upon the sacred tree, before a mob of concerned or indifferent men; of Dionysus, another sacrificial son, and seed, the horned child who himself, like Osiris, must escape the wrath of Typhon; and, of course, by extension, the legend of Persephone. But Dr. Paterson has made it explicit that he has read "Frazer's Golden Bough" (P, 74), as surely as has Eliot, and that he recognizes its recurring myths to be neither an intellectual or emotional model nor traces of some

---

53. I borrow here Michel Foucault's striking figure, though perhaps in a sense not altogether consistent with his meaning. See his *Madness and Civilization*, trans. Richard Howard (New York: Random House, 1965). This is a translation and abridgement of *Folie et déraison: Histoire de la folie à l'âge classique* (Paris: Plon, 1961).

initiating archetype. That is, the myths all emanate from one paradigm, the paternal metaphor and its immediate declensions. These myths in turn conceal the myth of the "lover" who assumes with his "eternal bride" the built-in paradox of his marriage, whose betrothal is centered upon the "bride's/ comeliness, and terror" (P, 75). It is the myth of the father whose inevitable violation of his bride is carried over into the displacement and violation of his sons. It is what anthropologists call the "familial constellation," which functions like language. The wanderer Cain and the builders of cities, Romulus and Dedalus, also murderers of a brother, are mythical types of the paradigm which the poem never needs to mention, since all cities are founded by wanderers (afflicted Ishmaels) out of a need for social or communal order (interpersonal law) which emanates from violence legislated by a fraternal crime.[54] But the fraternal crime only mirrors the

54. For example, in *Finnegans Wake* (New York: Viking, 1947, James Joyce weaves into his tale his father's story of Buckley's killing the Russian general, a story of war that applies to "epochs more cainozoic." It is a story of insult to the Irish fatherland, and also a timeless tale of original violence, of revolt against authority. It is another version of the original murder of the father-authority figure (of "Buckleyself who struck and the Russian generals, da! da!"). The Russian general had insulted Ireland when, in front of a rather compassionate Buckley on the battlefield, he had defecated and then wiped his bottom with a piece of grass, the Old Sod. The "cainozoic" story is repeated with variation throughout the *Wake*, in the figure of the builder Finnegan who is replaced by H. C. Earwicker, himself divided by two sons, Shem and Shaun, themselves echoic of a "cainozoic" time. Richard Ellmann notes that Joyce's use of the Shem-Shaun relationship is connected with his translation of Lord Byron's play, *Cain*, in which the light-bringer, artist-figure Cain is opposed to the conformist Abel, artist and critic. See Richard Ellmann, *James Joyce* (New York: Oxford, 1959), 640.

Finnegans Wake is obsessed with the violence of origins, including the poet's own inaugural violence: the "poeta, still more learned, who discovered the raiding there originally. That's the point of eschatology our book of kills reaches for now in soandso many counterpoint words" (p. 482). Joyce's "riverrun," like Williams', becomes a "stolentelling," a raid upon origins: "Every dimmed letter in it is a copy and now a few of the silbils and wholly words I can show you in my Kingdom of Heaven"; "And what's more rightdown lowbrown schisthematic robblemint" (P, 424). Somewhere between the poet and those origins he robs reigns the god Thoth. See Derrida, "La pharmacie de Platon," *La dissémination*, for a discussion of Thoth, the god of the alphabet (and for Derrida a "son," of Ra) as the *logos* and supplement (96 ff.).

initial paternal crime, the violation of the virgin which is the marriage itself. This may explain the role of the wanderer Audubon in *Paterson*, Book Five, who claims to be the "lost Dauphin" and claims to have seen a "horned beast" or Unicorn in the American interior (P, 210–11). He saw what was missing.

The full realization of *Paterson*, Book Four, then, is that the "nine months' wonder,/ the city, the man, an identity," is a metaphor for man as time, as desire, as historical. Recognizing their place at the threshold of history, poets desire "wholeness," an "Oceanus" (P, 201), which is the first dream of the figuratively original poet, Homer. They desire to make a poem which is a "temple" on the "rock." But recognition forces the poet to perceive himself as the son of an original violence, as a wanderer whose fall into history demands that he found a city and, in Stevens' terms, *try* to bring the whole world round. Only the "effort" is real because it is tainted and tainting. In *Paterson* it is finally recognized that the circle of the eternal return is itself the fiction concocted to repair original violence, and that the poet's desire to build the temple must be sacrificed to his discovery of the temple of art, the museum, that can be set within the labyrinth of the city. *Paterson*, Book Five, with its paradoxical view of the fiction which survives, of the virgin who must be whored or the Unicorn which is destroyed when captured, is only another version of the Dionysian dithyramb of beginnings, the ek-stasy of *beginning* to begin again. *Paterson*, the place lifted to expression, becomes one more piece of writing on the palimpsest of historical interpretations, one more fiction of the city composed upon the center of a temple, a fiction housing a fiction. The poet escapes nostalgia by refusing to believe that he can recover lost origins. He only aspires to write, to begin again by repeating man's original act of locating his freedom in the labyrinth of his own violation.

2

"There is one thing God Himself cannot
do," I said. "He cannot raise the arm and
lower it at the same time. . . . Therefore
duality, therefore the sexes. Sex is at
the bottom of all art. He is unity, but to
accomplish simultaneity we must have had
two, multiplicity, the male and the female . . .
acting together, the fecundating principle."

(A, 373)

Or to sum it all up there's the legend
in gold letters on the window of the
abandoned saloon:

O L   M P I   (Imag., 304)

From Mathematics
to Particulars

I

In *The Walls Do Not Fall*, the first of her little known "war trilogy," H.D. inscribes the problematic role of the Modern poet. It is, of course, a terribly ancient role, fundamental and arcane like the secret and secretions of language. Standing in the present scene of war, amid crumbling walls, the contemporary poet dreams her original place and writes her dream of the Dream. Confronted by "smashed" gods, she meditates the presence of the Word in words:

> . . . the ancient rubrics reveal that
> we are back at the beginning:
> . . . .
> for gods have been smashed before
> and idols and their secret is stored
> in man's very speech,
> in the trivial or
> the real dream . . .[1]

Words and things alike, the natural and the artifact, the imaginative or the trivial,

> grape, knife, cup, wheat
> . . . .

1. Hilda Doolittle *The Walls Do Not Fall* (London: Oxford University Press, 1944), 16. The other two poems in the "trilogy" are entitled *Tribute to the Angels* (1945) and *The Flowering of the Rod* (1946).

every concrete object
has abstract value, is timeless
in the dream parallel
whose relative sigil has not changed
since Nineveh and Babel.[2]

Timeless, however, only in the "dream parallel," in the "abstract value." Like a hieroglyphic, words exist in the closed pyramidal space of the poem as at once presences and signs of a deferred "secret." In his utterance the poet "takes precedence of the priest,/ stands second only to the Pharoah [sic]." [3] In the poem, words recover the abstract value that was originally tied to their concreteness. In the moment of writing, "Thoth, Hermes, the stylus,/ the palette, the pen, the quill endure . . ." [4] and we stand in the beginning of the first writing. The "ancient rubrics" concealed within the concrete reveal that we "are back at the beginning."

The beginning, however, as H.D.'s legend of legends reveals, is the departure from origins, the inaugural mediation of being thrown into history:

Without thought, invention,
you would not have been, O Sword,

without idea and the Word's mediation,
you would have remained

unmanifest in the dim dimension
where thought dwells,

and beyond thought and idea,
their begetter,

Dream,
Vision.[5]

2. Doolittle, The Walls Do Not Fall, 25.
3. Ibid., 17.
4. Ibid.
5. Ibid., 18–19.

As Dr. Paterson expressed it, "Thought clambers up,/ snail like, upon the wet rocks," from out of a "moist chamber" which is "shut from/ the world," and cloaks itself in the shroud of utterance (P, 39). The son's speech at once expresses and conceals its father. As H.D. sees it, every poet is a son—or, in her case, as she reveals in *Tribute to Freud*, a daughter, desiring to be her father's son and therefore her symbolic "father" Sigmund's son-daughter. And Sigmund, whom she calls the "singing voice," further conjures up Siegmund, "the victorious mouth or voice of utterance." [6] Every son (daughter) desires reunion with "the One, Amen [the Egyptian god, Ra, whose messenger was Thoth], All-father." [7] Whether male or female (and in H.D.'s case, the female, phallus-less and thus a "wingless Nike," suffers an even greater subjective distance from the All-father, and therefore is more an Isis than a Thoth-Hermes), the place of the poet is at the place of original speech, a place outside of or expelled from the place where God or the principle of simultaneity is *said* to be. The poet's place, like Thoth's, is the place of original desire and of action, the place of original dispersal, of duality rather than the "One, Amen." It is the "place" of language. The poet desires but

6. Hilda Doolittle, *Tribute to Freud* (New York: Pantheon, 1956), 133–34. In this remarkable passage, H.D. is recalling her analysis of a "Leitmotiv" dream, which Pound called her "Asklepios" dream. It is a recurring vision of a block of stone with two figures, identified as a serpent and thistle, carved on it. The "language" of this vision, a figure she had come upon once more at the Louvre in the form of a design on a Hellenistic signet-ring, concealed all of the significations of language itself, including especially the physician-father and daughter (son) relation of Word to word:

My serpent and thistle—what did it remind me of? There was Aaron's rod, of course, which when flung to the ground turned into a living reptile. Reptile? Aaron's rod, if I am not mistaken, was originally the staff of Moses. There was Moses in the bulrushes, "our" dream and "our" Princess. There was the ground, cursed by God because Adam and Eve had eaten of the Fruit of the Tree. Henceforth, it would bring forth thorns, thistles, the words conjure up the same scene, the barren unproductive waste or desert. *Do men gather grapes of thorns, or figs* of thistles? Another question, another question-mark, a half-*S*, THE OTHER WAY ROUND, *S* for seal, symbol, serpent certainly, signet, Sigmund.

7. Doolittle, *The Walls Do Not Fall*, 31. See also, pp. 28–29.

does not yet possess the phallus (the linguistic signifier) through which she might utter the "timeless."

Williams rarely names the gods as such; they are not among the apparent detail of his local, not a readily identifiable part of the "roar" of Paterson's present speech. We encounter them, however, in the recesses of his language, as in the irrational night of *Kora*, where a lost Eurydice is recalled and momentarily reclaimed in the poet's eternal hope, or in the suggested "ground" of Tenochtitlan, unnameable yet manifestly "extra-human" in the size of the idols devoted to their mystery (IAG, 34). But, of course, they are there in the "ground" of Paterson the place, in the gaps and folds of a language scattered to the peripheries of incoherence. They can be reclaimed only in the necessary "silence," in the gaps and folds of a language of place new measured, and named *Paterson*, myth and poem. Homer and his Oceanus; Odysseus and his dog; Rip Van Winkle and his; the nurse-girl Curie; the Virgin and her Word; the Unicorn and the cave paintings of Altamira; Dionysus, Osiris, and Ra—they are all there, some of them named, others only suggested, in the single plane of *Paterson*'s language. But they are not there as a structural a priori, the frame of a recognized myth by which to roll up some modern "sum" or frame some "whole poem." They are not, as Eliot once suggested of Joyce's Odysseus, an appropriation of some lost order that might redeem a present disorder.[8] On the contrary, "their secret is stored," as H.D. says of the "smashed" gods, "in man's very speech," an old "rune" commonly disguised.

8. T. S. Eliot, " 'Ulysses,' Order, and Myth," *The Dial*, LXXV (November, 1923), 380–83. Though Eliot later repudiated the idea that the mythic frame could, or should, provide a kind of allegorical frame of order for the Modern artist, this essay had a powerful influence on subsequent critical interpretations of *Ulysses* and *The Waste Land*, and also on subsequent creative activities of Modern writers appropriating myth as form. H.D. and Williams are working *contra* this tradition, assuming that the inherent form of experience (and language) is really the author of the myth, past and present manifestations, and that it is this form poetry seeks to release from historical language.

Words are "anagrams, cryptograms,/ little boxes, condi-
tioned/ to hatch butterflies. . . ." [9] Present disorder is a
failure of recognition, a failure to read what is there, dispersed
and concealed in the chaos of common speech.

In the beginning, the poet has an incoherent gathering of
local particulars, unmeasured and therefore nowhere:

> To make a start,
> out of particulars
> and make them general, rolling
> up the sum, by defective means—
>
> (P, 3)

The well-known beginning of the poem discards *archè* and
telos, and with them the mathematic of design, for a "field"
theory of language. The poem will move, then, from "mathematics to particulars" (P, 5). The phrase echoes Alfred North
Whitehead's distinction between the mathematic or subjective
and the realistic, or the "provisional realism" of related things
in a "perceptual field." In the latter, no one thing composes the
field, but the concrete, objective field suggests the world:
"every location involves an aspect of itself in every other
location. Thus every spatio-temporal standpoint mirrors the
world." [10] Whitehead, whose *Science and the Modern World*
was acknowledged by Williams as an inspiring book, called
equations of applied mathematics the "complete expression" of
the belief in a world of common subjectivity.[11] But Williams'
discovery of the subjectivity of a mathematically conceived
world did not need the bolstering of philosophical respectabil-
ity. Language was his problem and problematic, and speech
denied the mathematic of prescriptive law. Speech was the
particularity of words, not words in isolation but words

9. Doolittle, *The Walls Do Not Fall,* 44.
10. Alfred North Whitehead, *Science and the Modern World* (New York: Signet,
1948), 87.
11. *Ibid.,* 84.

coming into the particularity of relation. Speech drives a
particular motion through the general laws of grammar. It
momentarily suspends truth, as something that it exists to
convey, for its own act. The "means" are "defective" because
they are the discovery of the act—mean, mediation. In
mathematics, the sum stands outside, is greater than, the parts,
and therefore is subjective. Similarly, that ultimate myth of
Western onto-theological metaphysics, the "cogito ergo sum."
Paterson's "plan for action to supplant a plan for action" (P,
10) anticipates another kind of sum.

To begin with particulars, then, is not to repeat the
empiricist's law, and thus his mathematic, but to repeat the
myth of Chaos: of a shape "rolling up out of chaos" (P, 3).
The myth of the city ("a nine months' wonder, the city") is
not only the myth of the wanderer and the labyrinth, of
dispersal and gathering, but a fundamental retelling of the
Orphic myth of Time. In the beginning, Orpheus sings, was
Time, and out of Time came Chaos, the mist which Time
spun into the egg of creation, the two halves of Heaven and
Earth centered upon Eros. It is the myth of the "fecundating
principle," of "multiplicity" or "duality," retold as the myth of
language:

> Rolling in, top up,
> under, thrust and recoil, a great clatter:
> lifted as air, boated, multicolored, a
> wash of seas—
> from mathematics to particulars—
>
> divided as the dew,
> floating mists, to be rained down and
> regathered into a river that flows
> and encircles:
>
> shells and animalcules
> generally and so to man,
>
> to Paterson.   (P, 5)

Here is Orpheus' legend interpenetrating with Homer's, the lyric with the epic. And they in turn are interlayered with the primary myth of Cronus, of a father like Oedipus' who fails to destroy his son who is destined to displace him: it is the myth of the birth of the gods, of Jupiter-Zeus who is spared by his mother, the sister of his father and the queen; it is the myth of the father who devours his offspring, thus holding time in the presence of his own signification until the son manages to escape and supplant him, initiating the original division of the world. Did Williams think in such terms, or design his poem to retell primary myths in the modern idiom? Of course not, though such intentions are provocatively moot. He was surely discovering, on a present ground, the myth of birth, or origins, "obverse, reverse," dispersal and "interpenetration," the "fecundating principle" as original division and ceaseless dissemination and regathering. The "general" of "particulars" is the reflexive legend of language itself, revealed in the silences, gaps, and folds of its own original cleavage: "Or to sum it all up," as he says at the end of *A Novelette*, "there's the legend in gold letters on the window of the abandoned saloon: O L   M P I" (Imag., 304). This is the *legend* of the first place of gathering of the gods and hence of every place. But here it is a place barely recognized, manifest in a few faded letters or signs. The place of the modern gods, of a language, is only the sign of a lost significance. Language is only a trace of a preexisting "sum" and a dispersal of that Idea.

II

The original place of the gods is the place of original "sense," sense which "destroys 'God' " or the poetic word for the "unobtainable." Clarity of apprehension is always simple, not only in the outline or edges of related things but in the reduced distance of the "I" and the "other." The closer we get to words, to their shapes, their sound, their tumbling in the throat and mouth, the closer we get to their reality and their problematic. Touching them, we touch ourself, for words are, as Heidegger says, the house of our being. Standing in the presence of speech, we sense the priority of neither the speaker nor the thought he is speaking. The "idea" is nowhere locatable behind and before the speech, but is the residue speech leaves behind. "Obverse, reverse," we reflectively place *logos* first in the order of priority, but such reflective placing only deceives because it is subjective. No amount of experience can reveal the Word behind the word. Significance, and place, is only there between words. The irreducible particulars of speech, Ferdinand de Saussure has shown, are two phonemes lying side by side, and the irreducible particulars of the poem are two contiguous things:

> How to begin to find a shape—to begin to begin again,
> turning the inside out   : to find one phrase that will
> lie married beside another for delight . ?   (P, 140)

Man and woman, city and park—"What should we be without the sexual myth . . . ?" Wallace Stevens asks, in a poem enigmatically titled "Men Made Out of Words." [12] The "duality" of sex is not Cartesian, not a duality of mind and world or self and other. It is not a dualism in which subject precedes object. It is a primordial difference, diacritical. We have lost this original pairing in the history of reflection. And it is recoverable only in the violent reversal of the given language. In *Paterson*, the "fecundating principle" lies somewhere beneath the contiguous manifold of local particulars, within the "roar of the great beast," within the "multiple seed" of words "packed tight with detail" (P, 4). The poet begins by interpreting, by turning the speech of his place "inside out," by bringing into question the self-evident representations of common speech.

12. *The Collected Poems of Wallace Stevens* (New York: Alfred A. Knopf, 1954), 355.

Williams devotes a late chapter of his *Autobiography* to "The Practice," where he explores the analogy between his profession as a doctor and his avocation as poet. It is an analogy that also asserts a reciprocity, the interpenetration of a complex and an "elementary world" (A, 357). He treats the relation between physician and patient as that of opposing roles, so that one can slip into the situation of the other in a mutual struggle toward a solution. The interpenetration cures and rests doctor as well as patient. It cures him of self, takes him into the "underground current" where the "moving detail of a life" exists. The doctor penetrates the stereotype to the particularity of a life; he penetrates the surface of the patient's "inarticulate" struggle to express his illness, penetrates to the language that "reveals some secret twist of a whole community's pathetic way of thought" (A, 359). The "underground current" and "underground stream" suggest a continuity moving through discontinuity, a music running within a dissonance. It is poetry within prose, a "stream which for a moment has come up just under the surface" (A, 359).

The stream, however, is not made up of concealed words, but of a force coming "near the surface" which must be dis-covered, or brought to the particularity of utterance. He describes what he hears as "words being born," and the physician as "words' very parents":

After we have run the gamut of the simple meanings that come to one over the years, a change gradually occurs. We have grown used to the range of communication which is likely to reach us. The girl who comes to me breathless, staggering into my office, in her underwear a still breathing infant, asking me to lock her mother out of the room; the man whose mind is gone—all of them finally say the same thing. And then a new meaning begins to intervene. For under that language to which we have been listening all our lives a new, a more profound language, underlying all the dialectics, offers itself. It is what they call poetry. This is the final phase. (A, 361)

Like the commentary in *Kora in Hell* quoted in the previous
chapter, which names a "hidden language" beneath the
language of our day's affairs (Imag., 59), this passage speaks of
the poet as one who sets down the language as "heard" by the
"full senses" (the imagination) rather than by any one sense
and thus records "the poem which their lives are being lived to
realize" (A, 362). He brings to light the "rarest element," not
the revelation of the poet's imagination but of what is there "in
fact." And the facts are the words: "The poem that each is
trying actually to communicate to us lies in the words. It is at
least the words that make it articulate. It has always been so.
Occasionally that named person is born who catches a rumor
of it, a Homer, a Villon, and his race and the world perpetuates
his memory. . . . By listening to the minutest variations of the
speech we begin to detect that today, as always, the essence is
also to be found, hidden under the verbiage, seeking to be
realized" (A, 362).

"The poem *springs* from the half-spoken words" of the
inarticulate; the physician "observes" the "life" in the "pecu-
liar, actual conformations"; "he strives as best he can to
interpret the manner of its speech"; therein "the *secret* lies" (A,
362—my italics). This is the tentative language of a poetic
ontology. For the poetry of the poet's life is his act, his
interpretation which penetrates to the realm of the "secret"
and reveals it, or allows it to "spring" forth. Moving amid the
"scattered" voices of the Park, the poet of Paterson adds his
"useless voice" (P, 60), "his voice mingling with other voices"
(P, 56). The "voice in his voice" opens "his old throat" (P,
56), until he is moved to sleep and dream. And there "moves
in his sleep/ a music that is whole, unequivocal" (P, 60). The
two languages, the scattered and the whole, the prose and the
poetry, are ultimately both irreconcilable and inseparable,
folded upon each other like the convolutions of a sea-shell or

superimposed in their field like the hieroglyphs of an ancient palimpsest. Only in the poem can they be held momentarily separate, can the synchronic "music" be revealed within the diachronic and historical flow—only in the poem, which is a "homologue/ triple piled/ pulling the disparate together to clarify/ and compress" (P, 20).

The composition of such a homologue takes a form analogous to cubist construction. That is, it is also the "obverse, reverse" of construction, and therefore a kind of archeological excavation or deconstruction. What Williams calls "descent"—whether as with a Daniel Boone's "descent to the ground of his desire" (IAG, 136) or the mythic descents implied in Williams' uses of the Kore legend—is to be understood not so much as a physical or even a mental action; rather it is the doubling of its opposite, of ascent or lifting to articulation. The "descent beckons," as he writes in that famous sequence in *Paterson* (P, 77), reversing the historical order of descending, of moving from a higher or superior order to a lower order, of passing from the logically prior or the initiating source to the comprehensive particular. On the contrary, "descent" retains its spatial and moral implications only by an interesting irony; its verticality is relative only to the assumed superiority of the evolutionary higher stage from which it descends. One descends from the known and multiple to the source, the unknown, by way of that which he came. For he came via the word, itself a descent (or a declension) of an original order. Descent in Williams' poetry, like the young initiate's advent in "The Wanderer," involves a reversal of whatever direction one is moving in. It is itself reversal and bears within its motion its own obverse; thus language comes to be, in the function of single words or in the measure of phrases, a convolution (see P, 32, 37), turning upon itself until the etymological traces utter a secret concealed within the field of its current, like the giants living in the "silence" of the

"talk" of two lovers or the "back country" into which Garret
Mountain (figuratively, the woman whose head is the Park)
reaches (P, 8). That secret is not, however, a revealed truth, a
unity, a master word, a One, but original violence itself.

Kora in Hell, for example, thematizes descent as a breaking
up of prescribed or historical language, but not the annihilation
of speech. It dissolves the given set of relations, the governing
syntax and its moral law, in search of an original (and
originating) syntax. And it does this, as Williams would do so
often later, by violent juxtapositions: "that gentleness that
harbors all violence,/ the valid juxtaposition" (CLP, 29). This
is a hermeneutical violence, a reduction not to one but to two,
a reduction to the concept of "field." To make a word the
obverse of itself, as Williams does throughout *Paterson*, for
example, in the anagrammatic play of the dog as an obverse of
god, is to define the elemental "ground" of language as
binary.[13] Every word carries within itself its opposite, if not
semantically then structurally, and within the field of those
opposites lies the silence or zero degree in all its purity. Indeed,
"divorce" in *Paterson* is just the sad distancing (or scattering)
of self from other, man from woman, city from nature, and
words from other words, and therefore from themselves. This
dissolves space, definition, measure, and therefore the "fecundative principle." How can words be divorced from themselves? Well, in one way, by taking God as the eternal,
disembodied concept of the origin, as the word for the Word
that precedes all things, thus failing to see that in the mirror of
its own signature God is the word for a very earth-bound thing

13. *Paterson* is filled with anagrams and acronyms of which the god-dog mirror
image is only one variation. The "dog," of course, serves the thematic of the dead
gods, and thus of man's self-division, a theme exemplified best, I suppose, in the dog's
exclusion from the park (the forced restraint of the senses) and the dog's oneness with
the tribal chieftain. As one of my students has suggested, even "The *D*elineaments *of*
the *G*iants" tempts one to identify a residual acronym. But puns, both semantic puns
and sound puns, are more important in the poem than anagrams.

itself. In the consonantal reversals of its sound, the two beings lie side by side reversed at the root of the tongue. The one is the Word; the other sniffs only the signs of things. But between the two lies the whole enigmatic gap of man, separated from the god because he is also divorced from his world, his place. *Logos* thought, onto-theological metaphysics, separated words from themselves at the beginning.

Williams, of course, could hardly have consciously designed the total ramifications of his puns, of the freedom he felt it necessary to take with a language "resigned" from all the priorities of the "University." But there is no doubt he did feel concretely about the meaning of divorce as distance, and perceived the essentially homologous structures of language and human relationships. "Language is in its January" (Imag., 280), he says in *A Novelette*, and the very discovery of its Janus-face is a discovery of its original power; for its original power is really what the classics discovered, and what such experimenters as the surrealists were seeking. At the point of original duality, he suggests in *A Novelette*, language had both the power of meaning and the power of discovery, of being as *logos* and being as *physis*. It carried the power of the signature and the potential for speech to "reverse" that signature. In Williams' poetics there cannot be less than two particulars, two words, two sounds; and there is nothing more real than the moment when an end twists upon itself into a beginning, the two held there face to face in a revealing oppositeness and similarity.

III

One of *Paterson*'s dominant themes, which goes back to *In the American Grain*, is the futility of transplanting a received tradition upon an alien place. Williams rejects the mathematic of design, the preimposed "sum" that underwrites history as repetition of

the same, as eternal design. Denying the priority of the fecundating principle to the advent, Williams conceives of the principle as
that which is realized in the advent, like the "multiple" seed
which is "packed tight with detail" (P, 4). In the beginning was
the many. "Design," then, is not a logical precedent to any one
manifestation. It is not an *archè* but, as Heidegger says, the
cutting of a "trace," cutting a "furrow into the soil to open it
to seed and growth." [14] If *Paterson* is an epic, it is an epic of
beginnings, of discovery; and if the identifiable mythic frame
which appears and reappears occasionally near the surface, like
an underground stream, is the myth of Genesis, it is a myth
identifiable in the multiplicity and variety of the forms it takes:
forms which roll up and rebound upon themselves like a
"triple-piled" homologue, like an Eisenstein montage, like any
of the other possible similes for the "shelly rime" (P, 143) that
brings the design, abstract as it is, into appearance within the
multiple and discrete particulars of, say, a Gris painting (see
the commentary on the painting in *Spring and All*, Imag.,
110–11).

Book One of *Paterson*, indeed, is a book of Genesis, in the
sense that any book, attempting to penetrate to the ground of
its place must necessarily involve itself in a language about
language and thus become itself a metapoem. The poet's
sufferance of the language of the tribe, the common language
which speaks him from the billboards on busses as surely as he
speaks it, barely conceals the primordial roots of language.
Filled with local detail, the recorded history of a place, the
poem offers this local history as in itself an interpretation, a
moral mathematic or rhetoric, within which exists a more
original "sum," a more original design now lost. The poem,

14. Martin Heidegger, *On the Way to Language*, trans. Peter D. Hertz (New
York: Harper & Row, 1971), 121. Heidegger is speaking here of the "design" of
language, its "unity of being," the "whole of the traits of that drawing which
structures and prevails throughout the open, unlocked freedom of language."

then, serves to break down this specific detail toward its base—a base, one notes, that lies like an abstract within the particulars of everyday speech or the distracting details of recorded history. Paterson, New Jersey, with its location and history, might seem to offer a gratuitous landscape for a poet bent upon inventing (dis-covering) a mythic order moving beneath its mass of detail: river and falls, city and park, mountain and the opening to the sea, each in its way tied to a Romantic iconography. But Williams' point is that every *place* reveals this order; and the history of every place, if penetrated to the ground of its design, unveils this "hidden language." Yet it is not the abstract design, isolatable from its particular detail, which is real. It is not the archetype, but the texture or field in which it inheres, that must be recovered. The local is the universal for Williams, not just another repetition of the pattern, but a kind of mathematical "position" or place, the inter-section of manifold lines of force or differences.

The selection of historical detail, then, may well be made with the eye to its mythic resonances, resonances long since lost in the rhetoric of his history which has lost touch with those primary utterances. But it cannot be selected as an allegory of any ur-pattern; each repetition is another layer of the "shelly rime." That Paterson, named after a former governor, may be made to reveal the mythic order of beginnings and ends and thus the primary linguistic code may seem more than gratuitous. That Newark, a place too far downstream from the source to be at the point of a falls and thus at the place where history originates, as Williams once explained—that the place-name Newark, the "home" of the Hopper Cummings, bears within its own history the mythic lesson of a failed new beginning—is enough to reveal Williams' method. For Newark took its name from the American dream of renewal, of the place as a new "ark," and thus stands as the embodiment of a dream unfulfilled, a repeated act of naming/pairing or belated genesis. The irony of Mrs. Cumming's

vertigo, from atop the "Hundred Steps," just at the moment
when her husband has said that "it is time for us to set our face
homeward," (P, 24), lies in the lost meaning of "home" for her
and her husband. For if the relationship of the Cummings can
be discussed in terms of Williams' anti-Puritanism, as a failure
of sexuality, it is no less an example of a failure of language.
The official rhetoric describing the fall cannot penetrate the
"sublime curiosities of the place" as it says, and thus cannot
penetrate to the death that ensues when the coexistence of
selves in communication is broken. Mrs. Cumming's return to
Newark (in death) is the fulfillment of her husband's setting
his face homeward, a return to silence and, for her, an ironic
reversal of the thwarted "desire" to fulfill her (sexual) nature.
For that nature depends on the coexistence of its (her)
opposite, of the duality and marriage of the "fecundative
principle."

Williams sets the prose fragments of Paterson's history into
the flow of his or Dr. Paterson's rebounding thoughts, thereby
thematizing that history in a way its official language cannot
reveal. The poet's selections of that history may be arbitrary,
but they are of a piece, and what they thematize is not simply
the existence of an apocalyptic pattern of genesis beneath the
local ground of his place, but the danger of living as if the
human had escaped somehow that original cleavage. Even
Hopper Cumming's name, one is tempted to say, unveils the
obverse of his relations with his wife, in a rude sexual pun of
impotence and rootlessness. But the point of this is that the
sexual pun, even if rejected as that, has roots in the problematic
of language, in the dangerous inarticulateness of human
relatonships. Unlike her namesake, Sarah Cumming never
begat a son, and her metaphysical swoon from atop the
"Hundred Steps" (at the apex of "the Jacob's ladder")
becomes a perfect inversion of the primal myth she might have
lived had she submitted to the "ground" of her desire.

Other detail in Book One of *Paterson* reveals a similar thematization. "David Hower, a poor shoemaker" discovers the mussels of "Notch Brook," but neither he nor his fellow citizens understand that they have touched the center of an original event (P, 8–9). Despite his prophetic first name, his quest is abortive; the "Unios (mussels)" are sought for commercial value, and the most valuable pearl of them all is disintegrated by boiling. Hower is the prototype of the new world man's failure of recognition. He destroys the "Unios," the spiral of unity wound upon its secret origin, just as he is unaware to the sexual impulse that drives him to seek in "Notch Brook." Hower does not question; thus he fails to discover his roots in the "back country" or to realize his name. Similarly, the historical legend of Sam Patch, whose assumed guise of Noah Faitoute Paterson provides an obvious irony that prepares for his demise in the Genesee River, discloses an original denial. Patch's initials are an inversion of *Paterson*, which name he assumes. It is Paterson's cleavage (thus his own) which his dramatic act, a leap rather than a fall, seeks to bridge, an act he perverts into an end in itself. He literally misplaces himself for commercial reasons, and fails in his fall back into the Gene*seme*. His assumed name, Noah, embodies the obvious suggestions, as previously noted, of that surrogate father of us all, the maker of the original ark in which renewal demanded an original pairing of opposites, and the father of the American language whose dictionary Williams called a "radically subversive thesis" (SE, 136). Sam Patch remakes himself in the language of an ideal or imaginary subject, in words that have no relation either to his act or his place, or which violate that original relation. And he is undone by his betrayal of language—giving the word priority of the deed—and returned to the undifferentiated silence of his genesis.

The point to be made, however, is not the cleverness of Williams' linguistic games but his purpose in maneuvering

local history and language into a measure which discloses its
primary language. The original myth of genesis is found
reembodied, however obscurely, in the texture of Paterson's
(the city's) history, and is disclosed in Paterson's (the poet's)
recurring speech. The language prophetically warns of the
consequences of man's ignoring his loss of origins; yet, at the
same time it warns that he can only partially recover them, in
the trace marked by the silence of conversation, in poetry.
Like Patch's "confused" leap, our descent toward our genesis
is meaningless only if undisclosed, only if we fail to understand
that our genesis is language and that we are at once the speaker
of the word and spoken by the word. Otherwise, we become
another version of the monster, or what Williams called in an
early version of the poem, a "paralytic hydrocephalic" or
"waterhead," divided from ourselves and left at the mercy of
Cartesian vortices—either that, or an object dead. The
"monster in human form" (P, 10), visited in Paterson by
General Washington and other dignitaries, is the double of
those who, like the Puritan of *In the American Grain*, seek the
"miraculous" or revelation in a new reign of "wonder."
Worshipping the "natural curiosity" as a revelation of some
supernatural origin, they deny the ground of their desire.
What they miss, of course, is the revelation of the monster,
tied to its source in nature or literally filled of that (water)
source: that man's origins are indeed chthonic, and that he is a
mutation in nature's game of difference. Theirs is the opposite
of Madame Curie's curiosity, which leads to disclosure, not of
herself as subject but of the light of the elemental ground. That
is, her curiosity brings to light and thus enlightens. The need
for "wonder" which haunts the citizens of Paterson, and
haunted them from the beginning of their history, is contrasted
throughout the poem with the autochthonous roots of the
Indian and the dislocations he has suffered at the hands of
civilization.

The prose of *Paterson* is rhetorical only in its measure with the poetry. It can be interpreted moralistically not by some prescribed measure of the deeds or misdeeds of historical subjects, but because its language, whether recorded in *Historical Collections of the State of New Jersey* or in personal letters to a poet living in the present, relates to the etymological ground of Paterson's primordial myth. That Paterson is the historical place where Hamilton planned to realize his grand design for an industrial empire, by harnessing the power source of water, is a matter of fact. Yet, Williams' personal antipathy for Hamilton, a dominant theme of *In the American Grain*, only partly explains the appropriateness of the prose relating to Hamilton in *Paterson*. For Hamilton's vision of a Society for Establishing Useful Manufacturers, or SUM, as it was in fact called (P, 73), is only another "obverse" of the poet's original desire to take particulars and roll "up the sum" even if by defective means. But Hamilton lacked curiosity, and thus disregarded the particulars of place; he would import a foreign architect to impose his "sum" upon the place, a design, say, like that of the nation's capitol, the idea of which originates outside history and is its Law.[15] SUM was not a disclosure but an im-position, an acronym of the *archè* as pure mathematic. Hamilton tried to harness the language of Paterson to his own economic syntax, denying its source. When the economic theme of *Paterson* functions most integrally, it is as an analogy with language. Hamilton's SUM (his Word) is the very antithesis of the ritual disclosures of the Indian dance, the Kinte Kaye, which incorporates the restorative powers of water and fire. For the Indian ceremonies throughout the

15. Hamilton's chosen architect was Pierre L'Enfant, whose plans were called, in one of the historical inclusions in the poem, "more magnificent than practical" (P, 74). L'Enfant had designed Washington, D.C., according to a neoclassical or formalist mathematic of design. As Hamilton saw, L'Enfant's designs expressed a SUM or law that originated outside the place of its application, a universal law which reflected the order of the cosmos brought to bear upon the natural world.

poem celebrate not only man's relations with the "back country," but the survival of the tribe in the death and resurrection of its king-father. The ritualistic passing of the signifier from generation to generation in the Indian dance of life-in-death bridges the gaps of a discontinuity which Hamilton's rationalism ignores.

Dr. Paterson moves always between these two inseparable levels of language, the apparently random particulars and the invisible (authentic) speech unlocked by a syntactical shift in their arrangement. He can thus deny traditional symbolism, with its historically accrued meanings, as a product of waterheads who deny their bodies, while revealing that what the symbol truly discovers is its own origin, its obverse echo of the indifferent sea. If David Hower was oblivious to the meaning of his discovery, it was because he thought of universality as apart from particulars. If the Christian tradition appropriated the myth of the Unicorn as a figure of its own holy hunt, as in the tapestries of the Cloisters, it tended to deny the mythic origins and to stress the allegory of a prescribed vision. Only the poet could reroot meaning in the field of particulars, and rediscover authenticity (the "general") in the particulars. But to do so, the poet must suffer with those who "neither know their sources nor the sills of their/ disappointments" (P, 6). He is always at the "falls" and must share in the inevitable failure of language; to stand in the proximity of the source is to know one's departure from it. But that, after all, is to survive the divorce and to grasp the "design" of the "fecundative principle":

> It is the ignorant sun
> rising in the slot of
> hollow suns risen, so that never in this
> world will a man live well in his body
> save dying—and not know himself
> dying, yet that is

the design. Renews himself
thereby, in addition and subtraction,
walking up and down.   (P, 4)

The design is repetition, of beginnings and ends, relating man to the cycle of nature, but obversely. Man renews himself by wandering, "walking up and down." The phrase, of course, evokes Satan, Job's adversary; just as one following a few pages later in "The Delineaments of the Giants" evokes Moses: "PISS-AGH! the giant lets fly! good *Muncie* too . . ." (P, 10). The mountain-hill Singac is the giant, and the local Pisgah; the falls, his evacuation, like Job's protests or "roarings . . . poured out like the waters." Paterson, split across the stream, is "good *Muncie*," another Middletown, like the one studied by Helen and Robert Lynd.[16] And like the original Muncie, which took its name from a tribe of Delaware Indians driven from the eastern shore to Indiana (the tribe in turn, according to legend, sold this new home to the white man), Paterson is a recurrent instance of bourgeois cleavage, a repetition of the myth of dislocation. Satan and Moses—they are two more avatars of the poet concealed within the language of the "place," and retrievable only in the "addition and subtraction" of a local detail which will not speak with the symbolic authority of God. For Satan and Moses, however different they are, are interpreters of God, and they speak a law that is mediated in language; they seek a meaning, a place, in the earth. They can only bring meaning to earth, and in that gesture they deny its purity. They are interpreters, like the Lynds, and must interpret because they no longer stand in the presence of the unmediated word.

16. Williams has confessed to his plan to take his "place" as a kind of "Middletown." And as Mike Weaver notes, Williams' friend Horace Gregory, to whom he at one time was going to dedicate "The Delineaments of the Giants," had taken the Lynd's two studies as the "most reliable description of an American 'audience' " he could recommend. Mike Weaver, *William Carlos Williams: The American Background* (Cambridge, England: Cambridge University Press, 1971), 127.

The Paterson poet mounts neither a Pisgah nor an Olympus; he cannot delude himself, as could Moses, about promised lands. He stands in the presence of a distanced "wonder," in a thoroughly *middle* world, displaced: like the "OL MPI" (Imag., 304) of that "legend" which stands as epigraph to this chapter and the conclusion of Williams' *Novelette*. There is trace enough there to suggest a lost whole, a world where power and form were one, without mediation. But the "name" suggests as well an absence, a loss, a fall, and hence the "obverse, reverse" of naming, of the trace. The poet's measure, his names, function more like a Mendelief table of discrete and known differences, in which elements are arranged according to an arbitrary norm of relative atomic weight. The table not only measures known valences but predicts the presence of the unknown: the unknown element's "presence had been predicted by a blank in the table" (SL, 243). The poet, like the Lynds, like Moses, seeks such a law, and generates such a table of particulars. Like the Lynds, and even like Moses, he desires a law that will reveal a true presence, a more authentic light:

> adept at thought, playing the words
> following a table which is the synthesis
> of thought, a symbol that is to him,
> sun up! a Mendelief, the elements laid
> out by molecular weight, identity
> predicted before found! . . . (P, 179)

This is a chemistry of invention which takes the form of destruction, or deconstruction, of the ordinary, of breaking back toward the origin; it is, therefore, a parallel of the search of the wanderer for "home" or for a "city" which will replace those lost origins, allowing him a place to begin again. A breaking down to the elemental, however, is not a return to an original unity, to the "God" before or behind "sense." On the contrary, it takes the form of interpretation which breaks up the idea of a fixed center and opens the field to a "playing" of the "words." It is the creation of a poem, modeled on the idea of a unified or total structure (like, say, a dream or a heavenly city), but which, by the very virtue of its multiple and discrete particulars, asserts itself as the obverse of any closed and centered structure. It asserts itself as a metaphor for what cannot otherwise be named, an open field. When Williams breaks down the local detail of Paterson to the elemental language of the Pentateuch, or to the elements of a Homeric cosmos, when he reduces the "detail" in four books to the suggested analogy with the primary elements of earth, air, fire, and water (perhaps in direct response to Eliot's structuring of the *Four Quartets*), he is engaged in an ironic allegorizing that calls attention to its own reduction. For what it reveals is not a presence but the presence of an absence in language. The ground of being is revealed to be a structure in which the ruling law is a mystery suffused there in the "blanks." The poem is an interpretation, the creation of a grid or table wherein the fiction of presence can be maintained. In that fictional field, a linguistic field new measured, man stands in the proximity of those origins he has left behind, where he can lie married beside the woman whose "monstrous hair" reaches into the "back country." The figure recalls once more the original co-presence of nature and culture that defines man's autochthonous beginning. Here also, as we will see later, rests the key to Williams' anti-historicism—that is, his argument with the cleavage and the distance history has opened up between nature and culture, word and thing, man and woman. For the original duality of the "fecundative principle" was not a divorce but a necessary pairing of opposites. It is this origin into the proximity of which the poem takes us, if only to reveal that the creative principle itself depends upon a rejection of the nostalgia for origins and defines invention as the game.

IV

It is possible now to understand the nature of Williams' repeated attacks on metaphor, symbolism, and especially simile: "No symbolism is acceptable. No symbolism can be permitted to obscure the real purpose, to lift the world of the senses to the level of the imagination and so give it new currency" (SE, 213). He defers a language of substitution (metaphor) for that of a relation of differences (metonymy). Metonymic detail, however, does not render a thing in itself; it is not a naïve realism, or a language of presence in opposition to metaphor's language of absence. The metonymic defines itself, according to Jakobson, by succession and contiguity, and thus asserts the order of a diachronic or temporal sequence, an economy in which each thing exists to be displaced by its successor which defines and annihilates it.[17] Yet, this "new currency" of progressive description can itself be turned upon itself, and indeed must, since the metonym cannot exist without its opposite, the metaphor. Thus metonymic contiguity and successivity (diachrony) ultimately tends to unfold over itself, just as Williams' multiple, discrete, and contiguous detail is rebounded in the poet's thoughts until it discloses a design of elemental relations, thereby becoming a metaphor for this elemental order (synchrony). But a metaphor that is the substitution of what? Of lost origins, perhaps; that is, of the elemental principle of duality or freeplay.

I have made this excursus, with the help of Jakobson's theory, not to assert the complexity of Williams' thinking about language, but to affirm the elementary nature of it. There are symbols, even apparently traditional symbols, in his poems, despite his protests against a symbolic mode. Those symbols are invariably employed with a self-consciousness that

17. Roman Jakobson and M. Halle, *Fundamentals of Language* (The Hague:Mouton, 1956).

negates their traditional context and thereby asserts the primacy of the signifier to the signified. The symbol appears as an allegorical object which, when recognized as a sign, supersedes what it signifies and instantly reweaves itself into the fabric of relations which confer on it a significant place. It is only afterward that we *remember* its ties with an ancient and elemental story, and thus recognize it as a metaphorical substitution of a recognized allegory. The primary myth is thus lifted to expression in a present ground—as, for example, in the conclusion to *Paterson*, Book Four, where Odysseus, Rip Van Winkle, and the poet awake from their dreams (and hence from their separate wanderings) on the same ground and are brought into the presence of the myth of the Hanged God. The poem, then, does not offer its "hidden language" as a myth, but on the contrary calls attention to itself as an interpretation of the myth. It is a tapestry of all the myths it interweaves. It therefore demythologizes and thus calls attention to itself as a "fiction" of fiction.

What Williams attacks in *Spring and All* as "crude symbolism," the "empty" association of "emotions with natural phenomena," is a kind of naïve realism which makes language transparent and destroys its authenticity. A literary symbol, or cultural symbol, can be moved arbitrarily from context to context without altering its value, its meaning which lies somewhere apart from it and of which it is the recognized and imperfect vehicle. Men normally deceive themselves into thinking language is stable, because if it is, then the truth it represents will itself be stable and they will be tied to their origins by an authentic mediation. They will be given its power. But "Language is not stable," Williams could assert in the late 1920s: "Leaks occur and—though they are clearly aware of it or not—the lives of people are modified by accidents of language. And men instinctively feel it. There is a self-preservational dread of changes in language. For after all

aside from the language that is understood more or less
commonly by everyone we should soon find ourselves lost in a
howling wilderness where there should be nothing 'holy.' " [18]
And nothing whole. For what one notices here is that holiness
depends on the interpersonal understanding, on a coexistence
in language. When the poet sets down the ordinary language
as heard, so that poet and reader "mingle" there in the "dance"
(Imag., 59), he sets down the ordinary as an allegory of the
"hidden language": "In the imagination, we are from henceforth (so long as you read) locked in the fraternal embrace, the
classic caress of author and reader. We are one" (Imag., 89).
The language of myth totalizes; the language of poetry at once
totalizes and calls attention to the fiction of the whole. Poetry
turns language inside out and creates its own time-space, only
to step outside itself once more and demystify that space by
calling attention to its fictiveness. It demystifies symbolism,
since it demystifies the idea of the subject: "Whenever I say,
'I' I mean also, 'you.' And so, together, as one, we shall begin"
(Imag., 89). The subject is revealed not as a priori, an origin,
but that which arises in the field of coexistence, a field of "talk"
where the subject is reciprocally the object and the two exist together in their transactional difference, as in Stein.

From the beginning, Williams was drawn to the avant garde
art which demystified symbolism. As early as the famous
Prologue to *Kora in Hell*, he had borrowed Marcel Duchamp's
argument that an arrangement of things "conventionally
composed *in situ*" (Imag., 8) tended to reduce the particularity
of its component elements to the point of annihilation, making

18. William Carlos Williams, *"The Embodiment of Knowledge"* (MS in the
Beinecke Library of Yale University, New Haven, Conn.), 15; works in this
collection will hereinafter be cited as Yale MS. This essay on education was written in
the late 1920s, addressed to Williams' children, as a kind of propadeutic for an
education which would escape the secondary knowledge of formal, classroom
education. It has never been published. But it contains some of Williams' most
fundamental thoughts on education, literature (especially Shakespeare), and history.

the particulars arbitrarily represent a thing, a meaning, a value apart from any situational function. Duchamp had used the example of the stained glass window which had fallen out of its frame in the church as his exemplum of a sign regaining its original significance by being detached from its expected symbolic code. The window lying on the ground became a "valid juxtaposition," art laid beside nature, which asserted the particularity of each and returned to the object not only its presence but its meaning. For its meaning as sign depends on its discontinuity with nature, just as its signification in the situation of church architecture and iconography is appropriated by a center lying somewhere outside its immediate and contiguous relations. Moreover, the particulars of the thing itself, the arrangement of colors, regained their particularity; the window became art, not symbol.

"Crude symbolism" or the "strained association" and "lateral sliding" of simile, like the "complicated ritualistic forms designed to separate the work from 'reality'" (Imag., 102), compose the distancing style of the "Traditionalists of Plagiarism" (Imag., 94). These symbolists or traditionalists separated the desired holiness of art from the detritus of life, in order to reconstitute the illusion of a world ordered by an authority, by a presence recoverable in the work of art's ceremony of innocence. But Williams' opposing theory does not collapse art and life, or word and thing; on the contrary, the separation is fundamental. It is only a question of distance and relation. The prose of *Spring and All* repeatedly marks the difference between art and nature, words and things, poetry and prose—and therefore between presentation, which Williams calls "imitation," and representation, which he calls "copy" (Imag., 95, 107, 121, 122). From *Spring and All* to "The Desert Music" (PB, 109), as well as in his critical prose, he employed the terms with an unaccustomed consistency.

Imitation, he would argue, "involves the verb" (SL, 297),

while copy implies the "adjective" (SE, 303). To write a story, one must learn "not to place adjectives," but "to employ the verbs in imitation of nature" (SE, 302) and drive an action into a form—called a "plot." Not representation, then, but the *projection* of an activity of some "natural object" or "creation," is the artist's work: "It is perhaps a transit from adjective (the ideal 'copy') to verb (showing process)" (SE, 303). If works of art are natural creations, they are also *"additions* to nature" (SE, 302). Such additions are a "clarification of form" (SL, 226), and hence a subtraction from the chaotic manifold. They are movements from "the actual to the formal," the emergence of "culture" on the model (imitation) of nature (process coming to form).

The work of art is mimetic of process, of "active invention" and hence of making a "thing advanced and apart from" nature (A, 241). Williams' imitation is an act that is also a metaphor for demystifying metaphor. Imitating nature, we "become nature or we discover in ourselves nature's active part" (A, 241); or in a happier figure, from "The Desert Music," in the poem we "dance/ two and two with him—/ sequestered there asleep" (PB, 109). The dance here takes place around the fetal, "Egg-shaped!" form of an old drunk on the bridge between Juarez and El Paso. But the place is more primordial yet, the place where form begins its advance out of "inhuman shapelessness." At this "bridge" motion takes its measure against motionlessness, sound breaking out of silence. Or as Williams puts it in *Spring and All*, the "rock is split, the egg is hatched, the prismatically plumed bird of life has escaped from its cage" (Imag., 97). It is the place defined by "music" which "supersedes his composure," where the dance "wakens" from the music, where culture emerges and folds itself back over nature as in an original satyric dance. The poet *remembers* this as the lost time of authentic speech; the poem, as verb, imitates it, and makes it present once more in the musical time of the dance or fiction. It is in this sense that the Modern poet, like Lorca, can discover "in the old forms the very essence of today" (SE, 226).

Crude symbolism, forced metaphor, "the searching about in the daily experience for apt similes and pretty thoughts and images" (Imag., 120)—these are testimony to a subjectivist, representational, and associational poetics, because they either deny the discrete yet contiguous and homologous planes of language and nature or evoke an origin (and hence, a reality) in which the two are one. Williams experienced what he himself called an Imagist period and professed to have wanted to declare his own Vortex in relation to Pound's earlier adventure, but in his revolt from Imagism in the 1920s he regularly misconstrued the more fundamental theories of Imagism. By the late 1920s he felt he had to move from Imagism to Objectivism because, as he said, "Imagism was not structural" (SE, 283): "Note: Imagism, which had a use in focussing the attention upon the importance of concrete imagery in the poem, lost its place finally because as a form it completely lacked structural necessity. The image served for everything so that the structure, a weaker and weaker free verse, degenerated finally into a condition very nearly resembling that of the sonnet. The objectivists attempted to remedy this fault by fusing with each image a form in its own right. . . ." [19]

Disregarding Pound's careful distinctions between the visual image and the Image as "an intellectual and emotional complex in an instant of time," Williams came to define Imagism as mimetic, visual, static, and in the strictest sense, abstract because it had no "structural necessity." He seems never to have addressed himself to Pound's own antisubjectivist, anti-

19. William Carlos Williams, "The Basis of Form in Art" (MS in the Lockwood Library of the State University of New York at Buffalo), Env. 45; works in this collection will hereinafter be cited as Buffalo MS.

130 THE INVERTED BELL

visualist theory, nor to such theoretical pronouncements as
May Sinclair's on the distinction between Imagism and image
or imagery: "Presentation, not representation, is the watch-
word of the school. The Image I take it, is Form. But it is not
pure form. It is form *and* substance." [20] Pound's insistence on
"direct treatment of the 'thing' whether subjective or objective," indicates that the thing treated was the thing disclosed,
or projected, and not an object meditated, revolved, and
transcribed in a subject. The presentational, antivisual basis of
Pound's theory, however, easily became confused with the
pictorialism suggested by the words *image* or *imagery*. And the
direction this took, Pound called Amygism, the representation
of sentimental effects in patterned transparencies. His own
move from the Image to the Vortex indicates something more
than his recognition that the Imagist poem might tend to be
static, to lack the dynamic of speech and thus the form of
energy transference of the "verb" which Ernest Fenollosa had
found intrinsic to the Chinese written character.[21] Though the
Image emphasized a "complex" or gestalt of intersecting
forces, and Pound offered the analogy of a geometrical
equation in which the separate entities had value only in the
completeness of their interrelations as contrasted to the
invariable and prescribed value of number in an arithmetical
sequence, Pound was hard put to escape the visual, representational prejudice: "The defect of earlier Imagist propaganda,"
he was to write in the 1930s, "was not in misstatement but in
incomplete statement. The diluters took the handiest and
easiest meaning, and thought only of the STATIONARY
image. If you can't think of imagism or phanopoeia as
including the moving image, you will have to make a really

20. May Sinclair, "The Poems of H.D.," *Fortnightly Review*, n.s., CXXI (March,
1927), 329. See also her "Two Notes," *Egoist*, II (1915), 88.
21. See Ernest Fenollosa, "The Chinese Written Character as a Medium for
Poetry," included in Ezra Pound, *Instigations* (Freeport, N.Y.: Books for Libraries
Press, 1967), 357–88, esp. p. 363.

needless division of fixed image and praxis or action." [22] Phanopoeia was in one sense analogous to what Pound understood in 1916 as "cinematographic," a flow of images creating the effect of "super-positions." The cinema realized a synchronic time within the flow of diachronic successivity, until the work issued as a total Image, as a "radiant node or cluster," or "Vortex" ("planes in relation").[23] The poem as Image de-symbolized the world, and thus presented rather than represented.

Williams did indeed take the part of a "diluter" of Imagism. And when he and Louis Zukofsky set about their revisionism of the Image, which they came to call Objectivism, they pushed earlier Imagist doctrine more in the direction of a "structural" analysis. But they did not radically alter the premises of Pound's Vortex: "Poetic form . . . may be said, negatively, to comprise every use of the word beyond and including its literal prose sense. It relies on structure. Structurally the form itself is a 'word,' the most significant of all, that dominates every other word in the poem." [24] This is the poem's "being" beyond its prose meaning, the ontology of its primary language within the everyday language: "The poem as an object, an object which had a significance, by its form, in addition to what the prose phase of the poem had to say. . . . Imagism presented an image. You'll see that's all inside the poem. And trusted that to say something. But objectivism has to do with the structure of the poem as a metrical invention." [25]

22. Ezra Pound, *ABC of Reading*, New Classics Series (Norfolk, Conn.: New Directions, n.d.), 52.
23. Ezra Pound, *Gaudier-Brzeska, A Memoir* (New York, New Directions, 1970), 89–92.
24. Williams, "The Basis of Poetic Form," Buffalo MS, Env. 45.
25. Williams, "Concerning Modern Poetry (Columbia College Talk)," Buffalo MS, Env. 60. Another unpublished paper, "Dartmouth Talk," Buffalo MS, Env. 45, includes a similar passage: "Every poem has a prose meaning along with something else called form which together, under certain conditions, transform the whole into

If the poem is made exclusively to say something, then it speaks for something besides itself. For this reason Williams could argue that symbols, similes, and images denied at least one of the unique properties of words, either by pointing backward to the consciousness or subject who speaks itself in them or by pointing forward to some idea that transcends them, toward which they yearn. The point was that words could not avoid either of these properties, and that indeed to divorce their subjectivity from their objectivity was to upset the balance of language. Prose did this. Only the made poem, the invention, in which language brings to light its own nature, achieves the "structural necessity" of a new reality. Thus Williams can call the poem "a machine made of words" (CLP, 4). Structure, isolating the relations of words in contrast to their philological valence, makes the machine and nature homologous: "Nature is the hint to composition," a structural analogy, but nature and art are not continuous; nature "is [not] opposed to art but apposed to it" (Imag., 121).

The structural law of language rejects the priority of perception, and thus representation, just as it rejects the philology of symbolization. Williams insists on the diachronic dimension of language (the poem is "words at flow," SL, 175) as at least one of its undeniable properties, since words cannot be simultaneous and yet be different. But diachrony is only one dimension of the total structure, and perhaps not the major one. The sequential movement of words in the poem is essential to prevent words from collapsing into each other and thus destroying the "word" of the poem; yet "Either to write or to comprehend poetry the words must be recognized to be moving in a direction separate from the jostling or lack of it which occurs within the piece" (Imag., 146). In the interview with Mike Wallace, included in *Paterson*, Book Five, Williams

something which exists in neither of the elements," a *"complete significance"* (my italics).

denies that E. E. Cummings' well-known "c-a-t" poem is in fact a poem because its typographical gimmickery violates the relations of words, their essential difference, by making more than one word occupy the same place. The words cannot exist simultaneously. Words ex-ist only in place, and place means discrete difference. His own "grocery list," however, is a poem because he realizes not only the successivity but the measure of words in their interrelations (P, 224–25).

It is incorrect to read Williams' tree poems as copies of the tree, as visually thin like a tree and thus a picture poem. The analogy between "Young Sycamore" (CEP, 332) or "The Locust Tree in Flower" (CEP, 93–94) and the natural object lies in the structural parallels, and thus in the difference between art and nature. The young sycamore is a relation of parts, both systemically and spatially; and a poem is a relation of words, a "field." Cocoons are related to branches, branches to trunk, trunk to ground and top, and the whole to a place itself defined spatially and texturally "between the wet// pavement and the gutter." But it would be wrong to see the poem as an "image" of a tree or even of a place. The poem begins as a story, an address: "I must tell you." It does one of the things language can do, speak or address an other; it is manifest coexistence, a conversation. But in doing this, the words of the poem realize something more than the linear dimension of language. The words move from left to right and the lines from top to bottom; sounded, or spoken, they realize the distinctness of each part, particulars which exist only in relation to each other. The telling interprets, *relates*. The address of "I" to "you," neither of which exists without the other, creates a space or circuit in which the whole system of language is complete. Yet at the same time, the complete poem has meaning only when set beside nature. It is a homologue of utterance, or "talk," as the tree is a homologue of the structural necessity of nature. But one must not misconstrue nature's structure as an essence. It is nature as seen or understood, nature as interpreted and known, nature as experienced and lived in. In short, nature's order is a conception, a language. Nature is a metaphor for the poem; the poem is a metaphor for nature. Reciprocally, each becomes a metonymic substitution for the other. For neither can exist without the other, because they maintain within the space of their difference the enigma of their originary multiplicity.

Such a theory of language justifies a rhetorical poetry, like "Yachts" or "Impromptu: The Suckers," on the same grounds that it justifies an Objectivist structure like the shorter version of "The Locust Tree in Flower" (CEP, 93), in which the descriptive images and generally orderly syntax of the long version are abbreviated into one-word lines, giving a new significance to prepositions and adjectives. To use the implied pun of Zukofsky's book of criticism, it nominalizes pre-positions.[26] "The Locust Tree in Flower" names neither the parts of the tree nor their sequence of connections; nor does it offer the kaleidoscope of a consciousness moving from part to part of a tree, without connectives or logical sequence. On the contrary, the poem makes a statement, which is nothing less than a cliché, out of the fragment of an observation. But the important thing is the made poem, the new syntax of relations which catch in their instant the analogy between flowering tree, and the semioclastic law that seems to structure both language and nature. The poem is a disclosure of this principle, in language as in nature; just as one might say that a poem like "Yachts" (CEP, 106), with its oblique social commentary, draws its power from the discovery of a conflict between culture and nature. Its resort to what might be called the

26. Louis Zukofsky, *Prepositions* (New York: Horizon Press, 1967). Zukofsky therefore can draw upon the double meaning to help define poetry as placing: "A desire to place everything—everything aptly, perfectly, belonging within, one with, a context—" (p. 23).

pathetic fallacy in the concluding lines is justified apparently
by the need to see the conflict from within the experience of
one of the contenders. The "horror of the race" which staggers
the "mind" is the horror of a disclosure that can only be
spoken in the mood of the victim—that is, in the mood of man
discovering the depth of the void between culture and nature
and the violence that engendered their difference. That the
poem is also a disclosure of the violence within the economic
structure of capitalism only reinforces its nonrhetorical theme.

Williams' stress on *"tactus eruditus"* (CEP, 63), on the
primacy of contact as opposed to the secondary distancing of
the "eye," is basic to his awareness that the poem must
establish itself at the point of discovery or disclosure. Just as the
senses kill God, they kill the "explicit sentence" of the
"schoolmen" (P, 189), and rediscover language in its infinity, as
prior to the subject and to logic. The poem, Williams wrote
to Henry Wells, is a "social instrument," an "assertion,
always, of a new and total culture, the lifting of an environment to expression" (SL, 286). The poem does not express a
culture of the future, but discloses a "total culture," and thus
the original setting apart and gathering together that differentiates culture from nature. It totalizes by revealing the
infrastructure of an e-vent and thereby disclosing, in its own
totality, that a culture is "total" only in its primordial
structures. But this, of course, is a fiction maintained in
language. Until an environment is lifted to "expression," that
is, disclosed structurally, it has no being. *"Tactus eruditus"*
objectifies not because it is raw, undifferentiated, or naïve
experience, but because it differentiates in the primary sense of
setting side by side. Like the sniffing of dogs, it particularizes,
interprets, measures. The erudition of touch is a structure, and
as we will see, an abstraction.

"The structural approach," said Williams, "has two phases,
the first, the selection of forms from poems already achieved, to

restuff them with metaphysical and other matter and, the second, to parallel the inventive impetus of other times with structural concepts derived from our own day. The first is *weak*, the other *strong*." [27] The first is the way of Modernism, the "Traditionalists of Plagiarism"; the second is an avant garde return to an ancient and original art. The structural concepts of our own day are derivable from the "new physics," [28] particularly Einstein's theory of relativity with its constant of light: "Einstein had the speed of light as a constant—his only constant—What have we? Perhaps our concept of musical time" (SE, 286). It is a concept of totalization, to use the favorite term of structural anthropology, and it is a remarkable fact that Williams' "musical time" anticipates the methodological discovery that Lévi-Strauss sets forth in his Overture to *The Raw and the Cooked*. Music, says Lévi-Strauss, is like a myth in that both are "languages which in their different ways, transcend articulated expression, while at the same time—like articulate speech, but unlike painting—requiring a temporal dimension in which to un-fold." [29] Music and myth, then, are diachronic or linear in movement, but, according to Lévi-Strauss, they are diachronic in the very special sense that both "need time only in order to deny it":

> Both, indeed, are instruments for the obliteration of time. Below the level of sounds and rhythms, music acts upon a primitive terrain, which is the physiological time of the listener; this time is irreversible and therefore irredeemably diachronic, yet music transmutes the segment devoted to listening to it into a synchronic

27. Williams, "The Basis of Poetic Form," Buffalo MS, Env. 45.

28. Williams, "Notebook," Buffalo MS. This notebook contains important notes on *Paterson* and an early draft of the lectures Williams was to give at the University of Washington, later published in part in essay form under the title "The Poem as a Field of Action" (SE, 280–91).

29. Claude Lévi-Strauss, *The Raw and the Cooked*, trans. John and Doreen Weightman (New York: Harper & Row, 1969), 15. (Translation of *Mythologiques I, Le cru et le cuit*, 1964.)

totality, enclosed within itself. Because of the internal organization of the musical work, the act of listening to it immobilizes passing time; it catches and enfolds it as one catches and enfolds a cloth flapping in the wind. It follows that by listening to music, and while we are listening to it, we enter into a kind of immortality.[30]

Without attempting to pursue the intricacies and complexities of Lévi-Strauss's argument, which sharply distinguishes between music and the arts of poetry and painting, one can say that the anthropologist's view of poetry is what Williams would call traditional, and that the poet tends to interpret poetry and abstract painting in terms not unlike those Lévi-Strauss applies to music. What is important here, however, is not the relation of the two theories, but the way in which Lévi-Strauss throws light on Williams' search for a constant in "musical time," for an authentic language. For Williams' measure, like Straussian myths, implies the anonymity of the poem, a language which speaks the underlying totality of the culture which those individuals living in the culture cannot hear. The illusion of diachrony in the language of the poem is only that, for what the time of the poem discloses is the origin of time. The constant in a Williams poem is the constant the poem must disclose, the structure of the "hidden language." "Musical time," for Williams, is the synchronic "design" of particulars, the "time" of their real relation rather than the time of their perceived relation. It is the constant that must be assumed if one is to assume a structure, for structures are not centerless though the center may be anywhere and nowhere. Musical time holds us in the temporality of legend, the dream of wholeness. And yet, because a poem is *told* in words, it tends, unlike music, to bring its medium into question, to demythologize its "musical time." Unlike Lévi-Strauss, Williams cannot embrace the musical

30. *Ibid.,* 16.

analogy of interpretation, or hold out nostalgically for a recovery of an absolute, a presence in poetry. He continues to embrace the painterly metaphor, though it be cubist deconstruction.

In speaking of the art of his friend Charles Sheeler, Williams revealed what is perhaps the clearest key we have to the structural nature of his poetics. The world, he said, "is always seeking meanings! breaking down everything to its 'component parts,' not always without loss" (SE, 233). This movement toward abstraction, or de-composition, was evident in early Sheeler, said Williams. Later, he "turned, where his growth was to lie, to a *subtler particularization,* the *abstract* if you will but left by the artist integral with its native detail" (SE, 233—my italics). The early style decomposes a recognizable world of things into the elementary abstraction of lines, shapes, masses, and colors, like analytic cubism; while the later brings identifiable things into a single plane of relations which preserves the particularity of the thing even as it reveals the "subtler particularization" of relations, like synthetic cubism.[31] "Only where the eye hits does sight occur" (SE, 234), writes Williams, echoing the Objectivist manifesto of Louis Zukofsky: "An Objective: (Optics)—the lens bringing the rays from an object to a focus. That which is aimed at. . . . Desire for what is objectively perfect, inextricably the direction of historic and contemporary particulars." [32] The focus, one notes, is on a plane which is neither that of the particular object nor that of a constituting subject. In optics, the particular is drawn out of its context and brought to focus against the

31. The distinction between the two kinds of Cubism is well made by Daniel-Henry Kahnweiler, *Juan Gris: His Life and Work,* trans. Douglas Cooper (New York: H. N. Abrams, 1969), 141. Kahnweiler describes the relation of Gris' "signs," the objects or emblems of things he brings together on his canvases, as "rhymes," which "reveal certain hidden relationships, similarities between two apparently different objects." See also Jerome Mazzaro, *William Carlos Williams: The Later Poetry* (Ithaca, N.Y.: Cornell University Press, 1973), 50.

32. *Prepositions,* p. 21.

blurred or deflected background of the context it once existed in.[33] The lens literally draws the object into focus, discloses it—at once breaks up a familiar unity and gathers the rays into a new "objectively perfect" being. Measure in the time of a poem does this, creating a "subtler particularization" or focus for materials we commonly know on another (common-sense) plane. The subtler particularization, then, is a disclosure, like the Gris painting discussed in *Spring and All*, which maintains the outline of details as truly as if they had been photographed but runs them together in a simultaneous plane of relation, "detached" from the ordinary perspective of a privileged viewer.

"The local is the universal" (SE, 233) in the focus of an artist who can "look past the object to 'abstraction' " (SE, 234), a kind of "glandular perception" of the "uniqueness" of things in their field: "To discover and separate these things from the amorphous, the conglomerate normality with which they are surrounded and of which before the act of 'creation' each is a part, calls for an eye to draw out that detail which is in itself the thing, to clinch our insight, that is, our understanding, of it" (SE, 233). Getting rid of what Charles Olson[34] calls the "lyrical interference of the individual as ego, of the 'subject' and his soul, that particular presumption by which western man has interposed himself between what he is as a creature of nature . . . and the other creations of nature which we may, with no derogation, call objects"—the poet steps outside his

33. See James Guimond, *The Art of William Carlos Williams* (Urbana: University of Illinois Press, 1968), 95–96.

34. Charles Olson, "Projective Verse," *Selected Writings*, ed. with introd. Robert Creeley (New York: New Directions, 1966), 24. See also "Letter to Elaine Feinstein," 28, where Olson comments on the "double axis" of present-day poetry: "the replacement of the Classical-representational by the *primitive-abstract* . . . I mean of course not at all primitive in that stupid use of it as opposed to civilized. One means it now as 'primary,' as how one finds anything, pick it up as one does new—fresh/first. Thus one is equal across history forward and back, and it's all levy, as present is, but sd that way, one states . . . a different space-time."

"I" to the point of focus beyond reflection. He stands on the other side of the object. The "musical time" of the poem is a counterpoint of the two sides of language, an "abstraction" like those of "Arabic art" which, as Williams says in *Paterson*, Book Five, are at the beginning of all art and thus the beginning of a "cure" of historical cleavage (P, 222).

V

Paterson, as its epigraph indicates, is ordered on one level by the cycle of seasons, "spring, summer, fall and the sea" (P, 2); and on another, the first four books evoke sequentially a world reduced toward the primal elements of air, earth, fire, and water. Yet, just as one might argue that the first two books feature respectively earth and air rather than air and earth, and that in reality the dominant element of any one book (say, the fire of Book Three) is consistently complemented by the other three (the flood, tornado winds, and earthquake of the same book), so can he argue that the successive books only generally subscribe to the movement of seasons.[35] But this is simply to say that Williams does not use such basic formal devices as devices, or as "crude symbolism." The elements and seasons define each other and contextually embody the elemental ground upon which all human experience is lived; they define the irreducible field of man's historical departure into complexity. Each successive book indicates the systemic continuity of season flowing into season and not the arbitrary meaning of an allegorical sequence. It is a complete cycle which we understand, however, only in the language of distinct and discontinuous seasons. Time is the field of *Paterson*, the musical time enfolding historical time. And this time is the mythic time of interpretation reinterpreted. It is a parody of the "eternal

35. Louis L. Martz, "*Paterson*: A Plan for Action," *Journal of Modern Literature*, I (May, 1971), 512–22, rejects the idea that Williams' "plan" can be reduced, either theoretically or texturally, to external designs like the seasonal cycle.

return." Considered as a response to Eliot's *Quartets* in particular and the "Traditionalists of Plagiarism" in general, the naturalness of Williams' elemental ground is credible precisely because it is not used literarily or symbolically. It is allowed to emerge as the basic and irreducible abstraction one discovers when he penetrates either the plenitude or aridness of his experience to an interpretation of it. Though Williams is as conscious as Eliot of the symbolic lode of the alchemical elements, and of their role in the history of thought and literature, he is willing to accept mythic structures on their own totalizing terms. He does not use them, like Eliot, to shore up another (superior) mythology or body of belief that in turn absorbs and demythologizes the original myth.

Williams does not admit to a hierarchy of myths referring to an origin outside their various degrees of purity. Eliot views the elemental reduction as a kind of language by which alone man might imperfectly understand truth, or that which stands beyond myth and language, beyond knowledge, at some unknowable "still-point." For Williams, however, the elemental is always with us, as surely as our reality is inherently structured and moves from the invisible to the visible. Man lives his reason without knowing it, without knowing the design of his life. But ultimately his life is his understanding, his capacity for seeing the design disclose itself through him. That is, it is his movement from inarticulateness to speech. Man in his life is the measurer. Every place must have its poet, be lifted to expression and thus be totalized—except that historical man is simultaneously involved in the interpretation and demystification of the "dream" that he can know totally.

It is in this sense that the seasons function in *Paterson*. They are there in the poem as in the life of a resident of Paterson, both concretely and abstractly. They are successive and thus temporal, yet cyclic and repetitious. But in turn, the seasons are in themselves a language, the syntax of a continuous and renewable disclosure, of sameness and difference. As Williams put it in *Spring and All*, nature is a plagiarist, condemned to repeat itself. Unlike art, however, nature cannot raise itself to a new set of particulars. The expression of the seasons, then, constitutes the mythic time of the poem, the universal time that Williams calls structure. Man builds his particular (cultural) time, his city, upon this natural time. "The place where the time-lag is still adamant—is structure"—this, he says, is the last "dream" the poet has "clung to"; but reluctantly, the post-Modern has had to awaken to a new "reality": "How do we know reality? The only reality that we can know is MEASURE" (SE, 283). The cycle of seasons is the basic, primordial measure of the poem, the time in which all the particulars are measured, as opposed to the perspectival and sequential order in which they are arranged in the recorded history of the place. The "field of action" is the place of musical time, of a mythic order, of a "structure" ruled by "Einstein's theory of relativity." Structure is the ground of irreducible difference to which all complexity is referred.

Book Two is an exemplary phase of this subtler particularization, the more so because of the metapoetic level to which the language occasionally rises and the apparent "nul" it discloses as its source. *Paterson*, Book Two, is the summer poem, or more accurately, the "late spring" poem, as the opening lines announce (P, 43). Its time is the time of myth, ritual, holiday, a "Sunday in the Park," centering about the rituals in the "pubic grove" that has replaced the "sacred wood" (P, 53). It is a world which the poet experiences as "Outside/ outside myself," yet "subject to my incursions":

               —a world
                        (to me) at rest,
                                which I approach
          concretely—
                        The scene's the park

> upon the rock,
> female to the city
> —upon whose body Paterson instructs his thoughts
> (P, 43)

Dr. Paterson is the language, the verb of the scene who effects the transit from point to point in the park; his thought instructed upon the rock is the thought of musical time, a rhythm that measures event from event, sound from sound in the park, yet enfolds each one upon the other. *Walking* is the primary verb of Book Two, and Dr. Paterson's walk in his world is as elementary and as mythic as Satan's. It is the gesture of curiosity. Getting outside himself is an act of disclosing, of bringing himself and his environment to expression: he "seeks to induce his bones to rise into a scene,/ his dry bones, above the scene, (they will not)" (P, 80). Like Eliot's Tiresias he sees all, but does not suffer all, for unlike Tiresias he does not speak what man cannot hear, but hears what man cannot speak. Like the evangelical preacher in the park, he is a "voice, one among many (unheard)/ moving under all" (P, 56), the profound poetry running beneath the "roar" of the "great beast." *"What do I do? I listen, to the water falling. . . . This is my entire occupation"* (P, 45). Among the multiple of voices there is "the movement of one voice among the rest" (P, 54). Paterson alone hears this voice and speaks it in turn. It is the emerging "new mind" of the place:

> Without invention nothing is well spaced,
> unless the mind change, unless
> the stars are new measured, according
> to their relative positions, the
> line will not change, the necessity
> will not matriculate; unless there is
> a new mind there cannot be a new
> line   (P, 50)

This rhetoric, or metapoetic reflection, is justifiable within the role of Paterson as doctor and poet, listener and talker. For Dr. Paterson recognizes that language, like his anatomy chart of man walking, is the structure of our understanding; and until we have generated a new model, respacing the jumbled entities, there will be no new knowledge. The voice moving beneath the voices, unheard, is an invisible language on the verge of disclosure. The poem itself, a late spring poem, is like the famous first poem of *Spring and All*, the rhythm or action of this agonizing forthcoming.

Dr. Paterson's walk in the park is random. The particulars or fragments he sees and hears are like the "distorted subjects" of the Greek "choliambi"; they demand a "deformed verse" (P, 40). But de-formation is only a prelude to invention, an in-rushing of "Voices!/ multiple and inarticulate" to be spoken as one voice, the new line of the new mind. Thus Dr. Paterson's walk becomes a descent, a pursuit of the "nul" that is the center of "all/ equations," the "N" that signifies the differential of mathematics and particulars (P, 77). The nul is "past all/ seeing// the death of all/ that's past// all being." It is not a nihility, then, not an absence, but an elemental reduction, to the point (that is not a point) at which one system torques into another. Like the variable of Riemannian geometry, the "N" is the presence of an absence in any local field that will allow one to move from that field to another and to the universal field theory.[36] It is a sign of difference.

36. Whether or not Williams has in mind the Riemannian theory (as Charles Olson in fact does in an essay review and again in his "Mayan Letters," *Selected Writings*, 46, 84), his reference to the "N" offers a number of suggestive analogies. For example, one of Riemann's contributions to geometrical theory was the idea of studying the properties of geometrical space locally, rather than universally or absolutely. Riemann's theories, of course, lie behind modern theories of relativity, and introduce such mathematical possibilities as geodesic structures. And most significantly for Williams' new measure, the entry in the *Encyclopaedia Britannica* (1964), XIX, 302, offers the following: "One type of generalization of Riemannian geometry is that in which there is no assigned metric, but the basic concept is a generalization of geodesic lines."

The context of this crucial passage, which opens the third part of Book Two, is all important. The imperative to "Look for the nul" is enigmatic. Beyond all being there is either non-being, nothingness, or the unknown, a world where all recognizable laws are suspended, a world where the old Euclidian or Cartesian mathematic is changed. It could be a world of full presence, or a nothingness. But it is in the face of this new opening, and hence this death of the old, that the poet offers his answer to the "Traditionalists of Plagiarism": "But Spring shall come and flowers will bloom/ and man must chatter of his doom . . ." (P, 77). Rejecting the old mathematic, and the wasteland vision, Dr. Paterson launches into descent rather than despair. It is revealing that the passage which immediately follows ("The descent beckons/ as the ascent beckoned . . .") discovers what Williams would later recognize to be the basic tripartite line of his own new measure, his own new differential equation, that can lead from a world lost to a new world "unsuspected." For it is precisely a differential equation of language that is signified by the "N," that "blank" or "rock" which when pulled away reveals the zero-degree of language.

The "N" of all equations allows one local field to curve upon another, discovers parallels between curving vectors, and allows the kind of systemic shift from one plane or space to another without collapsing the two, as man sentimentally collapses nature and culture at the beginning and end of his teleological myths or radically separates them in his nihilistic despair. The "nul" passage, in other words, is one of several metapoetic asides in Book Two, passages which instead of prescribing any new measure or mathematic confirm the urgency of moving beyond the known into "that nul// that's past all/ seeing" (P, 77). To seek is to affirm neither presence nor absence but openness: "the world it opens is always a place/ formerly/ unsuspected" (P, 78). Dr. Paterson's walk, his search in the park, pursues traces of a new world. Those traces are not relics of some ideal past, but of man's act of seeking:

> Loiterers in groups straggle
> over the bare rock-table—scratched by their
> boot nails more than the glacier scratched
> them—walking indifferent through
> each other's privacy   .
>   —in any case,
> the center of movement, the core of gaiety.
>   (P, 56)

The scratches on the rock, whether by glacier or boot nails, are as elemental as the language of place, traces on "the blank/ that holds them up" (P, 77), and thus the opposite of indifference. They are the "trace" of an unremembered desire to discover new worlds. Paterson's walk up the mountain and down again discovers the "musical time" which binds the present scene to the timeless. The Dionysiac dance of the immigrant Italian picnickers, its origins now unrecognized, reminds him of the "old, the very old, old upon old,/ the undying: even to the minute gestures,/ the hand holding the cup, the wine" (P, 57). The immigrants begin again on their new ground by repeating mindlessly the timeless dance of their origins. And just as Dr. Paterson sees in that dance the "air of the Midi" and the juvenescent intoxication of "the old cultures," he hears in the silences of the evangelist's shouting and recalls in his own memory of Eisenstein's lost film the trace of a center which nihilism denies. His "Sunday in the Park" discovers the recurrent rhythm of the Dionysiac dithyramb underlying the "orchestral dullness" that "overlays their world" (P, 62). He brings to expression a "subtler particularization."

Dr. Paterson's walk is necessitated by the distance and unrelatedness of the multiple voices, "scattered over the mountain/ severally" (P, 60). For though the park is centered upon an "observation tower" standing within "its pubic grove" (P, 53), a phallic tower as many critics have suggested, it is seen only "in the middle distance." It is the signifier of a centerless field, and of events perspectively scattered like the random detail of Paterson's history. The "scattered" voices recall the legend of Babel and God's scattering of the languages of the human tribes who had built a tower dedicated to their own and not His design. The random activities of the park, whether the meaningless sexual activity of the young or the blurred signification of old Mary's ritual dance, accompanied by a young man "playing a guitar, dead pan" (P, 57)—the random voices can only be heard as "one voice" by a poet who does not establish himself at a fixed center but who moves through the "musical time" that is the equation of all the separate vectors. Walking up and down, the poet sees what is there and what is not: "Time! Count! Sever and mark time!" (P, 56).

Eisenstein's lost film becomes the structural model for gathering once more the scattered voices into a montage of sharply distinguished detail, into a "complex" (P, 60). The scene must be presented as a "deformity" to be "deciphered" (P, 61). On the surfaces of this scene there is "blockage," the failure of language and therefore the failure of coexistence, which marks the frustration of sexual gesturings and individual expression alike: the poet Cress's hysterical allegations; the young people aimlessly and automatically fondling each other in the park; Klaus Ehren's harangue; the official mediation of the church between man and nature; the economic exploitation of the bomb; Hamilton's "Ass*um*ption"; the legal exclusion of unleashed dogs from the park and therefore the official suppression of the fecundative principle; and, not least, the suppression of Eisenstein's film and therefore of the kind of mythical consciousness by which a culture might survive.

The lines on Eisenstein's lost film are a good instance of the musical time of Paterson's walk.[37] They are suggested by association in his "dream" with the satyric and "undying" dance of old Mary. He recalls the "lost" film—"Que Viva Mexico"—as an instance of life affirming itself even though suppressed, and of the coexistence of parallel contraries. (The film depicts the modern suppression of ageless instincts; and the film itself was suppressed.) The dancing "peon" of that "lost" negative is a "Heavenly man!":

> —the leg raised, verisimilitude
> even to the coarse contours of the leg, the
> bovine touch! The leer, the cave of it,
> the female of it facing the male, the satyr—
> (Priapus!)   (P, 58)

Here is Plato's myth denied. The "leer," that visual separation of subject and object that confines man to the cave of representation, is overcome in the dance of opposites, the male entering the female cave, fulfilling the "fecundative principle." In the measure of a remembered dance, the poet thinks of Priapus, son of Dionysus and Aphrodite, an embodiment of phallic power. Memory brings him once more into the presence of an original violence. Like silence within the shouting of the evangelist, whose "harangue hung featureless/ upon the ear, yet with a certain strangeness/ as if arrested in space" (P, 70), the remembered and the real dance, both that of art and that of life, reveals the "principle" that holds in place differences. Eisenstein called his film a "weave" of parallel

37. In Sergei Eisenstein, *The Film Sense* (New York: Harvest Books, 1947), 251, Eisenstein wrote that the structural principle of his film was based on the Mexican "serape" or "striped blanket" which, he said, is a "symbol of Mexico": of its "contrary cultures" which run parallel to each other, contiguous though "centuries" apart. Thus the six separate episodes of the picture represent the different colors of the blanket: "different in character, different in animals, trees and flowers. And still held together by the unity of the weave—a rhythmic and musical construction." The blanket is a manifestation of historical synchronism.

fields, like the colors of a serape, a figure that will become even more crucial with the appearance of the tapestries, first in Book Three and then centrally in Book Five. The film's "musical construction" holds together differences of time and place. Thus its "place" in Williams' local.

Beneath the evangelist's shout, his rhetoric of self-denial, Paterson hears the rhythms of rebirth:

> —the spirit of our Lord that gives
> the words of even such a plain, ignorant fellow
> as I a touch of His Own blessed dignity and
> strength among you . . .   (P, 66)

It proclaims the presentness of a presence (the Word) where there is now an apparent absence:

> The gentle Christ
> child of Pericles
> and femina practa
>
> Split between
> Athens and
> amphyoxus
>   (P, 72)

But the voice reveals only the presence of an absence:

> The gentle Christ
> weed and worth
> wistfully forthright
>
> Weeps and is
> remembered as of
> the open tomb
>   (P, 72)

The Word-made-flesh here is the son of the eloquent speaker of the word (Pericles) whose law is implanted in the body politic of history. He incorporates Athens, the highest civilized state, and amphyoxus, the elemental sea animal; he connects in the "word" the absolute difference between "man" and "animalcules" (P, 5). But most important, his power is in his absence; his presence is revealed only in rolling away the "rock," exposing the "empty tomb" that is the perfect figure for language. The tomb, like the sarcophagi at the center of Egyptian pyramids,[38] contains the fundamental mystery around which all language moves; and the poem opens this tomb only to reify the mystery, the absence that sustains the myth that holds up the "rock." The remembered Christ and the remembered film—both are evidence that "Memory is a kind/ of accomplishment/ a sort of renewal/ even an initiation, since the spaces it opens are new places" (P, 77). Like Christ's tomb, a descent leads to an opening, and on that opening all meaning depends. Descent inaugurates by decentering.

38. One recalls here the remarkable figure of Georg W. Friedrich Hegel, *The Phenomenology of Mind*, trans. with introd. and notes J. B. Baillie, and introd. George Lichtheim (New York: Harper Torchbooks, 1967), in regard to "Spirit" as a "form of the artificer." Spirit, he says, builds its own house, the pyramids being the earliest and most abstract manifestation of this building. Pyramids therefore are not yet "endued with spirit." Such works "only receive spirit into them as an alien, departed spirit, one that has forsaken its living suffusion and permeation with reality, and, being itself dead, enters into those lifeless crystals." Derrida, in his essay, "Differance," included in Jacques Derrida, *Speech and Phenomena: And Other Essays on Husserl's Theory of Signs*, ed. and trans. David B. Allison (Evanston, Ill.: Northwestern University Press, 1973), takes another text of Hegel's from the *Encyclopedie*, "where he compares the body of the sign to an Egyptian pyramid. The *a* of differance, therefore, is not heard; it remains silent, secret, and discreet, like a tomb." Derrida's reading emphasizes the *A* shape of the pyramid, the crypt of which when opened is empty, as an example of the substantive emptiness of language—in this instance, he spells difference with an *a* (thus *différance*) in order to accentuate the nature of graphic difference, that writing marks a break with presence that is characteristic of all language, including speech. In a more literary and post-Hegelian vein, one might also recall Melville's passage in *Pierre*, ed. Harrison Hayford, Hershel Parker, and G. Thomas Tanselle (Evanston, Ill.: Northwestern University Press, 1971), 285: "But, far as any geologist has yet gone down into the world, it is found to consist of nothing but surface stratified on surface. To its axis, the world being nothing but superinduced superficies. By vast pains we mine into the pyramid; by horrible gropings we come to the central room; with joy we espy the sarcophagus; but we lift the lid—and no body is there!—appallingly vacant as vast is the soul of a man." Melville's interpretation, of course, anticipates Nietzsche's denial of the origin, his view that man must "suspect behind each cave a deeper cave, a more extensive, richer world beyond the surface, a bottomless abyss beyond every 'bottom,' beneath every 'foundation'." See Friedrich Nietzsche, *Beyond Good and Evil*, trans. Marianne Cowan (Chicago: Regnery, 1955), 62–63.

Man's descent is as futile and as meaningful as the eagle which, making himself small, attempts to return to the egg though he "would not—for all/ the effort of the struggle, remain/ inside" (P, 73). The poet's search for the "sum" is destined to reveal his origins only as emptiness, or silence. It reveals the essential "nul" that is the equation of "all being." His wandering is like "foot pacing foot outward/ into emptiness" (P, 63). Unlike Hamilton, who violates the memory of the "Assumption" by making it the "assumption of the Federal Government of the national debt" (P, 67), the evangelist, or speaker of the word, discovers the good only by divesting himself of worldly goods just as he empties his words of everything but the silence at their center. Hamilton imposes his SUM (*S*ociety for *E*stablishing *U*seful *M*anufacturers) upon the place, by generating the *N*ational *U*sury *S*ystem, itself an inverted acronym of the origin of light. Hamilton's economics have produced Paterson the city, and its multiple divorces. And now a poet must come to seek the sum once more, but with defective means and with the awareness of his inevitable defeat. For the words he inherits speak only of the violation of origins: the empty tomb, the lost film, the "nul" that "defeats it all," the "world" that is "gone," the city "reversed in the mirror of its/ own squalor" (P, 81), the "history" which is pandered.

He desires to create the poem as "rock and temple" and "induce his bones to rise into the scene" (P, 90)—that is, to create in the closed and sacred space of art a true presence that will express a "total culture." He desires to make language flower once more. He desires to bring the silence of an "unequivocal" music which he hears "scattered over the mountain" (P, 60) to a new expression. But he can only "remember" loss, "remember when as a child/ I stopped praying and shook with fear/ until sleep—your sleep calmed me—" (P, 74). The "you" is the "eternal bride and/ father," the miracle of presence or the word in the world. To remember what is lost, however, is to re-member the scattered and fragmented present upon a center that is not fixed. If language will not flower and bloom with revelation once again, as spring does, it can be made to flower in the fictional space of the made poem. But invention calls attention to its own fictiveness:

> without invention the line
> will never again take on its ancient
> divisions when the word, a supple word,
> lived in it, crumbled now to chalk.
>
> (P, 50)

The enduring hope of one's walk in the world is to find something there, "lost among the words" (P, 84), a hope that sustains itself by calling each invention into question and opening the search once more. It is the allegory of language and history, of the "open tomb." It is a double opening, the poetic resistance to history's closure.

3

history follows governments and never men. It
portrays us in generic patterns, like effigies
or the carvings on sarcophagi, which say
nothing save, of such and such a man, that he
is dead. . . . History must stay open, it is all
humanity.   (IAG, 188–89)

Everything exists from the beginning.
                              (Imag., 158)
the imagination
         knows all stories
                     before they are told
                              (PB, 61)
Everything we do must be a repetition of
the past with a difference.   (Imag., 210)

Poem and City: The Sarcophagus of Time

I

"I conceived the whole of *Paterson* at one stroke and wrote it down—as it appears at the beginning of the poem. All I had to do after that was fill in the details as I went along, from day to day" (SL, 333). Williams was speaking, probably, of the epigraph and its multiple paradoxes; or perhaps of the Preface, with its differences ("obverse, reverse") multiplying into a reduction to one; or even perhaps of the delineation of the giants, those basic opposites (man and woman, city and park) which divide into the initial utterance of the poem. Then again, he was very likely speaking of none of these, but rather was articulating the problematic of all conception. In the beginning, everything ex-ists—always already; or better, the "design" of the poem is "centered" upon a manifold. It is polytropically a-centric. All subsequent details, added and subtracted day to day, refer to that mysterious conception. What is important here, however, is that this conception or beginning is not necessarily a point of time before the time of the poem. Though it is, like all beginnings, a "stroke" immediately left behind, it is nevertheless a time which the details in their flow and rebound circle and enfold, repeat and recapitulate. It is that stroke which the poem desires to bring to light. For it is to this moment, of the appearance of the design, the poem incessantly returns and from which it simultaneously recedes. Thus the stroke is also a "past" which the poem repeats, but always with a "difference" (Imag., 210).

That is not, of course, how poems are conceived or written historically, but is itself a "myth" or perhaps simply a "story" of creation, the "fecundative principle" as Williams elsewhere called it. Again, polytropic difference decenters the design: man and woman, "A man like a city and a woman like a flower/ —who are in love. Two women. Three women./ Innumerable women, each like a flower" (P, 7). The opposites really are culture (city) and nature (flower), or perhaps history and innocence, design and body, *logos* and *physis*. In his epigraph to Book Three, taken from George Santayana's *The Last Puritan*, Williams reinforces the problematic of history which haunts the poem: "Cities, for Oliver, were not a part of nature. He could hardly feel, he could hardly admit even when it was pointed out to him, that cities are a second body for the human mind, a second organism, more rational, permanent and decorative than the animal organism of flesh and bone: a work of natural yet moral art, where the soul sets up her trophies of action and instruments of pleasure" (P, 94).

The Puritan of *In the American Grain* is Williams' figure of man twisted by the tyranny of history. The Puritan subordinates himself to a distant and rigid center and suffers the confusions of the manifold world until he can relate them all back to that original unity from which they have fallen. There is no flowering for the Puritan, no continuity between culture and nature; nature represents for him the manifestation of loss or the absence which is really himself, his flesh. Nature signifies its and therefore man's nothingness. Just as Cotton Mather takes the language of nature as providential signs, he takes those signs as evidence of their own emptiness, the veil cast between man and the Word. For the Puritan, God's wonder-working providences are ample testimony to the distance of man from the source, his fallenness and scatteredness; the symbolic opaqueness of language only increases man's awareness of that distance, and of the veil which has fallen between him and the center he would know. When Williams sets down Mather's providential descriptions verbatim, he reveals the distance between word and thing that constitutes Mather's divorce from the world and the emptiness of his curiosity and desire. The world is a "riddle" for the Puritan, a riddle only partly decoded by an original Word or Text, the Bible. Even man in a state of grace is condemned to interpretation. Characteristically, Williams concludes the Mather section with the following remark: "Unriddle these Things" (IAG, 104). On the other hand, Boone and Rasles, Burr and Houston suffer no such distance; or when they do, they depart from the place which distances (civilization) toward some yet undiscovered "back country" or some as yet untouched wonder. For Mather, "wonder" is supernatural, some remote lost perfection apocalyptically recalled by natural sign; for those in the truer American grain, "wonder" is openness, made manifest by the step they take into the silence of their desire. For Mather, truth lies out of time; for the wanderer, his truth is his temporality, his discovery of his historicity in his act.

The laying of man beside woman, city beside park, or culture beside nature suggests that the original conception of *Paterson*, that "one stroke," was in itself a thematizing of the poem as a poem of time. If man is a city, "one man like a city," and woman a flower, they constitute two different but interpenetrating times. Nature is multiple ("Innumerable women"), but each part repeats its time, its flowering and scattering of seed, at once independently and systemically. Nature is one in many. Culture, in contrast, is a labyrinthine and historical organism which is at once a gathering of diverse parts and a system of indissoluble differences. Culture is many in one. Woman-nature is irrational; man-city is rational.

Nature's time is synchronic; culture's time is diachronic. Yet
nature evolves by a sequence of repetitions that is a plagiarism;
culture evolves by a sequence of concentrated places (cities)
which in their difference repeat the same pattern of organization and decay.[1] In their necessary difference, they incline
toward each other. Like man and woman, they are locked in a
"desire" for each other, and incline toward a marriage,
suggesting an original, lost unity. Their essential difference is,
indeed, a "marriage riddle" (P, 105) as Williams puts it in
Paterson, a "riddle (in the Joycean mode— . . .)" which
holds the enigma of death at its center:

> What end but love, that stares death in the eye?
> A city, a marriage—that stares death
> in the eye.
> . . . .
> Sing me a song to make death tolerable, a song
> of a man and a woman: the riddle of a man
> and a woman.   (P, 106–107)

Love, like Eros which married Heaven and Earth in the
original myth of creation out of Chaos, suggests the presence
of an original unity. Yet it is also the sign of man's historicity,
his temporality and therefore his movement toward death. And
only "love," the "song" of the possible restoration of that
origin, can make "death tolerable," remarry man to nature's
deathlessness. Modern history, however, is the history of
"corrupt cities,/ nothing else, that death stares in the eye,/

1. One might compare the metaphor of Brooks Adams' book, *The Law of
Civilization and Decay* (New York: Alfred A. Knopf, 1943), which so influenced Ezra
Pound. Adams is mentioned in *Paterson*, in one of Pound's letters (P, 138). Adams'
economics, and the "law" he discovers, predicts "oscillations between barbarism and
civilization, or, what amounts to the same thing . . . movement from a condition of
physical dispersion to one of concentration" (p. 59). Nature's energy and primitive
force are dispersed; civilizations move always toward a centralization of this energy
(Pound's Vortex). At the point of utmost concentration inertia threatens and a
"stationary period may supervene" (p. 61), but inevitably a new motion of
decentralization and decay ensues, and a "reversion may take place to a primitive form
of organism" (p. 61).

lacking love" (P, 107). It is history as "divorce," of man deprived of his sources. History is the increasing cleavage of culture from nature, of city from the park and therefore from her whose "monstrous hair" reaches into the "back country" (P, 8), into the primal scene of originary Chaos.

The history of the West, as Williams had conceived it in *In the American Grain*, had been the history of divorce which has provoked a senseless plagiarism, the repeated attempt to transport one tradition into an alien place in order to confirm the continuity of history. The destruction of the "barbaric city" (IAG, 27) of Tenochtitlan by adventurers bearing the will of the "royal name" and the "true church" (IAG, 29) is his primary historical instance: the violation of the original interpenetration of city and nature in the name of a superior idea. For Williams, Cortez is only the incarnation of "instincts, ancient beyond thought," which launch the adventurer into the "recreative New"; but the "instincts" for "adventure" are subordinated to the "name" of a higher presence (God or king), and discovery is followed by destruction in the name of that authority because the world is "evil" (IAG, 27). Thus westering itself reverses the dependency of *logos* on nature; adventure in the name of emptiness violates the pagan ecology: "the tribe's deep feeling for a reality that stems back into the permanence of remote origins" (IAG, 33). "It was the earthward thrust of their logic," Williams argues, "the realization of their primal and continuous identity with the ground itself, where everything is fixed in darkness" (IAG, 33–34), that defines the original city dweller and marks the city as a flower. Tenochtitlan revealed a "religious sense," sacralized in its icons and temples and manifest in its vortex of forms. These forms "drive upward, toward the sun and the stars" (IAG, 35). That Tenochtitlan was a flowering city, a complexly advanced culture, a place of "genius" (IAG, 27), is just Williams' point. The poet of *Paterson* is at once like the natives of this city, in that he recalls his sources, and yet like the inhabitants of the modern city, "divided as the dew" (P, 5), a *genius* which has lost its *loci*.

The urgency of "love" in *Paterson*, and the debasements of sex, are in one sense at least a thematization of the "riddle" of history. For what the modern city represents, in its distance from that time when a "wild and cultured life grew up together in the Ramapos" (P, 12), is the disappearance of that *presence* or constitutive center which Western man has always assumed in his "assumption" that he lives in a purposeful history, that he lives teleologically. Hamilton's "SUM," indeed, is the economic design of a confirmed presence, of a world with a deistic center and of nature as a creative presence.[2] Any rational design impressed upon nature could only coincide with the immanent design of nature itself, the coincidence of reason with reason. For Hamilton there was no cleavage of culture and nature, for nature simply did not exist. Nature was presence, power. But the modern city is the testimony to Hamilton's design, the systematic imposition of reason to channel power, the tyranny of reason which divides and multiplies both vertically and horizontally. Nature becomes the forgetfulness of reason, and the city lies "forked by preconception and accident" (P, 6). Nature exists to be subdued, channeled, used, spent.

Only the poet remembers the original union, or better, the original marriage, and the catastrophic birth of original division.[3] The poet is the suppressed androgyne, a male

2. See Jean Starobinski, *The Invention of Liberty, 1700–1789*, trans. Bernard C. Swift (Geneva: Skira, 1964), *passim*, for the eighteenth-century view of nature and language. Also, Michel Foucault, *The Order of Things: An Archeology of the Human Sciences* (New York: Random House, 1970), especially on the imagination of representation and on the discourse of nature.

3. The metaphor here refers to Williams' poem "Catastrophic Birth" (CLP, 8), a poem about destructive violence at the heart of nature. It is also about creative violence, the volcanic fury of the origin. One might also point to "The Monstrous Marriage" (CLP, 53) for another instance of the violent tie of women and nature.

seeking reunion with his lost female counterpart. He is the language of the place, the language of its history within which echoes the silences of a lost presence—not the presence of reason but the plenitude of the "first wife" herself. *Paterson* might well be called the poetic deconstruction of history, of the myth of history as the presence of reason (*logos*); and a reconstitution of history as poetry, as the search or the "effort" toward "virtue" (P, 188–89). But this presence-virtue is captured and held only in the time of the effort, in the "temple" (P, 80) of the poem which asserts itself as a "fiction" (P, 236), or a "museum" (P, 209) that is a "real" house of fictions. Therefore, it is not a recovered presence at all. *Paterson*, that is, may be called the demystification of history only because it ends by affirming the essential historicity of man, caught in the "riddle" of his desire, creating the "song" which celebrates a "marriage" that makes death meaningful. We might, indeed, recall that crucial passage concerning the "first wife":

> a flower within a flower whose history
> (within the mind) crouching
> among the ferny rocks, laughs at the names
> by which they think to trap it   (P, 22)

This history "grins" its enigmatic secret, its polytropic irreducibility. It is a "brother" to the "temple upon/ the rock," a poem whose "majesty/ lies in jungles" (P, 23). The poem, like the temple, becomes a cloister for this "history." It is also, then, a labyrinth, concealing the mystery of origins which lies at the center of all "marriages," of man and woman or culture and nature, the "riddle" which perplexes the one who would seek to affirm its self-conception, to "name" its own history and genesis. Thus the dream of a Pater-language is displaced in the "first wife" and her gathering.

Williams returns to this motif in the fourth book, recalling the poet to his "virgin purpose,/ the language" (P, 219) and thus to a search for "virtue" (perhaps, also, *virtù*[4]). Virtue is the "complex reward in all/ languages, achieved slowly" (P, 188), an "effort" (*"La Vertue/ est toute dans l'effort"* goes the "legend" baked into the "Venerian scallop" ashtray), an effort which "takes connivance/ takes convoluted forms, takes time" (P, 189). "Time" is the problematic, for time is the deprivation of virtue. Like language, time is brought into question by "thought." Time is the measure of lost innocence. To rediscover language is to recall the original time of "legend," enwrapped in the "sea-shell" (P, 189). Legend embodies a past in which the coexistence of form and power, nature and culture are revealed and our historical loss exposed. Dr. Paterson therefore recalls his (Williams') grandmother, his childhood, and her death which affirms his own mortality. He remembers, or dreams, the cycle of his own historicity, of the city and of the man:

> To bring himself in,
> hold together wives in one wife and
> at the same time scatter it,
> the one in all of them   .   (P, 191)

Both bringing in and scattering are necessary, a simultaneous effort to generate and gather. It is, as his subsequent remembrances of many loves indicates, an effort to restore himself at the violent origins of history, where he can once

---

4. See T. S. Eliot (ed.), *The Literary Essays of Ezra Pound* (Norfolk, Conn.: New Directions, 1954), 154. Whether or not Williams' "virtue" is comparable to Pound's concern with recovering *virtù* is a moot question. For Pound the medieval concept of *virtù* is the concept of "potency," a "magnet" of spiritualized force around which the cosmos arranges itself. *Virtù* implies a "radiant world," a "world of moving energies," a "Mediterranean sanity" balancing sentience and form in a "harmony of the sentient." *Virtù* is the presence that defines substance, the force that flowers. Pound's figure for it is the "rose" that "his magnet makes in iron filings," a figure that also concludes Canto 74. It is at once the center of attraction and the appearance of a presence around which things radiate. Williams' "virtue," one notes, is a presence only at the center of a field of activity ("effort") and therefore the law of freeplay.

more be held in the moment of originary sexual genesis, the time of the polytropic "first wife," a manifold "one," or one-plus. Without the recovery of this moment, time has no meaning. His many remembered loves recall the paradox of love and violence that constitutes all beginnings, the "riddle" that lies in the presence of time and language:

> All these [several loves]
> and more—shining, struggling flies
> caught in the meshes of Her hair, of whom
> there can be no complaint, fast in
> the invisible net—from the back country,
> half awakened—all desiring. . . .   (P, 192)

There follows immediately a prose passage on Peter the Dwarf, a poetic recall of the "serpent" river "Kra," the passage on the hurling of seed from the phallic "peak," and the onset of the long lyrical sequence on the history of Paterson from its beginnings as a village set amid the wilderness mountain up to the present. The sequence begins in violent scattering, is interspersed with violence, and ends with a modern renewal of violence, the Korean War:

> —you cannot believe
> that it can begin again, again, here
> again   here   (P, 200)

History begins in violence, an original cleaving, evident everywhere in nature. This violence negates the idea of a privileged source, and produces the nostalgia for wholeness which is the ultimate dream of historical man. Jacques Derrida may offer us a penetrating philosophical analysis of the way in which the language of Western thought conceals from itself the rhetoric of *presence* and therefore the fiction of its *telos*. I quote at some length:

> It would be easy enough to show that the concept of structure and even the word "structure" itself are as old as the *epistèmè*—

that is to say, as old as western science and western philosophy—
and that their roots thrust deep into the soil of ordinary language,
into whose deepest recesses the *epistèmè* plunges to gather them
together once more, making them part of itself in a metaphorical
displacement. Nevertheless, up until the event which I wish to
mark out and define [the recent event in the history of thought
which he calls a "rupture" or sudden break with the *epistèmè*,
identified in the "deconstructive" thought of Freud, Nietzsche,
and Heidegger], structure—or rather the structurality of structure—although it has always been involved, has always been
neutralized or reduced, and this by a process of giving it a center
or referring it to a point of presence, a fixed origin. The function
of this center was not only to orient, balance, and organize the
structure . . . but above all to make sure that the organizing
principle of the structure would limit what we might call the
freeplay of the structure. . . .

At the center, the permutation or the transformation of elements . . . is forbidden. . . . Thus it has always been thought
that the center, which is by definition unique, constituted that
very thing within a structure which governs the structure, while
escaping structurality. This is why classical thought concerning
structure could say that the center is, paradoxically, *within* the
structure and *outside* it.[5]

Therefore, Derrida continues, all events within a structure
(a "history") exist within a "history of meaning," and the
center, which is either inside or outside the structure, can as
easily be called "the origin as the end, as readily *archè* as
telos."[6] Thus Eliot's paradox, in the *Four Quartets*, is what
Derrida calls "contradictorily coherent," a paradox Williams
can demystify by parody at the beginning of *Paterson*. For
Paterson is nothing else but an attempt to step outside this myth

5. Jacques Derrida, "Structure, Sign, and Play in the Discourse of the Human
Sciences," in Richard Macksey and Eugenio Donato (eds.), *The Languages of
Criticism and the Sciences of Man: The Structuralist Controversy* (Baltimore: The Johns
Hopkins University Press, 1970), 247–48.

6. *Ibid.*, 248. See also Derrida's essay, "Differance," in Jacques Derrida, *Speech
and Phenomena: And Other Essays on Husserl's Theory of Signs*, ed. and trans. David B.
Allison (Evanston, Ill.: Northwestern University Press, 1973), 129–60.

of centered structurality—not outside of structure itself, note, but outside the tyranny of the center, of history as a "generic pattern" (IAG, 188). And one of its methods is to bring the old names for the center into question. For as Derrida says, "the whole history of the concept of structure . . . must be thought of as a series of substitutions of center for center. . . ."

> Successively, and in a regulated fashion, the center received different forms or names. The history of metaphysics, like the history of the West, is the history of these metaphors and metonymies. Its matrix . . . is the determination of being as *presence* in all the senses of the word. It would be possible to show that all the names related to fundamentals, to principles, or to the center have always designated the constant of a presence—*eidos, archè, telos, energeia, ousia* (essence, existence, substance, subject) *aletheia,* transcendentality, consciousness, or conscience, God, man, and so forth.[7]

History has always implied a difference that is ultimately repressed. *Telos* presumes *ousia,* and the ultimate return to the unity from which it issued. To begin to think the "structurality of structure," whether of history or poetry, is not simply to supply another metaphor for *presence,* another sign of the origin. It is to de-center, to defer the idea of a center.

One need not claim that Williams succeeds in escaping the lure of *presence* to recognize that his "effort" to free history from the dominance of the University, from the Library and the accumulation of Texts, or to invent a new measure, issues in a poetry that brings into question all ideas of priority and therefore of a fixed center. It suggests that any post-Modern concept of poetic form must include the thought of structural

7. Derrida, "Structure, Sign, and Play," 249. In "Differance" Derrida rejects the idea that to name the origin "différance" is to substitute another *sign* for *ousia.* His *différance* (with an *a*) is not a concept, but a deconstruction of the conceptualization of origin. It names the beginning as play, and writing as at the same time different and deferred.

freeplay suggested by Derrida as the alternative to the received idea of structure, and especially to the dominant idea of history as *archè* and *telos*. The post-Modern poem about poetry demystifies in a way analogous to a discourse on discourse. "Waken from a dream, this dream of/ the whole poem" (P, 200), the poet reminds himself just after the pastoral interlude on Paterson's history. The reoccurrences of "murder" at crucial points in *Paterson* reveal the kinds of displacements and ruptures which bring all ideas of order into question, and set into motion once more the scattering of the seed which generates a new beginning. When this occurs, we are confronted with a structure (poem or city), the center of which is everywhere and nowhere, the measure of which the poet can take only in terms of the variable "N" of all "equations." The paradoxical "end" of the poem, the death and the "blast" of seed, is only the most obvious instance of the decentering of the idea of wholeness. The "dream" of the "whole poem" is the dream of Eliot and the New Criticism, as it is the dream of Christian history. The "Traditionalists of Plagiarism" want to bring the violence of beginnings into the text of a redemptive myth, and with the Incarnation regather *archè* and *telos* and make "time" the adjunct of "history." For Williams, the poem must be a dream, an "effort" toward "virtue" which in its own time (musical time) deceives itself with its very plenitude. But in the end it must declare itself as a poem, a fiction, and step outside itself again, thereby revealing that the "virtue" is all in the "effort," in the "fiction" or "game" which replaces the old rituals.[8] It must end, therefore,

8. Compare Lévi-Strauss's distinction between rites and games in *The Savage Mind* (Chicago: University of Chicago Press, 1966), 30–32, particularly the distinction of the equilibrium achieved in ritual play between two opposing sides and the disjunctive effect of the game which ends in a difference between opposites, the difference of winners and losers. In the field of the game the preordained symmetry of the rules, which apply equally to each side, allow for individual variables (talent, chance, improvisation) which engender asymmetry and thus openness in the results.

with a return to time, by opening itself and thereby revealing history as open, as the threshold of "humanity" (IAG, 189) or culture.

II

Hugh Kenner, reconstructing what he calls *The Pound Era*, speaks of the period of Modernism which emerged in the last decade of the past century as a new classicism: "The second Renaissance that opened for classicists in 1891 with a shower of papyri was a renaissance of attention." [9] He is referring not only to the return to the primacy of detail, to the object, but to the archeological and anthropological recovery of fragments to shore against our modern ruin. In the "shower" of papyri, of course, were the newly uncovered manuscripts of Sappho's poems, those classical examples of a lost expression which had existed historically only in the recorded memory of scribes. Like the lost Algerian lake discovered by Frobenius (see SE, xvi–xvii), or even the lost city whose existence he predicted before it was dug up,[10] Sappho's uncovered manuscripts seemed to belie the distancing of history and the unavailability

---

Ritual, to the contrary, begins with asymmetrical difference between two orders (sacred and profane, for example) and moves toward a symmetry. In ritual everyone wins.

One is reminded here of Williams' resistance to the ritual definition of poetry (obviously *contra* Eliot, as he believed), of the idea of poetry's leading indirectly but surely toward some "patent 'end' ": this kind of poetry moves "away from pursuit" and is more the "case of those who follow than of the one who leads. 'Ritual,' too often to suit my ear, connotes a stereotyped mode of procedure from which pleasure has passed whereas the poetry to which my attention clings, if it ever knew those conditions, is distinguished only as it leaves them behind" (Imag., 314). Quest is distinguished from pursuit as a closed game from an open one.

9. Hugh Kenner, *The Pound Era* (Berkeley: University of California Press, 1972), 69.

10. See Ezra Pound, *Guide to Kulcher* (Norfolk, Conn.: New Directions, n.d.), 60–61: "Hence the yarn that Frobenius looked at two African pots and, observing their shapes and proportions, said: if you will go to a certain place and there digge, you will find traces of a civilization with such and such characteristics." For Pound, this meant that any part of a system could be made to yield the whole; any trace, properly studied, could lead to discovery as recovery.

of a remote and lost presence. But the presence they revealed was the presence of utterance, and the absence at its center. Similarly the opening of the caverns at Altamira (in 1868) and *Les Trois Frères* in the French Pyrenees (in 1917), those dis-coverings of Quaternary art which, according to Kenner, summoned T. S. Eliot to stand in their presence and inspired the interpretation of history that we know as "Tradition and the Individual Talent." [11] But if for Eliot, these monuments of a "lost significance" (to use Jean Starobinski's phrase for the melancholy of ruins[12]) can be interpreted as the evidence, however enigmatic, of a timeless presence doubly lost in language, for Williams they are the very stuff of the problematic of history itself. They stand as testimony to the universal of all art, to the nowness of all expression, which subsequently gets lost in the accumulated debris of history and appears, if at all, only as an unrecognized and enigmatic sign. To stand in the presence of the cave paintings of Altamira, or in the perspectiveless "time" of the medieval tapestries now housed in the Cloisters, or even to touch and translate the recovered manuscripts of Sappho, is to stand in the "place" or locus of man's originary scatteredness, that is, language. And

11. Kenner, *The Pound Era*, 30.

12. Starobinski, *The Invention of Liberty*, 180. Starobinski calls ruins the manifest "peace" achieved between two opposing cosmic forces: a "balance is achieved in which the opposing forces of nature and culture are reconciled and man moves on, when the traces of human effort are fading away and the natural wilderness is regaining its lost ground." "The ancient monument had originally been a memorial, a 'monition,' perpetuating a memory. But the initial memory has now been lost, to be replaced by a second significance, which resides in the disappearance of the memory that the constructor had claimed he was perpetuating in this stone. Its melancholy resides in the fact that it has become a monument of lost significance." Applied to Eliot's own shoring of fragments, Starobinski's interpretation reveals the nostalgia rejected by Williams; for Eliot's fragments do indeed represent a "second significance," which marks the present distance not only from the "memory" of the original maker, but the loss of significance received once (immediately) from the Word. Williams, on the other hand, sees the work of art as analogous to nature's "regaining its lost ground," to breaking down the human trace and its distancing. "Masterpieces," he has written, "are only beautiful in a tragic sense, like a starfish lying stretched dead on a beach in the sun" (SE, xvii).

therefore, it is to stand in the time of the "song" that makes
"death tolerable" and contains the "riddle" of "marriage."
" 'I am no authority on Sappho,' " writes one of Williams'
correspondents (A.P.), and the poet includes it at the
beginning of the second section of *Paterson*, Book Five: " 'She
avoided all roughness. "The silence that is in the starry sky,"
gives something of her tone . . .' " (P, 217). Williams then
proceeds to translate one of her poems which confesses her
"faltering voice" in the face of one she loves. It is precisely this
"silence" at the center of Sappho's "tone" that is recapitulated
in the *site* of her newly discovered manuscripts.[13] "Beauty," he
recalls "is a defiance of authority." For this moralists

> —burnt Sappho's poems, burned
> by intention (or are they still hid
> in the Vatican crypts?)   :
> . . . .
>   for they were
> unwrapped, fragment by fragment, from
> outer mummy cases of papier mâché inside
> Egyptian sarcophagi .   (P, 119)

Beauty defies authority, escapes subordination to a mediation that stands outside it, and reveals the enigma at its center.
Appropriately, Sappho's utterance enwrapped a "mummy"
case, the silences of death. The uncovered fragments disclose
the "layer after layer" of language's history, the accumulations
of time which increase the distances of man from his origins
yet tempt him to think he can recover them. A "defiance of
authority," then, is the first definition of "beauty"; beauty is

13. By *site* here I mean not only the historical context in which Sappho's poems
were found, but the significance drawn by Williams from those utterances which
enwrapped the silence of death and still today speak that silence. This, of course,
implies the Heideggerian meaning of the poet's site, previously mentioned (see Martin
Heidegger, *On the Way to Language*, trans. Peter D. Hertz (New York: Harper &
Row, 1971), 159–60). The *site* of Sappho's poems lies in the silence at their center;
and the *site* of Williams shares that centerless center by bringing Sapphic utterance
and Sapphic history over into his field.

that which lives outside the law, asserting itself as a presence
that brings into question all ideas of a transcendent law. The
survival of Sappho's manuscripts is evidence that beauty will
not be suppressed, and that it cannot exist as pure idea. Beauty,
the "Beautiful Thing," becomes the substitution for old ideas
of presence: "Let them explain you and you will be/ the heart
of the explanation. Nameless,/ you will appear . . ." (P,
123). Like the cave paintings, Sappho's recovered manuscripts
take us into the presence of the first expression and locate for
us the center of death from which all utterance issues and to
which all names of presence return. The old names reveal
themselves as simply substitutions for all the other names of
presence. For we must name the "Beautiful Thing" and in
naming it violate it, like whoring a virgin, by bringing it to
light, to time and place.

Unlike Eliot, Williams did not need to go to Altamira or *Les
Trois Frères* and stand in the presence of a first writing, but
from very early in his career he put himself in their
imaginative place. The twenty-fourth poem of *Spring and All*
expresses the ecstasy of the poet held in the "kiss" of nature,
that "wordless/ world/ without personality" where man might
commune. But it is no longer a "world" he can enter (Imag.,
142–43). His own place in nature can only remind him of
what he shares with her and his difference from her. It
provokes the reflection upon that possible past unity with her,
now lost:

> I ascend
>
> through
> a canopy of leaves
>
> and at the same time
> I descend
>
> for I do nothing
> unusual—

I ride in my car
I think about

prehistoric caves
in the Pyrenees—

the cave of
Les Trois Frères
                    (Imag., 143)

The thought which thinks of the prehistoric cave thinks in
the history that marks the distance from the place of original
writing. And yet, it is exactly there, in the space of
imagination, that the poet repeats that originary act and restages
the scene of writing, as descent from history. This poem is set
amid a number of prose commentaries on the essential
difference between prose and poetry, a difference which,
Williams argues, is not simply the difference of style (of
metrical characteristics, rhyme, meter, or whatever), but a
difference of origin: "There is a very marked difference
between the two which may arise in the fact of a separate
origin for each, each using similar modes for dis-similar
purposes" (Imag., 144). If words compose the medium of each,
the significance of each is not in the different way it uses the
words but in the different "source" from which the words
issue. The definition fails of definition because the origin itself
must remain silent. If Williams suggests a kind of emotional
recognition of poetry (like A. E. Housman's), it is because he
needs to insist on the "origin" of poetry in the irrational, which
no form of logical definition or analysis could touch. Or as he
says in an apt circular description of what makes Marianne
Moore's poetry poetic: "She is most constantly a poet in her
work because the purpose of her work is invariably from the
source from which poetry starts—that it is constantly from the
purpose of poetry. And that it actually possesses this characteristic, as of that origin, to a more distinguishable degree when it

eschews verse rhythms than when it does not" (Imag., 145).

This origin, otherwise indescribable, is a point of near simultaneity with nature—a "place" different from nature which makes that difference distinct, but not at a distance from nature. And despite the difficulty of locating that "place" (which is the site of original expression, as it were), Williams in another commentary on the poetry of Miss Moore is precise on the way poetry (as culture) must be set beside nature. In her poems, he says, one encounters a "garden" but a garden of "porcelain": "It is the mythical, indestructible garden of pleasure, perhaps greatly pressed for space today . . ." (Imag., 311). And he continues:

> I don't know where, except in modern poetry, this quality of the brittle, highly set-off porcelain garden exists. . . . It is this chief beauty of today, this hard crest to nature, that makes the best present work with its "unnatural" appearance seem so thoroughly gratuitous, so difficult to explain, and so doubly a treasure of seclusion. . . . what I wish to point is that there need be no stilled and archaic heaven, no ducking under religiosities to have poetry and to have it stand in its place beyond "nature." Poems have a separate existence uncompelled by nature or the supernatural.
>
> (Imag., 311–12)

Only in their recovery of this "source" can they be authentic language. Williams wants to define poetry as unmediated, but poetic language presents itself as original difference.

Williams clearly recognized that the reach of a truly original poetry would be through modernism back to the origin—a reduplication, as it were, of some "first" poetry. The "history" of literature is not the history of repetition but an "advance" of art, repetition with a difference. "You know . . . enough of me to understand," he wrote to Kay Boyle in 1932, "that I have no belief in the continuity of history. To me the classic lives now just as it did then—or not at all. . . . Everything we know is a local virtue. . . . In other words, art can be made of anything—provided it can be seen, smelt, touched, apprehended and understood to be what it is—the flesh of a constantly repeated permanence" (SL, 130). A decade earlier, in *Spring and All*, he had tried to distinguish the "constantly repeated permanence" of art from the evolutionary repetitions of nature ("EVOLUTION HAS REPEATED ITSELF FROM THE BEGINNING"), which is "a perfect plagiarism" (Imag., 93). He associated nature's plagiarism with that of "The Traditionalists of Plagiarism" (Imag., 94, 98), or that Modernism which views the present as an evolving, refined repetition of the past. Its "art" is tied to the "proven truths of tradition, even to the twice proven" (Imag., 98). To this teleology Williams opposed "art" as renewal, as "SPRING" or springing, "that colossal surge toward the finite" (Imag., 94), recognizable only in the stark nudity of some emergent new form, as yet unnamed but ripe for naming. The new art would be "inaugural naming."

Thus the new art will destroy "art," split the "rock." It will not repeat some past model or design, but will reduplicate the original mysterious act of splitting the rock, the act of naming itself. Destroying "symbolism," it destroys the tyranny of the transcendent Word, and frees itself of the mediating categories of bleak necessity. But ironically, this is to make the utterly "new" work a true repetition of the old: "It is no different from the aristocratic compositions of the earlier times, the Homeric inventions/ but/ these occurred in different times, to this extent, that life had not yet sieved through its own multiformity. That aside, the work the two-thousand-year-old poet did and that we do are one piece. That is the vitality of the classics" (Imag., 101). It is all the more revealing that he also called the classics a deformity, and in turn called Dada and surrealism the modern variant of classicism: "Long live dada! we are praising that which has already, in some one of its phases, long since outlived the pyramids" (SE, xvii).

"The primitives," Williams wrote in *Spring and All*, "are
not back in some remote age—they are not BEHIND
experience. . . . Time does not move" (Imag., 134). And Dev
Evans says of his search for pagany: "Greece is ahead of us, not
back. The Middle Ages are back" (VP, 113). "Time,"
therefore, "is a storm in which we are all lost" (SE, xvi). But at
the level of structure, "inside the convolutions of the storm,"
we stand in the place of all original poets: "Chaucer, Villon,
and Whitman were contemporaries of mind with whom I am
constantly in touch" (SE, xvii), not by a knowledge of the
tradition they comprise, but through the "art of writing." Both
Dada's destructions and Frobenius' archeological digging bring
structure to light. Discovery brings "knowledge" to an end, so
that it can begin again. Dev saw "all knowledge vanishing into
the apex of a hollow cone—spinning off" (VP, 92–93). Time
is a vortex.

Like Pound who asserted, in *The Spirit of Romance*, that "all
ages are contemporaneous," and who argued that the *Cantos*
moved through a fugal design of descending into the under-
world of structure where the "repeat of history" disclosed the
presence of the "divine or permanent world" of the "Gods," [14]
Williams entertains a cyclical view of history. But with a
difference from Pound. Here is Williams' Vortex: ". . . let us
never forget the lesson of the spiral, the Vorticists in England
discovered that though we do over and over the same things it
is never in the same plane but elsewhere in space. There is
always something new to be experienced if we have the wit for
it." [15] Pound's preference for certain of the planes to others, for

14. See D. D. Paige (ed.), *The Letters of Ezra Pound, 1907–1914* (New York:
Harcourt, Brace, 1950), 210. This letter to his father does much to reveal Pound's
enduring view of the presence upon which Western history is centered, and to which
all of its particular, recurring forms symbolically point.

15. William Carlos Williams, "The American Idiom," from his projected "Book
on Prosody" (MS in the Beinecke Library of Yale University, New Haven, Conn.);
works in this collection will hereinafter be cited as Yale MS.

the Renaissance model or the Confucian precision, very nearly denied anything like a modern Vortex, except in the isolated work of certain artists. For him no American city could approach the London of 1914, the Venice or even the Rimini of the Italian Renaissance.[16] No modern city any longer centralized the arts. Pound, regrettably, shared something with the traditionalists of plagiarism—an unequivocal faith in the meaningful evolution of culture out of nature, or so was Williams' view of his running off to "other centers" (P, 36). For Williams, on the other hand, "You must begin with nothing, like a river in the morning and make, make new" (VP, 98). The river, says Dev, is the "prototype of art." To remount the stream of time is to reduplicate the beginning (again) as a "spinning off," the descent or tropic return of writing.

III

Charles Olson has suggested that Pound's destruction of "historical time" constitutes the major advance in Modern poetics, the gathering up of history into a "space-field where, by inversion, though the material is all time material, he has driven through it so sharply the beak of his ego, that, he has turned time into what we must now have, space and its live air." The "primary contrast" for Olson "is BILL: his Pat is

16. See Eliot (ed.), *Literary Essays of Ezra Pound*, 220: "America has no capital," and thus no center for the artist. It, therefore, has no Vortex. On these grounds, Pound could accuse Williams of being interested in the "bloody loam" rather than seeking "after" the "finished product" (P, 50). This difference, which Williams finds thematically central to *Paterson*, reveals their different sense of the Vortex: Pound's centered upon a presence (that is nonetheless absent from modern history), Williams' upon an absence which predicates presence but which, on the contrary, really implies a principle of freeplay at the origin. The difference makes all the difference in the selection and use of detail, and in the openness and contingency of the poetic field. It also reveals the different senses of the city—for Pound it is the fulfillment of the Vortex, the point of concentration, a bringing of nature to form and thus to the intensity of culture; while for Williams it manifests the dispersal of man, alienated from himself and from nature, and the subsequent artifice of his attempt to recover some lost ground rather than seek a new measure.

exactly opposite of Ez's, that is Bill HAS an emotional system
which is capable of extensions & comprehensions the ego
system (the Old Deal, Ez as Cento Man, here dates) is not.
Yet/ by making his substance historical of one city (the Joyce
deal), Bill completely licks himself, lets time roll him under as
Ez does not and thus . . . contributes nothing. . . ." [17] There
are a number of problematical discriminations here. The most
obvious is Olson's distinction between Pound's ego-centered
field and Williams' more diffuse ("emotional") system which
spreads itself temporally because it takes space ("city") to be
constituted temporally (historically). Put another way, Williams' stress on local detail demands a metonymic and hence
diachronic view of that detail, extending his poem to the point
that it reveals no true center and thus no "field." Pound's
"beak" constitutes a "space-field" that asserts presence—the
presence not of any particular ego, but the presence of the
artist-imagination which constitutes the "Human Universe."
But Pound, for Olson, is still a nineteenth-century man,
ego-centered.

By concentrating on the dimension of Williams' poem
that asserts the priority of the detail (which exists successively
or temporally and therefore cannot appear simultaneously
or spatially), Olson dismisses Williams' "musical time," or
structure. Williams' one city is too specific to stand for all
cities, or for the city as "space-field." [18] What Olson disregards

17. Charles Olson, "Mayan Letters," *Selected Writings*, ed. with introd. Robert
Creeley (New York: New Directions, 1966), 82–83. If Pound's view of the ego-beak
is "mis-centered" (p. 112), Williams' view fails to define any space at all. Olson
insisted, above all else, that the poet must have a principle of selection, and that
principle constitutes his "personality" in the poem (p. 61). Again, in *Letters for Origin*,
ed. Albert Glover (London: Cape Goliard, 1969), 129, Olson pursues the distinction:
"if I think EP gave us any of the methodological clues: the RAG-BAG; bill gave us
the lead on the LOCAL/ Or put it that pat: EP the verb, BILL the NOUN
PROBLEM." This ignores Williams' repeated stress on the need of poetry to imitate
the process of (the verb) rather than copy (the adjective) nature (SE, 303).

18. Williams, according to Olson, "don't know fr nothing about what a city *is*"
(Olson, *Selected Writings*, 83). He takes Williams' "local" as a historical place which

or denies is the possible freeplay of structure or space-field, and thus the mythic dimensions of a single "period of time," the details of which are unfolded over each other. What he misses is exactly what Williams shares with Pound, the necessary "musical time" which is at once the reconciling equation of a space-time dichotomy and the time which dispels the ego-center. But what he recognizes is Williams' essential difference from Pound—not that Williams is rolled under by the time but that his poems end by opening the field they have composed, thereby revealing the "live air" of space to be its fundamental freeplay, its lack of a fixed center (or "beak").

"The old order changeth and lasts like the first," says the author of *Finnegans Wake*, parodying Tennyson who was indeed rolled under by time.[19] Old becomes different from ancient as time from timelessness. The change from an old order to a new recapitulates a first order and thus reveals what lasts, change. Williams and Pound may indeed have contended over which was most concerned with the authenticity of history, but the sources of their facts tell us little about whether one triumphed over time and the other succumbed. Time, indeed, seems to have been for both the chaos of particulars which was very like the chaos of images Geoffrey Hartman identifies as the riddle of origins haunting Romantic man. Both ultimately, if in different ways, were preoccupied with "space" and "field," with "structure," with musical time or repetition and reduplication, with the universal that pervaded the particular. And both were equally concerned that this universal not be mistaken with the old *epistèmè* of presence as an origin at once inside and outside the system. Their difference turns

provides him with an overabundance of detail, while Pound's city is figurative, or a concentration of forces. Olson, as we have seen, takes Riemann as a geometer who has helped overturn the fiction of a transcendentally centered cosmos, but cannot recognize in Williams' sifting of his local any principle of the "N" of all equations, as indeed he assumes his "Maximus" poems to constitute.

19. James Joyce, *Finnegans Wake* (New York: Viking, 1947), 486.

largely, as Olson did see, on what principle of selection each assumes.

Pound, as eagerly as Williams, turned back to the enigma of nature as the original energy of culture, and to the original marriage of the two in any existence or historical beginning. One has only to refer to that classical Imagist poem, "In the Station of the Metro," to recall that it is a poem of e-mergence. It is not simply the image of a crowd of faces emerging from a subway, the gestalt of light coming to light. Flowering is e-mergence, the coming to be of difference out of an unknown (in-different) origin: "Petals on a wet, black bough." And if Pound's "theme" from the beginning was the historicity of culture as difference (a "complex"), he would recall throughout the *Cantos* that his theme was the "constantly repeated permanence" of history as an original rupture and of space as the original place of time:

> H.D. once said "serenitas"
>   (At this, etc.)
>   at Dieudonne's
>   in pre-history.
> No dog, no horse, and no goat,
> The long flank, the firm breast
>   and to know beauty and death and despair
> and to think that what has been shall be,
>   flowing, ever unstill.[20]

Culture for Pound is not knowledge, or the accumulation of facts, but form: "Knowledge is NOT culture. The domain of culture begins when one HAS 'forgotten-what-book'." [21] Culture is Frobenius' Paideuma, the "tangle or complex of the

---

20. Ezra Pound, Canto 113, *The Cantos* (New York: New Directions, 1970), 787. More and more in his later poems, beginning with the *Pisan Cantos*, Pound returns to the plenitude of nature as origin. Nature had always been the ground and index of his economics, the ground of the reciprocal exchanges that allow culture to develop out of but never separate itself from nature.

21. Pound, *Guide to Kulcher*, 134.

inrooted ideas of any period." [22] Like Frobenius' archeological method, the poet's search for it is not "retrospective," a study of the past, but "immediate," a digging into his present to see what of the universal "complex" inheres there. Pound used the example of Frobenius' discovery of the African city, and again, the following: "the peasants opposed a railway cutting. A king had driven into the ground at that place. The engineers dug and unearthed the bronze car of Dis, two thousand years buried."

> It wd. be unjust to Frazer to say that his work was *merely* retrospective. But there is a quite different phase in the work of Frobenius.
> "Where we found these rock drawings, there was always water within six feet of the surface." That kind of research goes not only into the past and forgotten life, but points to tomorrow's water supply.[23]

At one point in *Guide to Kulcher*, Pound reminisces on the Prado he had visited some thirty years previously, and then of Whistler's visits there to study the remarkably self-mirroring paintings of Velasquez: "A dozen returns and each time a new permanent acquisition, light, green shadows instead of the brown as in Rembrandt, who has steadily declined through 30 years in his power to rouse enthusiasm. I don't mean ceased, I mean that the current in our past three decades has been toward the primitives, with a forward current, via Velasquez. . . . Our husky young undergraduates may start their quest of Osiris in a search for what was the PRADO." [24] Gaudier-Brzeska's drawings, he had recognized, were full of "reminiscence, Oceanic, Egyptian," and more important, were done while he was enthused about the "drawings in the Dordogne caverns and 'Fonts-de-Gaume'," which had become his "pace-

22. *Ibid.*, 57.
23. *Ibid.*
24. *Ibid.*, 110.

maker." [25] For Pound, art stood at the point where history and myth interpenetrated and metamorphosed into each other, the point of the vortex. Poetry invariably stands at the point of "primary form"; "music, sheer melody, seems as if it were just bursting into speech"; sculpture "seems as if it were 'just coming over into speech,'" that point where "form" comes "into being." [26] Or as Pound says of Jacob Epstein's sculpture: "The work is conceived from the beginning, slow stroke by slow stroke, like some prehistoric, age-long upheaval in natural things, driven by natural forces." [27] It does not mirror or copy nature, but is rather the "language of exploration." [28] One might well recognize that the "Metro" Image repeats the structure of Persephone's return.

Williams' tendency to linger on the surface of his detail, and on its difference (the "edges" of images) rather than its potentiality for metamorphic unfolding, leads to the kind of critical distinction Olson insists on: that time (really, the succession of things) overwhelms him. But it is a distinction that will not hold. Williams' "substance" is not "historical of one city" but the unearthed "design" of the city, the city as Vortex. The Passaic River flows from the mountains down through the New Jersey plain, over the falls at Paterson, and on to the sea, but lifted to expression in the single "plane" of one poem, the "time material" reveals a "design." As Dev Evans said of the Arno, the river flows forever new under the "old bridge," connecting the present with a "time before there was a city, teaching from the fields of Proserpine" (VP, 96–97). But Paterson's old bridge has fallen down, or is a span

25. Ezra Pound, *Gaudier-Brzeska, A Memoir* (New York: New Directions, 1970), 131–32.

26. *Ibid.*, 82, 88, 93.

27. *Ibid.*, 99. See also Eliot (ed.), *Literary Essays of Ezra Pound*, 92: "A return to origins invigorates because it is a return to nature and reason. The man who returns to origins does so because he wishes to behave in the eternally sensible manner."

28. Pound, *Gaudier-Brzeska*, 88.

tenuously made by such improvisations as Sam Patch's act. Or it blocks the destructive and renewing flood. The bridge of the Florentine masters, Pound's great Renaissance tradition and thus his ego-center, affirms only the mediations of history and blocks us from the source. Traditional forms are historical pure and simple, since they are interpretations, bridgings of time. To evoke them is to copy them. But to imitate them is to realize their true originality, their "time." It is to repeat their original interpretations.

The "history" of *Paterson* is made to speak its "constantly repeated permanence," that history is the freeplay of interpretation. Paterson's design, its significance, is unearthed in the archeological strata of a scattered language, a diachronous history. The "beak" of Pound's "ego," on the contrary, composes the center of the Vortex in which his world-engorging erudition is made to flow. Pound's "time material" speaks not a personal "ego" but the timeless "genius" of all poets foregathered; thus Pound the Modern poet is the present presence of that genius, the artist. His *Cantos*, as the form and force of culture once more coming to a head, is the *genius loci* where ideas move into action, or where history manifests itself: his Vortex (here he is speaking of the "great Roman vortex") is "an understanding of, and an awakening to, the value of a capital, the value of centralization, in matters of knowledge and art, and of the interaction and stimulus of genius foregathered." [29]

Williams would start from the opposite premise. Every historical city was a *locus*, an instance of original flowering and original gathering. And its history was the history of obscuring the original event, the design of opening. Its history composes the layers of explanation which at once obscure *genius loci* and entomb it there. The language of place and the place of

29. Eliot (ed.), *Literary Essays of Ezra Pound*, 220.

language are one and the same, a *genius* repressed by history's generic patterns and laid in the sarcophagus of time. Writing must be the act, then, of decentering the authority of time, and therefore of bringing into question the possibility of a "space" that is not open, that has a fixed center. Writing seeks a depth, the *locus* where *genius* originally manifests itself: "Today we know the meaning of depth, it is a primitive profoundity of the personality that must be touched if what we do is to have it. The faculties, untied, proceed backward through the night of our unconscious past. It goes down to the ritualistic, amoral past of the race, to fetish, to dream to wherever the 'genius' of the particular writer finds itself able to go"; there, "in the writings of genius, in the poems (if any) the released personality of the artist the very break with stupidity which we are seeking may have occurred. And this will always be in the *form* which the first writing has taken." [30] Every city is the monument of a lost significance, a metaphor for what was once a "new language" and the complex of tongues (time material) obscuring that "genius." Lifting the "local" to "expression" means bringing the *genius loci* to light. For Williams, any modern city might serve, if its poet were "local." Paterson's recorded detail, though more ordinary than Frobenius' lost city, Olson's Mayan glyphs, the ancient cave paintings, or even Pound's Rimini, concealed the same language and mystery.

IV

Williams' poem of the local may profitably be compared with what Lévi-Strauss calls a "reference myth," a myth that might arise from any of several discontinuous (both historically and geographically) places and manifest itself in radically different particulars. The "reference myth" is an abstraction

30. From William Carlos Williams, "How to Write," included in Linda W. Wagner's *The Poetry of William Carlos Williams* (Middletown, Conn.: Wesleyan University Press, 1964), 145, 147.

from the variety of its particular realizations and exists at the level of infrastructure. Myth is characterized by "repetition," the process of which discloses or makes apparent its structure. "Myth," says Lévi-Strauss, "grows spiral-wise until the intellectual impulse which has produced it is exhausted. Its *growth* is a continuous process, whereas its *structure* remains discontinuous. If this is the case, we should assume that it closely corresponds, in the realm of the spoken word, to a crystal in the realm of physical matter." [31] In a later work, *The Raw and the Cooked*, Lévi-Strauss likens the repetition-compulsion of myth to musical structure and offers a methodological procedure for studying it based on musical form. [32] The comparison holds, however, only if one does not force the analogy; *Paterson* is a poem, not a myth. Composed of the detail gathered in one place, the poem is a reweaving of that detail into the tapestry of its concealed myth, the structure within its history. Music, myth, tapestry—they are only analogies for the poem's "form," its "shelly rime."

Olson reads *Paterson* as a kind of serial poem, overwhelmed by the process of detail and the rush of history. But it is precisely through repetition that Williams works toward a "measure" that will lift the process to structure, de-signing time into a new significance. His poet is more the ethnographer than the seer, a gatherer of detail and a measurer (thus interpreter) of it. If the history of Paterson, New Jersey, is built up like a palimpsest in overlays of discontinuous but repetitive detail, as for example in local speech, the "genius" of that history has become more and more obscured. [33] The

31. Claude Lévi-Strauss, "The Structural Study of Myth," *Structural Anthropology*, trans. Claire Jacobson and Brooke Grundfest Schoepf (New York: Anchor, 1967), 226.
32. Claude Lévi-Strauss, "Overture," *The Raw and the Cooked*, trans. John and Doreen Weightman (New York: Harper & Row, 1969), *passim*.
33. One might compare here H.D.'s use of the "palimpsest" metaphor, especially in her three-part novel by that title (Paris: Contact, 1926). The title refers to the

repetitions in *Paterson* (in subject matter, in theme, in measure) are the process by which Williams discloses or decodes the structure. That is, the poem decodes and interprets history by revealing the primary myth of that history, by revealing the fiction of the "fiction" as *Paterson*, Book Five, makes clear (P, 236). The poem discloses the myth of place, the *genius loci*, by creating a sudden reversal of its history, a torque in the spiral, a dissonance in the harmony of its time material.

Paterson's repetitions, far from being evidence that its poet is drowned in the surge of time, opens the history of place to the "live air," and in that opening denies that history is concerned with the "dead" (see "The Virtue of History," IAG, 188–90).

> All rivers
> stem from the Nile!
> All poems stem from
> the Iliad as all life ends
> in the Bomb.
> Repeat it! [34]

This unpublished passage was once a part of "Asphodel, That Greeny Flower," one of the early versions of which was entitled, "The River of Heaven." In its early drafts, "Asphodel" was considered work-in-progress toward *Paterson*, Book Five; and "The River of Heaven" had once been used instead of "The Run to the Sea" as the title of *Paterson*, Book Four. The problem of time and the river haunted Williams, for it was the problem of history and language which frustrated man's desire for the universal. The poet who lived his life in

---

overlayed structure of the three discontinuous parts (though a single heroine runs through each), but of most importance is the metaphor of excavation or retrieval or discovery, by which the poetess seeks her pure self, her writing signature. To make this discovery, she must peel away the outer layers of her false (in this case, feminine) self, Raymonde Ransom, in order to arrive at her objective, masculine penname, Ray Bart. Thus Hilda Doolittle becoming her signature, H.D.

34. William Carlos Williams, unpublished stanza from manuscript of "Asphodel, That Greeny Flower," Yale MS.

Rutherford, New Jersey, did not choose Paterson, New Jersey, as his "local" because it was his physical home, but because it was a place (local to him, surely enough) through which all movement flowed. In its ground remained the trace of a mythic design partly apparent, partly residual, though certainly not self-evident to those who were living it. The city was neither at the source of the river nor at its mouth, neither at a beginning nor an end. It was, then, at the locus of discourse in history. The poet's task was to reveal that the beginning and end existed at the falls of every river, at the point where the energy gathers into a rush and simultaneously breaks into expression. Like the Arno which Dev Evans says existed before "Dante's city," the Arno which brought its message from the "fields of the Vernal gods," the Passaic flows on, "making, making, inviting the recreators" (VP, 97).

The Falls at Paterson is the point at which the river reaches its maximum articulation and energy, a place which had suggested its genius or power to Hamilton as an ideal capital, the center of a SUM. But the history of Paterson is the history of misplaced or misued potential. It was not Pound's prewar London, but a point in the spiral of a "new country" which like all such points incorporated that country's total myth. It is therefore like any point on a spiral which contains and yet conceals the laws of the whole. The city, that is, was a myth set upon a crumbling rock, a culture which had been built at the expense of nature. But the poet, exploring that "divorce" or "fall," could discover in it not the end but the beginning of history, a speech which even in its despair spoke the language of long-silenced gods, of making. For whatever the present state of this "vilest swillhole in Christendom" (IAG, 195), the place revealed a vortex of suppressed energy. Unlike the ethnographer, however, the poet could not speak from the end of or from outside the vortex. The myth he discovered was also the game he was living. The genius of language was dispersed, had no center. The city lacked its poet. The four books of the original poem, conceived as they were in one mythic "stroke," had to reveal the lack of *genius loci,* the decentralization so abhorred by Pound. Thus it had to look as if the poet were rolled under by time.[35]

Even Book Five of *Paterson,* which is discontinuous with the other four parts especially in its use of local detail, refuses to reclaim a center. Its theme is the survival of art, and therefore

35. One might compare Olson's argument about poetic time. Charles Olson, *Human Universe and Other Essays,* ed. Donald Allen (New York: Grove Press, 1967), 70: "a poem is ordered not so much *in* time (Poe's Poetic Principle) or *by* time (metric, measure) as of a characteristic *of* time which is most profound: that time is synchronistic and that a poem is the one example of a man-made continuum 'which contains qualities or basic conditions manifesting themselves simultaneously in various places in a way not to be explained by causal parallellisms'." This creates an interesting but not altogether convincing poetics of space which argues that if a poem creates a synchronous time it must create the time out of elements of different *places* or from different times which, defying causal or logical relations, are composed into a simultaneity. It suggests the possibility of getting back to the origin, to an original place (in the time of a projective poem). Apparently, Olson rejects Williams' use of different elements of different times occurring in the same historical place. In any event, Olson's main argument against Williams is his lack of selectivity, his desire to include everything at the expense of selective design. Olson's search is backward, through time material, to an ever more original point of departure from which one again comes forward into the present. (See his remarks on Melville, Chapter 1, note 3.) Olson's Maximus is the old Tyrian sailor, the figure of "forwarding" or the "figure of outward" as he calls Robert Creeley in the dedication to *The Maximus Poems* (New York: Jargon/Corinth, 1960), 2. This "figure" desires to be "the first human eyes to look again/ at the start of human motion (just last week/ 300,000,000 years ago"), p. 15. History for Olson is a Moebius strip, and the poet a historian who projects or throws together his knowledge into a kind of "map," a forwarding that also cuts backward toward the time when civilization had "ONE CENTER, Sumer," in order to recover the "primordial & phallic energies & methodologies which . . . make it possible for man, that participant thing, to take up, straight, nature's, live nature's force." See Olson, *Human Universe and Other Essays,* 19–20, 23. This world precedes the "generalizing time" of Western man, the time of the *logos* and its representations, of East *and* West, a dualism which America was destined to heal but did not. Olson, in other words, maintains a nostalgia for the center, for a recoverable power, and disdains the inaugural freedom of the beginning which, I will argue, makes Williams the more characteristic post-Modern poet. Compare Olson's figure of the "map" with Pound's "periplum" and H.D.'s "palimpsest." One might also recall the words of Edward Dahlberg, *The Carnal Myth* (New York: Weybright and Tally, 1968), 89: "Men travel in search of strange hemispheres, little suspecting that they are ransacking their origins."

it should have confirmed the retrieval of presence, the wholeness of time. The poem's conglomerate of local detail, the tradition of artistic genius (the history of innovators from Dürer and Leonardo to Picasso, Juan Gris, and Gertrude Stein), and the allegory of the medieval tapestries, is a measure of the "plane" to which *Paterson* has lifted its local environment. A dream of a dream, *Paterson*, Book Five, is Williams' assertion of his simultaneity with the pantheon of artist-dreamers, those who take their present ground as the measure of their desire and raise it to the level of a "complete little universe" (P, 224). Poets totalize, thus provide a *locus*. Like Peter Brueghel's "Nativity," which discovered the presence of the Word in the structure of German peasant life, or like the medieval tapestries of the Cloisters, which found It in the life of royalty, *Paterson*, Book Five, must speak of a "Baby/ new born!/ among the words" (P, 226). It celebrates the possible recovery of origins, the beginning of history, in the ex-centricity of any local ground, "whatever the detail" (P, 235). But at the same time, it deprives itself of this mythic recovery and ends in another decentering. It puts itself in question, affirming the "fiction."

Paterson, Book Five, is the poem of the dance and the flower—the dance which contrapuntally turns upon itself and the flower which hedges the field of the tapestries, like individual poems enveloping a totalized space which in turn reconstitutes a mythic center, the Unicorn. From beginning to end Book Five of *Paterson* is the poem as vortex, a spiral out of the other four books. From the center of the descending spiral at the end of Book Four, the death that is also a "blast" or dissemination, the "eagle" of the mind casts off into a new cycle, "rebelliously" (P, 207). Out of the discontinuity of violent death grows a new dream of continuity, the continuum that is the synchronic history of art. The center recovered by each new work is what Dev Evans called the "burning presence under the veneer of to-day" (VP, 109). But it is a presence only in a fiction that proclaims its fictiveness.

In the spiral of the poem, the end turns back into a beginning, like the reversal of Yeats's gyres, and thus moves, according to Williams, into a "new dimension." [36] This is the continuity Williams spoke about in his "Author's Note" to the larger poem. The "new dimension" is a new language, though it consists of the old words. One might even argue that *Paterson*, Book Five, is *Paterson*, Books One–Four, turned inside out, just as in the old man's memory the "museum became real":

> *The Cloisters—*
>   on its rock
>
>   casting its shadow—
>   "la réalité! la réalité!
>   la réa, la réa, la réalité!"
>   (P, 209)

The shadow becomes the reality, as the word becomes a *res* itself, becomes the house of being, the space of a marriage. The Cloisters, which houses the tapestries, is itself a former sacred space now transposed into an aesthetic space. It is a place where memory reconstitutes a lost significance in fictions. The museum itself, we know, was reconstituted of old religious ruins, transported to a new ground and reconstructed upon a nonfigurative rock. Like the authentic detail of the tapestries it

36. Compare the following stanza from an early typescript of what later became the Preface to *Paterson* (originally placed after the "multiple seed" passage):

> —today is tomorrow, is yesterday
> is time reversed, circuitous. So that
> that which enters, leaves and
> that which exists, enters and the city
>   (MS in the Lockwood Library
>   of the State University of New York at Buffalo)

This motif of the cycle of time—figured in Book Five of *Paterson* as the *ouroboros* or serpent with its tail in its mouth (P, 214) and in Book Four as the river Kra (P, 193)—is treated more extensively in Chapter 5.

houses, its own recomposed fragments evince the survival of particular things but also the retrieval of a lost significance in the space of the whole. But this significance is now brought into question. The museum is the space centered upon its fictions, the presence of an absence. And the artifacts it houses express in turn the problematic of the center. The museum is like a Chinese box.

Williams accentuates this series of decenterings even further by presenting his own remembered detail of the tapestries out of sequence, further depriving the legend they depict of the allegorical clarity they had in their original time and place. The relocation of the tapestries into a new place leaves behind the apparent fixedness of their historical "meaning." They allegorize, as is well known, the marriage of Anne of Brittany to Louis XII of France, making it a sacred historical repetition of the Incarnation. (But that story, Williams' poetic deconstruction of the tapestries back to the multiple ambiguities of an original myth, is the subject of the final chapter.) Of primary significance here is the undermining of the idea of the center, upon which all cloisters had been built and to which the intentionality of the tapestries was historical testimony. What is at issue here, and in Williams' memory, is the fiction of history itself, and the openness which only a deconstructive art can bring to those generic patterns.[37]

Thus Williams recalls the detail of the second tapestry:

—the birds and flowers, the castle showing through the leaves
of the trees, a pheasant drinks at the fountain, his shadow drinks
there also

   .   cyclamen, columbine, if the art
   with which these flowers have
   been put down are to be trusted
          (P, 215–16)

37. The observations of Jorge Luis Borges would appear relevant here: "Music, stages of happiness, mythology, faces molded by time, certain twilights and certain places—all these are trying to tell us something; that imminence of revelation that is not yet produced is, perhaps, the aesthetic reality." Jorge Luis Borges, *Other Imaginations*, trans. Ruth Sims (Austin: University of Texas Press, 1964), 5.

The field of the second tapestry centers upon the fountain to which the Unicorn is lured. The fountain is surrounded by the plenitude of nature shading away into a background of gathering hunters behind which appear the turrets of the castle rising in the distance. The encroachment of leashed dogs and hunters signifies the increasing incursion of man into nature and the increasing cleavage of the two. This civilized detail will continue to move toward the front and center until in the sixth tapestry, in which the Unicorn is wounded and brought back to the castle, culture veritably displaces nature.[38] Only in the final tapestry, where the Unicorn is reborn in the enclosed garden, is nature restored to her primacy, centered by the presence of the Unicorn. Even man, who as hunter was engulfed in natural plenitude in the first tapestry, has been vanquished—except, of course, that he is now rejoined to nature in the form of the Unicorn as Word, a center which at once is immanent and transcendent.

But Williams' detail of the second tapestry already catches the problematic of the Christian allegory and brings it into question. The fountain is a mirror reflecting nature as an infinite narcissism. Pheasant and shadow double each other and drink of a source which is both present and absent. The entire tapestry (of one rabbit emerging from the flowers while another disappears into them, of animals and men moving toward a center where a murder is anticipated, of castle protruding through leaves) reflects ambiguously beginning and

38. My colleague Fred See first pointed out to me the culture-nature theme and its ramifications in the Flemish tapestries now housed at the Cloisters. He finds the mythic design of the use of nature in the tapestries to provide an interesting analogue for the frontier thematic in American literature, more significant, in fact, than the explicit theme of the "hunt" and the allegory of the Word which is the story of the tapestries. See also Chapter 5. Louis L. Martz's "The Unicorn in *Paterson*: William Carlos Williams," *Thought*, XXXV (Winter, 1960), 537–54, is an indispensable essay treating the poem as tapestry; it is reprinted in a revised form in Louis L. Martz, *The Poem of the Mind: Essays on Poetry, English and American* (New York: Oxford University Press, 1966), 147–61.

end. It holds in suspension the purity of presence, and brings it
into question. The "cyclamen," the "columbine"—those particular flowers, which can be named by the old names, contain
within their very names the question of cycle and center. The
"columbine" is the name of the dove who, at least in the
Christian allegory, is reciprocal with the Unicorn. Williams'
measure of this moment of suspended violence, in which the
"brutish eyes of the deer" accentuate their difference from the
"eyes of the Queen" (P, 216), enfolds a mystery and brings
into question the very meaning of the unifying center which
the tapestries had presumed to affirm. That is, Williams
interprets the tapestries, and demystifies them, by increasing
the possibilities of their signification. He opens their history of
history by an act of imaginative doubling.

Almost every line in *Paterson*, Book Five, reveals the
doubling effect of the detail of the tapestries, where the primal
center is the reflecting pool: the flight of the mind-eagle; the
Unicorn's spiral horn; the "identity" of the "whore" and the
"virgin"; the "sphere, a snake with its tail in/ its mouth"
which is the "river . . . returned to its beginnings" (P, 214,
233); the Cloisters and its shadow which contains the tapestry
which contains the pheasant and its shadow; the jazz motif,
including the very name of Mezz Mezzrow who argued that
the white man could learn to play the black man's blues
without cultural dislocation; the poem within the criticism
within the interview which in turn is presented as prose within
the longer poem; the "enclosed garden" within the cycle of the
tapestries within the Cloisters, the museum that becomes real;
the theater which is a "reel house, a real house" (P, 214); the
title of Ginsberg's "SUNFLOWER SUTRA" which literally
points its leafy precepts upon a center that is absent; and its
author's annunciation of himself as the son of Paterson, who
when he returns to act and live there will have "W. C. Fields
on my left and Jehovah on my right" (P, 213). The poet's

names become the shadows of things, but in turn those shadows become things which turn the detail into a shadow. This doubling of image and sound is the counterpoint of a dance, the "rout of the vocables" (P, 222) which produces a "fiction" in which the center is everywhere and nowhere: "Anywhere is everywhere" (P, 235).[39] The poet sees "from the two sides: the/ imagination must be served" (P, 228).

Book Five of *Paterson* lifts the local detail of the earlier books to another (aesthetic) plane. As such, it is a doubling of the earlier poem, turning it inside out in order to disclose its synchrony with all the art which "has survived." What it discloses, therefore, is that this enduring art is the "fiction" of beginnings, and reflexively, a demystification of the logocentrism implied by fictions. The freedom of fictions is the absence of the subject. Speaking to Valéry Larbaud, in the Père Sebastian Rasles chapter of *In the American Grain*, Williams had protested that Larbaud was concerned only with sources and not the issue of history: "I seek the support of history, but wish to understand it aright, to make it *show* itself" (IAG, 116). That which shows itself comes to light; to come to light is to leave the origin behind. To know the source, then, one must reconstitute it as fiction. *Paterson*, of course, begins as a poem of those who do not "know their sources" (P, 6); but it ends by revealing that one can only know them, once they are

39. In his Notes for *Paterson* (Yale MS), Williams scribbled the following title page:

PATERSON
or
Any/Every Place
by
William Carlos Williams
---WCW-----------------DJL-----------------MN---
with the assistance of
DJL   AND   MN

"DJL" is David J. Lyle, the systems engineer whose letters Williams had once compiled into a pastiche of a dialogue between Noah (Williams) and Faitoute (Lyle); "MN" is Marcia Nardie, the Cress of *Paterson*, a number of whose letters are included in the poem.

lost, as fictions. To be free, to be historical, one must know the fiction of fictions. Therefore, the "dream" of *Paterson*, Book Five, is not a perspectival dream, drawing the four previous poems into focus and reconstituting their wholeness. It brings the others to the point of "dream" only to announce the dream as "pursuit." Again, the demystification of the tapestries reveals at once the universality of art and the illusion of its plenitude: "four petals/ one near the other to/ fill in the detail// from frame to frame without perspective/ touching each other on the canvas/ make up the picture" (P, 235–36). From tapestry to tapestry a blank space asserts itself, marking the discontinuities in the "legend." But it is this discontinuity, bridged by the recurring plenitude of a continuous nature, which constitutes the separate tapestries as a single "picture," yet a story. And "the cranky violet/ like a knight in chess" (P, 236) asserts itself as the implicit freedom within the field. Book Five reveals the play of interpretation, in history as in art.

Standing in the presence of the "legend," of a field of multiple detail the center of which is everywhere and nowhere, the poet is reminded of his freedom and his limitation. That is, he is confronted by his temporality, his historicity:

> Though he is approaching
> death he is possessed by many poems.
> Flowers have always been his friends,
> even in paintings and tapestries
> which have lain through the past
> in museums jealously guarded, treated
> against moths. They draw him imperiously
> to witness them, make him think
> of bus schedules and how to avoid the
> irreverent . . .   (P, 231–32)

Art mates desire and death, and discloses their interpenetrations. A man possessed by many poems is possessed by this discovery, of the reversibility of time in art. Poems move, but in a measure or "musical time" that winds upon itself, contrapuntally. As Roman Jakobson has pointed out, synchrony, which is the essential characteristic of language, should not be confused with the static:

> It would be a serious error to consider statics and the synchronic as synonymous. The static cross-section is a fiction: it is only a helpful scientific device, and not a particular mode of being. We can consider the perception of the film not only diachronically but also synchronically; however, the synchronic aspect of a film is not identical to an isolated image extracted from the film. Movement is also perceived in the synchronic aspect as well. The same is true of language.[40]

The tapestries incorporate in their seven panels the synchronic history of origins rather than the revelation of the origin of Christian history. And Book Five, the detail of which is as much from the history of art and myth as from the history of Williams' local, synchronizes its detail in a "memory" which is contemporary with the "memory" that structured the tapestries. For the tapestries are anonymous. That is, they are not simply the consciousness of their historical period, but the repeated utterance, for all their particularity, of a legend the origin of which precedes recorded history and is eternally lost. *Paterson*, Book Five, is the historical issue of this missing center. Or as it bespeaks its own project:

> The (self) direction has been changed
> the serpent
> its tail in its mouth
> "the river has returned to its beginnings"
> and backward
> (and forward)
> it tortures itself within me
> until time has been washed finally under:
> (P, 233)

40. Quoted by Lévi-Strauss, in *Structural Anthropology*, 88.

The "time" of Book Five is "once on a time" (P, 238), and it recapitulates the beginning, the advent of "The Wanderer." In this dream time, the "history" of *Paterson*, Books One–Four, is lifted to the level of a metamyth, for this was an "effort" to evolve a "myth," a "river that flows/ and encircles," gathering history into the circle of "oceanus." But the making continually reminded the poet that he could not encapsulate all time, that the consummation of the dream was to awaken from the dream. Not only does the detail of *Paterson*, Books One–Four, lack chronology, the *lift* of the poem raises it into a simultaneous flow and return. Like *Paterson*, Book Five, it spirals upon itself from the beginning. From the paradoxes and tautologies of the epigraph to "the spiral/ the final somersault/ the end" (P, 204), the poem doubles and redoubles itself both thematically and linguistically. As words double each other (dog-god; New-ark and the serpent river Kra) events double each other (David Hower's search for the Unios he does not recognize; Hamilton's dream of a SUM; the poet's "dream of/ the whole poem"). The "rigor of beauty" which is the "quest," announced in the poem's opening phrases, becomes finally the "effort" in which alone there is "virtue."

Every assertion of a recovered presence is demystified, and an inaugural difference is revealed. As the historical fragments of Paterson are rebounded upon each other, the old meanings which they were presumed to reveal are exposed as fictions, the testimony to a significance concealed in a dead "rhetoric." And even the poet's assertion that his "rhetoric/ is real!" (P, 145) comes at the end of a passage which presents language as the "visible part" of the "invisible," containing a "meaning" that brings all meanings into question. History, like the "song" of the "marriage" of a man and a woman, is a riddle which hides "death" at its center:

Here's a fossil conch (a paper weight
of sufficient quaintness) mud
and shells baked by a near eternity
into a melange, hard as stone, full of
tiny shells
—baked by endless desiccations into
a shelly rime—turned up
in an old pasture whose history—
even whose partial history, is
death itself   (P, 142–43)

Poems are at once mystifications of time as presence and demystifications of a totalized history.

It is in 'this sense that Williams could insist on the simultaneity of all original poems, which were at the same time quests after beauty (and presence) and the "shells" or secretions of a lost presence. If the *Iliad* was the model for his "new measure," it was not because the *Iliad* was a model epic, but because it contained the original riddle of a man and a woman: of violence and beauty, of desire, and of the necessity of utterance. The "riddle" is a tapestry that at once conceals and expresses the myth of history. "I have been able to 'place' the new in its relation to the past much more accurately," Williams wrote to Louis Martz about his search for a "new measure": "We have been looking for too big, too spectacular a divergence from the old. The 'new measure' is much more particular, much more related to the remote past than I, for one, believed" (SL, 299). Or as he put it in "Asphodel":

If we are to understand our time
we must find the key to it,
not in the eighteenth
and nineteenth centuries
but in earlier, wilder
and darker epochs   . .
(PB, 162)

The "new measure" is of a time which precedes history and

the language of self-consciousness. It is a primordial "time," the time of language at the moment of its origin, its fall. The "certain new rules" he has discovered turn out to be "ancient rules, profoundly true but long since all but forgotten" (SE, xiii–xiv).

"Asphodel," as was mentioned earlier, was begun as *Paterson*, Book Five, and projected as a poem speaking from the threshold of death. A "love" poem, it speaks from a plane beyond differentiation, from the site of memory where "all appears/ as if seen/ wavering through water" (PB, 162), perspectiveless like the time of beginning itself. It is a "cry/ of recognition" (PB, 162) which penetrates the veil of history to connect his "Approaching death" with his origins. Interestingly, it has been the poem most praised by critics because of Williams' late breakthrough, presumably like Stevens', to a new lyricism. And this signifies not simply an advance beyond *Paterson* but a reversal, perhaps, ironically, a return to the tradition. But the tradition to which "Asphodel" appeals is that of the "rituals of the hunt/ on the walls/ of prehistoric// caves in the Pyrenees" (PB, 174). As was suggested earlier, the caves offer man a present entry into time and place, of the primordial origins of art itself.[41] At the impending moment of his own death, the poet sings of origins: the "cave" which is both beginning and end, and the "hunt" or quest to which man is compelled in his desire.

These "rituals" are the beginning of language itself; for they are a "first" art, "rituals of the hunt" for some "secret word" (PB, 170) through which man recovers presence and the "dream" of his own renewal. This "secret word" is the desire of all art, like the "flower" Melville admired in his South Sea

41. See esp. Georges Bataille, *Lascaux ou la naissance de l'art* (Paris: Skira, 1955); and Georges Bataille, *Death and Sensuality: A Study of Eroticism and the Taboo* (New York: Ballentine Books, 1969). See also Chapter 5.

hunts. It is related to the poet's apocalyptic experience one day on the subway when he found himself confronting a man who was the image of his father. For the father is the keeper of the "secret" which the son can possess only by replacing him, and thus only in his "recognition" of his own inevitable violence. This "word" is the poet's only defense "against time" (PB, 154). It is, finally, the word that will inhere in his poem, if he makes it right, the "secret word" that inheres at the center of every poem that endures. It is a word that silently speaks the meaning of love. For love, like death, is his only escape from solitude, from discontinuity—that is, from his historicity.

"Asphodel" seems to go beyond the cry of *Paterson*, Book Five, that only art survives. It evokes the "light," that constant of Einstein's relativity principle, which existed once in the purity of the origin and is recoverable now only within the convolutions of his own "shelly rime." And "Asphodel" at its conclusion goes as far as any Williams poem in suggesting that the "virtue" transcends the "effort." It therefore comes very near to suggesting a poetics no longer resigned to failure or to the hermeneutical circle. It comes very near to insisting that the "secret word" has been possessed, the son reconciled with the father, and thus a language fully achieved—that the "place/ dedicated in the imagination/ to memory// of the dead" (PB, 177–78) has come to be more real than the world, and that the poem restores the presence of an original virgin. "Asphodel" was not appropriate to *Paterson*, then, because it was written from a point on the spiral of its author's history beyond, or nearly so, desire. It marries "love" and "death," those conflicting opposites of light and dark, in a new light, the restored presence of a first marriage. "Asphodel" is the poem of a condemned man, a "sexless old man" (PB, 166), and not like *Paterson*, Book Five, a poem of some ancient eagle, casting off once more. It is not a poem of quest or effort, but a dream of virtue recovered and held "against time."

In "Asphodel" Williams comes as close as he ever will in celebrating the transcendent: "Inseparable from the fire," the coda begins, "its light/ takes precedence over it" (PB, 178). The self-consciousness with which he reminds himself that the light, like the "radiant gist" of *Paterson*, must inhere in the world cannot prevent him from asserting the desired precedence of the one to the other. Yet, the "light" is "Inseparable from the fire"—and thus the light is also the act of bringing to light, the creative act itself. "Only the imagination is real!" this nearly disembodied man sings, and "love and the imagination/ are of a piece,/ swift as the light" (PB, 179). The poem becomes the odorless flower remembered in relation to the "light," the light that shone before him and his bride on their wedding day. It constitutes the "place" of that "time" the poet has begged for, the "time" to recall his life and restore its coherence. It becomes his book of flowers and his book of love, his poems created out of the desire of a love unfulfilled or violated. Its recovered "light" is the light of a beginning, an original marriage that thrust him into time and condemned him to whore the virgin.

"Asphodel" associates itself with that great poem of the "sea," the *Iliad*, and thus with "Helen's public fault/ that bred it" (PB, 158).[42] That is, it associates itself with the proto-myth of history made necessary by the public fault. Desire is the origin of history and language, and Man is Time with very little time. But the poem, if it is achieved, can be the sarcophagus of time:

> The poem
> if it reflects the sea

42. Compare H.D.'s *Helen in Egypt* (New York: Grove Press, 1961), which takes as its theme the legend that Helen was never at Troy, except as a "phantom" or Greek illusion, but was always at the island of Leuke, the realm of the dead. In H.D.'s legend, Helen in her temple ("La Mort") stands for the imagination in the sanctuary of the unconscious which contains the secret for what all historical symbols are at once manifestations and mediations (see p. 111). Myths, poems, artifacts, ideas, even history, are issues of the mystery, and like all issues, a falling away into some hieroglyphic trace that must be deciphered.

> reflects only
> its dance
> upon that profound depth
> where
> it seems to triumph.   (P, 165)

The "new measure" of any poem is the "time" it rescues from the sea, the deathlessness of the desire it catches in its "dance." In this sense, all poems are contemporaneous and copresent, enwound upon the silence of the "secret word." They are one with prehistoric man's original "rituals of the hunt," and they reveal the beginning as a "fault."

"Asphodel" could not be the metapoem of *Paterson*, Books One–Four, which Williams was seeking, perhaps because the personal urgency which demanded it (in particular, his catastrophic illness that all but denied him any more time) provoked a more nearly pure lyric than *Paterson*, Book Five, could be. In any event, "Asphodel" seems at times more closely related to the *Four Quartets* than to Williams' earlier canon, though its motif of art's survival is revived and completed in Book Five of *Paterson*. Both necessarily are a "celebration of the light" (PB, 181), of that father-idea which had disappeared from the world or that female-body which had been violated, leaving desire unrequited, love silenced, and culture languishing in the ruins of nature. Both are poems seeking the restoration of the enduring "word," which is the achievement of any poem truly achieved. But "Asphodel," unlike *Paterson*, Book Five, the later poem, cannot admit the problematic of its achievement. The imminence of death provokes the lyric nostalgia of the former; while the latter maintains to the end the motif of *Paterson*: the "hunt" which is the "fiction" of language itself and the original violation that throws man into "time." *Paterson*, Book Five, must end in the openness of the dance.

The "death" revealed at the center of the "fossil conch" in

Paterson is the freedom at the center of all language. Books, in *Paterson*, are the "cry" of the "pitiful dead," the "dream" of "dead men" who have sought to possess the "Beautiful Thing" (presence, or virtue, or whatever other name may be substituted for the lack at the center). Books, then, are the self-consuming allegories of their own enigmatic origin, in the surface nothingness of dispersed words:

> We read: not the flames
> but the ruin left
> by the conflagration
>
> Not the enormous burning
> but the dead (the books
> remaining). Let us read
>
> and digest: the surface
> glistens, only the surface.
> Dig in—and you have
>
> a nothing, surrounded by
> a surface, an inverted
> bell resounding, a
>
> white-hot man become
> a book, the emptiness of
> a cavern resounding (P, 123)

Every book has been an "effort" toward "virtue," an effort to contain the plenitude of the passion that made it necessary. The "Beautiful Thing" is the "dream of dead men" (P, 122), and their books are efforts to possess it. But what we now read is the trace or "ruin" of the effort, and what we hear, an "inverted/ bell resounding," is like the "open tomb" of Christ (P, 72) or the opened pyramid (or even, the silence at the center of Sappho's poems).

Books are the issue of history, and they must be demystified if history is to remain open. That is, they must be deconstructed, so that the presence they pretend to contain is

revealed as the inaugural fury of another "white hot man."
Paterson is surely a deconstructive poem, at once an "effort"
toward a "whole poem" and an act that brings the "whole"
into question. *Paterson* is, therefore, a poem of history—in
Stevens' words, "the cry of its occasion,/ Part of the res itself
and not about it." [43] And if we understand "cry" to be the
term for utterance and "occasion" to be the time of the *fall*
into time, as I think Stevens did, we can understand why
violence and destruction stand at the center of the creative act
for Williams. *Paterson* repeats all original poems, is one with
the *Iliad* and *Odyssey*, because it is an attempt to retrieve the
"cry" of the "pitiful dead" from old books, from given history,
and thus repeat that "cry" on a new plane. The poem becomes
a man, a city, the "locus/ where two women meet,"
regathering the "One from the backwoods" and the "other—
wanting,/ from an old culture" (P, 110). The poem does not
restore to history a "meaning"; it becomes a "relief from
'meaning' " (P, 111).

43. *The Collected Poems of Wallace Stevens* (New York: Alfred A. Knopf, 1954),
473.

4

destruction and creation
are simultaneous
                    (Imag., 127, 309)

I shall never be satisfied until I have
destroyed the whole of poetry as it has
been in the past.
        (Notes for *Paterson*, Buffalo MS)

The revelation is compact—
compact of regathered fury

By violence lost, recaptured by violence
violence alone opens the shell of the nut.
                    (CLP, 8)

The Game of Invention

I

There are, as we have seen, two senses of history for Williams, the closed and the open. The one is recorded and interred in books; the other is available in literature, the adventure of imagination. The one takes its meaning from an idea that precedes it, a remembered *presence* to which it repeatedly appeals as its origin. But the very perfection of this presence calls history into question. The other bears its presence within it and holds us in the openness of our origins. The history which Williams rejects, that which arranges us in "generic patterns," is in the words of Jacques Derrida the classic view of *historia,* or the "unity of a becoming," and is thus a "diversion between two presences": "History has always been conceived as the movement of a resumption of history." [1] Therefore, it takes place in the space connecting *archè* and *telos,* and any definition of it includes the classical opposition of culture and nature. The history to which Williams gives his homage is the history available in "good writing." Writing breaks up the "tyrannous designs" of those patterns which array man like the "effigies or carvings on sarcophagi" (IAG, 188). The history

1. Jacques Derrida, "Structure, Sign, and Play in the Discourse of the Human Sciences," in Richard Macksey and Eugenio Donato (eds.), *The Languages of Criticism and the Sciences of Man* (Baltimore: The Johns Hopkins University Press, 1970), 262.

Williams detests is the history of traditionalists; that which he
celebrates restores "virtue" (the chapter of *In the American
Grain* is entitled The Virtue of History), returns man to the
passion of "a springtime of the soul" (IAG, 196) and thus to
the openness of his freedom: to what he calls "immediacy" or
language before it has reached conceptual rigidity, categorical
mediacy. This is history and language in its "adolescence."

In *Paterson*, the tyrannous designs of history are manifest in
the stamp of Hamilton's SUM upon the place, in the moral
rhetoric that interprets the metaphysical vertigo of Mrs.
Cumming as an effect of the mysterious hand of God, or in the
closed and suffocating space of the Library, which, like the
ideas of the University, connected events to a meaning (an
origin) which lay outside them and the field of their occurrence. This history is also manifest in the language of place, as
a "blockage" that separates man from his origins and therefore
from other men, "blockage" being another term for mediation
and distance from origins. The poem, then, is an "effort"
toward restoring "virtue" or the other sense of history as open.
One of the ways it does this is by decomposing the grammar of
the other history's events, by demystifying their presence, by
short-circuiting the syntax of their chronology. To put it
another way, *Paterson* changes the succession of diachronic
events into the vectors of "musical time," generating in its
counterpoint, its rebound of sound upon sound and detail upon
detail, a simultaneity of things, a "field" that is ahistorical.

The analogy Williams chooses, whether musical time or a
tapestry, is a spatial figure which tries to incorporate into itself
the sense of a dynamic left behind in the concept of diachronic
time. Or in other words, to recall Jakobson's and Lévi-Strauss's
argument for the dynamic character of synchronic time
discussed in the preceding chapter, Williams' substitution of
literature for history moves us beyond mimetic theories of
literature to the problematic of a structural view of literature,

which claims that literature like myth can take us into the immediacy of time. In this view, poetry makes us stand in the presence of the original event, the event of rupture or catastrophe, in which a structure or field of "history" is generated by leaving its origin behind. Only in this moment of catastrophe (a Williams title calls it "Catastrophic Birth") can man stand in the openness of his freedom. In that moment he can reclaim the "nut" from the "shell" (CLP, 8), repossess the lost "virtue," stand once more in relation to a presence.

The figures are all Williams', and they bespeak a Rousseauistic drive toward innocence, toward a language of reclaimed presence—nut, virtue, radiant gist, new—which survives at the center of historical language, like the "hidden" language of poetry concealed within the "everyday language." This new language reveals a presence that precedes history, and is concealed by it. It is, therefore, ancient, timeless, and coexistent with original speech. To discover it, a Modern poetry must be like the first writing. It is a language not of mediacy or distance, but of immediacy, and therefore cannot be described in the language of language at all. It must be conceived on the analogy of "musical time." The Modern poem, then, must repeat an ancient poetry, at least at its oral interior. But at its own exterior, it speaks the language of history, the words of everyday. The function of the Modern (or, as we shall see, post-Modern) poem is not simply to speak of the one (the "gist") in terms of the other (the everyday, the detritus or pitchblende), which would imply a metaphorical or symbolist poem, but to disclose the presence concealed in history and therefore denied by historical language. "A presence there is," says Dev Evans in *A Voyage to Pagany*, "a thing that lives here always, always unaffected by man, always wild" (VP, 88). The function of the poem is, therefore, deconstructive and demystifying—deconstructive because of its unweaving of the accrued complexities which obscure the simplicity of origins, demystifying because it brings into question what Heidegger calls the onto-theological idea of history as presence.

Paradoxically, then, we might say that Williams' poetics only substitutes one idea of presence (aesthetic) for another (historical), and therefore there is something Modern but not radically post-Modern in his substitution of the one for the other. In a sense, this is true. To destroy the Library, or to celebrate the violent exposure of its closed space, is to celebrate the opening of a tomb, the exposure of presence as an absence—only to celebrate at the same time the immanence of a true presence, the elemental flame, the dynamic light. It is to substitute, in a sense, *energeia* for *telos*. Or to use another analogy, it is to displace the idea of a structure with a fixed center by the idea of a structure in which the center is decentered, broken free and floating, or suffused throughout the entire field. The latter incorporates an idea of freeplay, but a freeplay which nostalgically recalls the loss or disappearance of the center and seeks to restore it even in the awareness that its restoration will be a fiction. Still, this is not all that is implied by Williams' self-consciousness. Indeed, it may be a better description of Eliot, whose words circle the absent Word, whose music calls words and even its own sensuousness into question, and whose incessant naming of the still-point laments the ruptured immediacy words suffer in relation to the absent still-point.

There is no doubt that, at least in the most explicit terms, Williams' poetry asserts the true moment of experience as an immediacy, of words coexistent with things, of innocence and poetry as co-incident. But history is not innocent. It signifies that man can only know presence mediately, or in ceremonies of innocence. In other words, innocence is recoverable today in the most sophisticated game of art, like Klee's primitiveness which is achieved with only the most complex and conscious simplicity. But this is even more paradoxical when we see that

Eliot's poetic moment of redemption, in which the will-less self is held in the presence of the silence of poetry, only brings the weight of the Christian tradition to bear on the game, thus making the game an allegory and not a game at all. In this sense, there does not appear to be the distance between Williams and Eliot that Williams believed; and indeed, something less than the difference which would make the one's use of fragments to shore against his ruins different from the other's use of local detail. To say that the first implies things as metaphors, the second things as metonym, is to suggest a difference of opposites that even the structural linguists found to exist only because the two poles tended to slide into one another, or change positions.

But there is a more fundamental difference between Eliot and Williams, though perhaps not the difference Williams thought, and it exists in the radical nature of the game (of language) each had to play. For now I will call it the difference between Modern and post-Modern. It is not simply a matter of temporal priority that distinguishes the one from the other, but of the kind of priority (the kind of presence or origin) assumed by each. For the one is logocentered and recalls the distance of words from the Word, while the other celebrates the energy of the imagination which might rise once again into the immediate field of words, manifest as the "light" that is diffused throughout the poem, like the pure white implied in the spectrum of juxtaposed colors.

Williams' poetry begins, then, with an attack on logocentrism, on a system in which "Texts mount and complicate them-/ selves, lead to further texts and those/ to synopses, digests and emendations" (P, 130). This is Dr. Paterson's "stream" of time, his history which "grows leaden within him" (P, 130). It is a time of accumulated meanings which have led to blockage and from which man demands relief. "Until the words break loose" (P, 130), man is condemned to silence, and

the lilies of his Paradiso "drag." Like the suffocating air of the
Library (and this passage is from the same section of the
poem), the "debris" of "Texts" and "emendations," of a
language which distances meaning, must be exploded. The
means is writing: "writing/ is also an attack" and thus "a
destroying fire"; "to write/ is a fire" (P, 113). Writing is a
passion that is a "relief" from passion, the upsurge of elemental
force which reclaims the elemental from complexity. "Each
age," he writes in another poem, "brings new calls upon
violence/ for new rewards" (CLP, 8).

The refrain that runs through Book Three of *Paterson*, the
book of elements and the book of destruction, is the prayer "So
be it." It is a prayer of violence, a call for the elemental
reductions of fire, flood, tornado, and earthquake. It summons
nature to reclaim its priority and destroy the "made-arch"
which "holds." It calls up an original energy to break the
"unshaken" artifice of man's interpretations, those human
channelings of nature (P, 130). The "So be it" refrain occurs
at several points of blockage, calling forth the violence that
opens closed space or clears blocked time: at the point where
the "drunkenness/ of flames" consumes the Library (P, 117),
where the flood piles up debris against the man-made bridge,
or where books provide an ease of mind and the Library "is
sanctuary to our fears":

> Blow! So be it. Bring down! So be it. Consume
> and submerge! So be it. Cyclone, fire
> and flood. So be it. Hell, New Jersey, it said
> on the letter.   (P, 97)

If "So be it" is the translation of Amen, it is no less the
utterance of an action—of letting be, perhaps Heidegger's "let
it be." [2] Pound, indeed, singles out the phrase as something

2. See Martin Heidegger, *Existence and Being*, trans. Douglas Scott (Chicago:
Gateway edition, 1967), 305–307. Heidegger distinguishes between the usual sense of
"letting be" as standing off or leaving alone, a kind of indifference toward being, and

"less rhetorical" than Amen, as the translation of the Italian
Cosi sia which is associated with the Mediterranean prayer for
rain and for fair weather. This prayer, says Pound, exemplifies
"Mediterranean moderation." [3] "So be it" summons the mind
to acceptance, and to resignation, but it is no less a summons to
destruction and thus to the act of making or letting "be." Only
by destruction of the sanctuaries of "our fears" can the original
violence of language be disclosed, can the "perfume" of "locust
blossoms" concealed in the "cool of books" (P, 95) or the
"Beautiful thing" that lurks in the "rumor" of the falls be
released, by "reverberation" (P, 96). *Paterson*, and especially
Book Three, links creation with violence at every stage—the
violence that is hermeneutic, demystifying the winds of
doctrine which fill historical Texts in order to let "be" the
passion which is the gist of all utterance.

Poetry is murderous, Williams argued in his projected
"Book on Prosody," and poets are "image breakers." [4] From
the beginning, he celebrated the simultaneity of destruction
and creation: in *Spring and All*, the fifteenth lyric heralds the
"growth of movie houses" out of the "decay of cathedrals" as
something other than a moral disaster portending the decline of
culture; rather, it manifests not a schism but a rotation of
fundamental space, in which "light becomes/ darkness and

the "letting be" which is identified with "freedom" as a form of "participation in the
revealment of what-is-as-such." The truth "exposed" by unconcealment is "not the
mark of some correct proposition made by a human 'subject' in respect of an 'object'
and which then . . . counts as 'true'; truth is rather the revelation of what is, a
revelation through which something 'overt' comes into force" (p. 309).

3. Ezra Pound, *Guide to Kulcher* (Norfolk, Conn.: New Directions, n.d.), 141.

4. William Carlos Williams' projected "Book on Prosody" (MS in the Beinecke
Library of Yale University, New Haven, Conn.), 26; works in this collection will
hereinafter be cited as Yale MS. See J. Hillis Miller, "Williams' *Spring and All* and
the Progress of Poetry," *Daedalus*, XCIX (Spring, 1970), 405–34, for a treatment of
deconstruction. Miller's point of departure is Derrida's observation that one cannot
escape the language of the system or theory one is attacking, and therefore that
Williams' attack on Modernism and on the tradition participates in the language and
the idea of the system under attack, in Williams' case, the Platonic tradition of
presence which governs Western formalist theories of poetry.

darkness/ light," and the perpendicular reach of religious metaphor is rotated into a poetics of earth (Imag., 127–28). Of his "improvisations" (presumably, *Kora in Hell*), he could argue that their "excellence is . . . the shifting of category," the "disjointing process" (Imag., 285). "Joyce maims words" because their meanings have been "perverted by time and chance" and kept "perverted by academic observance and intention." But the maiming restores them: "The words are freed to be understood again in an original, a fresh, delightful sense" (SE, 89–90). Marianne Moore "gets great pleasure from wiping soiled words or cutting them clean out," giving them an "acid" cleansing (Imag., 315–16).

Modernism, by which Williams means the avant garde, attacks the mediacy of traditional art and arrives at "immediacy," even at the expense of the appearance of "disorder" (Imag., 308). Its counterlanguage demands its critic: "So it is that the present writers must turn interpreters of their own work" (Imag., 308). The phrase repeats one of the prose passages of *Spring and All* (Imag., 111), previously noted, and exposes the ironic doubling of any "new" writing. Williams clearly recognized what most avant garde expression at once acknowledges and tries to hide from itself, that its only available medium is the medium of an exhausted tradition which can be escaped only by the most radical inversion, a condition which irrevocably and ironically ties the new to the forms and values embedded or entombed in the old tradition. An avant garde art is necessarily an "attack," even if it is like Poe's originality, an "attack . . . *from the center out*" (IAG, 219). Even though this is "destructive!" it destroys "with the conserving abandon, foreshadowed, of a Gertrude Stein" (IAG, 221). Such an art is tied, whether by parody or allegory, to the tradition it attacks or demystifies; it is the style of a "conserving" radicalness. Ironically, it assumes its newness only when it finds its interpreter, even if that interpreter is itself, for only the interpreter can save it from the charge of anarchy and justify its "attack" as creative, as a "making new." Poe's destructions, he noted, derived from a kind of "algebra," a "sense of play" with words (IAG, 2 2 1).

Is this necessarily the result only of a literature which can be defined as an "attack"? Derrida, speaking of what he calls the "rupture" in the history of Western thought which occurred some time late in the last century and continued on into this one, describes that rupture in terms of a startling shift in the conception of "structure." The rupture, which leads as he says from the traditional metaphysics (the philosopher as a thinker of systems or structures) to the philosophy of deconstruction (the philosopher as the questioner of systems), began when "the structurality of structure had to begin to be thought, that is to say, repeated." [5] This produces a discourse on discourse. At this moment, he continues, "language entered the universal problematic," and man had to think of structure not as the result of some central presence but as his own need for a central presence. He recognizes that all the old names for presence (*eidos, archè, telos, energeia,* God, etc.) are merely substitutions for an idea that was never really questioned but always assumed: that all structure was the product of an origin, a form of *logos,* that stands outside and is unqualified by what it structures. But as soon as that idea is explored, and the center recognized as the unexamined presence which allowed for infinite substitutions, the "rupture" occurred. The rupture is manifest in what Derrida calls "decentering" and is historically evidenced in the thinking of Nietzsche, Freud, and Heidegger as the "critique" or the "destruction of metaphysics." All "destructive discourses and all their analogies," he says, "are trapped in a sort of circle," like Heidegger's hermeneutical circle:

> This circle is unique. It describes the form of the relationship between the history of metaphysics and the destruction of the

5. Derrida, "Structure, Sign, and Play," 249.

history of metaphysics. *There is no sense* in doing without the concepts of metaphysics in order to attack metaphysics. We have no language—no syntax or lexicon—which is alien to this history; we cannot utter a single destructive proposition which has not already slipped into the form, the logic, and the implicit postulations of precisely what it seeks to contest.[6]

Destruction here, as indeed in Williams, implies "deconstruction," which has become the preferred translation of the Heideggerian term. It bears within itself the distinction Wallace Stevens made when, borrowing from Simone Weil, he spoke of "modern reality" as "a reality of decreation" and defined "decreation" as "making pass from the created to the uncreated" in contrast with "destruction" which is "making pass from the created to nothing."[7] To decreate to the "uncreated" is to participate in an act of de-centering, of bringing the idea of the center which sustains any "created" into question. For Heidegger, deconstruction implies a questioning of the foundations of ontology, not to destroy the tradition but to loosen the rigidity of its logical structure so that we may have fuller access to the original sources which gave birth to the governing concepts and categories. It involves a questioning of the center:

> When tradition thus becomes master, it does so in such a way that what it "transmits" is made so inaccessible, proximally and for the most part, that it rather becomes concealed. Tradition takes what has come down to us and delivers it over to self-evidence; it blocks our access to those primordial "sources" from which the categories and concepts handed down to us have been in part genuinely drawn. Indeed it makes us forget that they have had such an

6. *Ibid.*, 250. Though Derrida dates this event as recent and offers the names of Freud, Nietzsche, and Heidegger as those who begin deconstructive thinking, his view rejects the "history of ideas" approach. The modern examples cannot be taken with historical literalness.

7. Wallace Stevens, *The Necessary Angel* (New York: Alfred A. Knopf, 1951), 174–75.

origin, and makes us suppose that the necessity of going back to these sources is something which we need not even understand.[8]

It is precisely this "blockage" which provokes Williams to his view of writing as an "attack," and provokes the need for a work that clarifies by self-criticism. For poems (or books) like *Spring and All* were products of the repeated act of decentering, of a poem which progresses by its repeated declarations of its freedom from the tradition. This freedom, however, characteristically results in the parodic mirroring of the very tradition being subverted. The discourse on discourse that characterizes Williams' early "prose-poems," *Kora in Hell* and *Spring and All*, is a discourse that looks both inward and outward, toward the primordial source and toward the historical audience and its tradition. And what it repeatedly brings into question is not simply the tradition, but its own place, the assumed presence of art itself, or the fiction that literature accrues to itself: that it reconstitutes order, the center, and holds it there in its sacred space. Like cubist painting, Williams' poems simultaneously center and decenter; and their self-awareness thrusts them beyond Modernism (which, after all, in its Eliotic, or symbolistic, manifestation reconstituted presence as an absence or still-point) toward post-Modernism (and the freeplay of the center). To this I will return at the end of the chapter.

Williams, then, thought of his Modernism as a return to immediacy; and of the recovery of "sources" as a form that must inevitably remind the traditionalist of "disorder." In other words, he thought of Modernism in terms of its fundamental contrariety, the freedom of its internal order from the fixed centers of traditional literature:

8. Martin Heidegger, *Being and Time*, trans. John Macquarrie and Edward Robinson (New York: Harper & Row, 1962), 43.

If one come with Miss Moore's work to some wary friend and
say, "Everything is worthless but the best and this is the best,"
adding, "only with difficulty discerned" will he see anything, if he
be at all well read, but destruction? From my experience he will
be shocked and bewildered. He will perceive absolutely nothing
except that his whole preconceived scheme of values has been
ruined. And this is exactly what he should see, a break *through* all
preconception of poetic form and mood and pace, a flaw, a crack
in the bowl. It is this that one means when he says destruction and
creation are simultaneous. . . . Miss Moore, using the same
material as all others before her, comes at it so effectively at a new
angle as to throw out of fashion the classical conventional poetry
to which one is used and puts her own and that about her in its
place. The old stops are discarded. This must antagonize many.
Furthermore, there is a multiplication, a quickening, a burrowing
through, a blasting aside, a dynamization, a flight over—it is
modern, but the critic must show that this is only to reveal an
essential poetry through the mass, as always. . . .

(Imag., 308–309)

That "essential poetry," lying nearer the sources, would
presumably be a recovered presence. It would be "authentic"
language. Does Williams' poetics, to repeat the question, do no
more than participate in the substitution of one idea of
presence for another? If so, is its "destructive" function
nothing other than repetition, and thus traditional? These are
questions not easily answered, because of what the poems tend
to conceal from themselves. And one can offer a tentative
answer, and an argument for the truly radical nature of
Williams' experiments, only after an exploration of the
destructive and creative vectors, both thematic and linguistic,
that characterize those experiments. What is involved, crit-
ically, is a determination of the freeplay in Williams' poems—
the concept of the game, and how this game is opened
originally by writing. Poe's "sense of play," the algebraic
breakup of "literary habit," is also a sense of a beginning
(IAG, 221–22).

II

If *Spring and All* is, as Williams said, the "book" of

"imagination" (Imag., 89), it is also a book of violence; for the "imagination" is the "single force" which can take man into the "eternal moment" when he is "what he is" (Imag., 89). This is a moment of beginning, of contact. "There is a constant barrier between the reader and his consciousness of immediate contact with the world" (Imag., 88), and the imagination is a force resistant to that barrier. Art as it is traditionally known, and especially literature, has been a part of the "barrier between sense and the vaporous fringe," because art has been a "search for 'the beautiful illusion' " (Imag., 89). Art, thus defined, is symbolic, metaphoric, mimetic, and tied to a "world" in the past or future. The very word *poetry* bears within itself the assumptions of the "beautiful illusion." And Williams, dedicating himself to return toward immediacy, accepts in this moment the charge that his poetry is "antipoetry" (Imag., 88) and that his poetics, as he would later express it, advocated a "pre-art" (CLP, 5).[9]

The very language of art conceals its own assumption of presence. Williams' book of imagination exists to bring the idea of the "book" into question, to wipe out the mediacy of time, and destroy the barrier of the "world" as alien other. It will "kill" for "love," which is to say, destroy mediacy to restore immediacy:

> The imagination, intoxicated by prohibitions, rises to drunken heights to destroy the world. Let it rage, let it kill. The imagination is supreme. To it all our works forever, from the remotest past to the farthest future, have been, are and will be dedicated. . . . To it now we come to dedicate our secret project: the annihilation of every human creature on the face of the earth.
> (Imag., 90–91)

9. This not to ignore Williams' repeated irritation with those like Stevens who call his poetry antipoetic, as we have seen. "Pre-art" here means a view of art which precedes definition, an art, however, which would not necessarily be logocentered or subject-centered or otherwise assume the priority of presence which defines the Western onto-theological aesthetic. The "new" art, Williams knows, would come into being as an anti-art, but he wishes to identify it with original or first art, which would be pre-art.

Drunkenness, as we shall see later, is related to the elemental
fire which consumes the old logic, destroying the logocentrism
of the "world" and of "poetry." What occurs, however, is not
destruction but a reversal, a violent torsion of the expected
which brings it into question yet leaves it fundamentally as it
was: "Yes, the imagination, drunk with prohibitions, has
destroyed and recreated everything afresh in the likeness of
that which it was" (Imag., 93). The violence produces an
unexpectancy, a disruption of the accepted syntax of things,
suddenly revealing the priority of the thing and its immediate
relations to any general grammar. *Spring and All* proceeds, like
so many of Williams' other early experiments, by the "valid
juxtaposition," which is a "gentleness that harbors all violence"
(CLP, 29). It exposes the blindness of the "poetic," its
assumption of symmetry, center, association: "the/ anti-poetic
they say ignorantly, a/ disassociation" (CLP, 28).

"Violence and/ gentleness, which is the core?" asks one of
Williams' poems, even as it refutes the moral of traditional art:
"The lion/ according to old paintings will/ lie down with the
lamb" (CLP, 24). But the old paintings tended, in their
centeredness of the Word, to deny the violence implicit in the
lamb's centeredness. The poem of imagination, on the contrary, must be a poem of decentering, setting itself against the
logocentric texts of "poetry" or "art." Thus the elements of
parody, satire, surrealism, and verbal play which characterize
Kora in Hell and *Spring and All.* The deconstructive art of
these poems functions linguistically, thematically, stylistically,
structurally, to embody as well as exemplify the violence of
aletheia: springing, unconcealing, flowering, bursting out,
e-merging, and thus the simultaneous breaking down of some
previous unity, idea, concept, "World."

If *Kora* progresses by the alternation of improvisation and
commentary, the latter does not clarify or illuminate the
former. On the contrary, the commentary more often compli-

cates than simplifies the improvisation, by giving it a meaning which distorts its original openness and opaqueness. As it brings the improvisation to the order of explanation, it destroys the coherent nonsense of the verbal play, that unity of sense which is the concealed unity (passion) of expression itself. To put it another way, the commentary often allegorizes the improvisation, thereby exposing the improvisation as an allegory. The question of which precedes the other, a question perhaps of narrative development or of development in general, is suspended. *Kora* breaks down language, and experience, toward its origins, in order to recover an immediacy which disallows both temporal and moral distancing. But then it immediately submits this immediacy to interpretation. Yet, neither improvisation nor interpretation escapes the doubling effect; they become reciprocal mirrors of the interpretive process and two sides of a language which must incessantly comment on itself:

> The frontispiece is her portrait and further on—the obituary sermon: she held the school upon her shoulders. Did she. Well—turn in here then:—we found money in the blood and some in the room and on the stairs. My God I never knew a man had so much blood in his head! —and thirteen empty whisky bottles. I am sorry but those who come this way meet strange company. This is you see death's canticle.

> *A young woman who had excelled at intellectual pursuits, a person of great power in her sphere, died on the same night that a man was murdered in the next street, a fellow of very gross behavior. The poet takes advantage of this to send them on their way side by side without making the usual unhappy moral distinctions.* (Imag., 37–38)

It would be a mistake, however, to take the first passage as unmediated experience, the second as interpretation. Both are interpretations, and reciprocally demand each other. The second stands as surrogate for the self-explanation which Williams said modern or avant garde art demanded. Yet, the improvisation, which is "death's canticle," is also a critique, by the valid juxtaposition. It is the immediacy not of sensation but of interpretation, the experience of bringing to light the meaning of a relationship which moral distinctions based on the logic of good and bad conceal. It is an interpretation of violence, by violence, by a rotation of the syntax of things that eliminates the moral distancing. Death's song reveals a violence, but repudiates a judgment.

In this sense *Kora* and *Spring and All* are exemplary avant garde art, and thus deconstructions of the tradition. Even the famous Prologue of *Kora*, that contentious attack upon contemporary traditionalists in the name of the new, Adamic art, becomes a function of the text, to the point that some of the commentaries initially written for the improvisations are transposed back into the pre-text. In their new context, they extend the contentiousness of Williams' argument against his contemporaries toward an assertion of an indefinable new art. The doubling effect, therefore, illuminates the method of Williams' attack, which employs the violence of the valid juxtaposition with examples of the new art which is composed by valid juxtaposition. The example of Duchamp's *Nude Descending a Staircase*, the stroboscopic effects of which created such a stir in art circles, for all the wrong reasons, or the exhibit of the porcelain urinal with a rose lying in the bowl at the "Palace Exhibition of 1917," indicate the "novelty" that is essential for "good art" (Imag., 8). The novelty is a new syntax of relations, not simply a rhetorical shock. It is generated by the displacement of a center which might confer meaning and relation upon the parts. The symbolic rose is violently uprooted from the system of meaning which defined it and disclosed by opposition: red against white, flower against porcelain, nature violated by culture.

But a part of the "meaning" of the exhibition is Duchamp's dependence on a language of taste, the emptiness of which he exposes when he exposes the violence with which its source is concealed and protected from questioning. Williams' examples in the Prologue are consistent: the stained-glass window which defines itself as art only when it has fallen out of the church frame; Walter Arensberg's picture of the *Nude Descending a Staircase*, itself a violation of moral expectancy, being reproduced as a "full-sized photographic print . . . with many new touches by Duchamp himself," thereby becoming another "novelty" (Imag., 8–9). The "novel" is that which at its disclosure cannot be referred back to a meaning which precedes it; "novelty" appears as immediate, a presence that is the virtue without a presence. *"The act is disclosed by the imagination of it,"* goes one of the commentaries; *"But of first importance is to realize that the imagination leads and the deed comes behind. First Don Quixote then Sancho Panza"* (Imag., 64). The "rose is obsolete," (Imag., 107), to recall one of the poems of *Spring and All*, when its symbolic role subsumes it and detaches meaning from thing. Only a juxtaposition like rose and urinal can destroy that symbolic repression and restore thing to itself.

If the imagination comes first, however, we must be cautious in defining this in terms of traditional concepts of the imagination, as shaping spirit whose origin lies in some transcendental spirit or even as the human presence of mind, a point of departure or constitutive subject. The imagination precedes the act, and freedom, what Derrida calls freeplay, may be said to precede any definition. The imagination named here is the imagination which in *Spring and All* Williams calls a "force, an electricity or a medium, a place" (Imag., 150), all terms suggesting its priority as a presence. But the halting, and necessarily failing, attempts at defining the imagination in that book are indeed the only possible definitions. For as the poet conjectures, the names are "immaterial" (just as the imagination is immaterial), but its effect is its definition. And the effect of imagination is to "free." I will return to the implications of this view of imagination, as the name for something that precedes either presence or absence, as a synonym for freeplay, at the end of this chapter. For now, however, it should be kept in mind in regard to the deconstructive function of the "new" art, whose vitality lies in the game it keeps open and advances, so like the useless game of poem twenty-six of *Spring and All*. For only the game, like the dance (for Williams always the dance of two), can maintain the sense of fundamental pairing at the origin, and thus expose the full meaning of the freedom of imagination. In *Kora* Williams stumbled toward this definition which would contradict all the terms he had to use in defining it. And thereby he reveals, as Derrida said of deconstructive thought, that one can only define the new in terms of the old:

> this loose linking of one thing with another has effects of a destructive power little to be guessed at: all manner of things are thrown out of key so that it approaches the impossible to arrive at an understanding of anything. All is confusion, yet it comes from a hidden desire for the dance, a lust of the imagination, a will to accord two instruments in a duet.   (Imag., 18–19)

> Thus a poem is tough by no quality it borrows from a logical recital of events nor from the events themselves but solely from that attenuated power which draws perhaps many broken things into a dance giving them thus a full being.   (Imag., 16–17)

III

Spring and All, as we have seen, begins in the conventional rhetoric of the avant garde, setting Modernism against tradition, the "eternal moment" or "now" against the past or future, immediacy against the mediate. There is no question who is under attack as the "Traditionalists of Plagiarism." What we commonly think of as the Modernist movement of Eliot and Pound, and of the New Criticism, stands indicted at its beginning as the last breath of historicism. Its logocentrism is exposed, and it is tied ironically to what seemed (especially to Eliot) to be its opposite, evolutionism and progressivism. Williams properly exposes the rhetoric of Eliot's Modernism as another substitute for the history of presence; the "Traditionalists of Plagiarism" are advocates of an art of repetition and thus, like nature, are involved in copying. Eliot's metaphor of the individual talent as the stenographer of tradition is interpreted, like the duplications of evolutionary advance, as a "perfect plagiarism" (Imag., 93).

Williams offers in contrast the recreations of a "new day," an art in which consciousness of the past is wiped away so that we stand in the immediacy of a new understanding of art:

> In fact now, for the first time, everything IS new. Now at last the perfect effect is being witlessly discovered. The terms "veracity," "actuality," "real," "natural," "sincere" are being discussed at length, every word in the discussion being evolved from an identical discussion which took place the day before yesterday. (Imag., 93)

This would appear to be yet another instance of the hermeneutical circle which ties present to past in an endless, regressive series of interpretations. But in fact it is a demystification of the terms, breaking them loose from their philological destiny. The words remain the same, only they are "recreated . . . afresh in the likeness of that which . . . was" (Imag., 93). That which they are like is words, not meanings.

The history of Modernism in literature, Paul de Man has argued, cannot simply be recorded either as the period of some near end of history or as the synonym for some privileged break off from history, some avant garde countermovement.[10] Yet, the rhetoric of Modernism, as de Man also shows, has

10. See esp. the chapters "Literary History and Literary Modernity" and "Lyric and Modernity," in Paul de Man, *Blindness and Insight: Essays in the Rhetoric of Contemporary Criticism* (New York: Oxford University Press, 1971), 142–65, 166–86.

popularly employed both the language of periodization (Decadence; Dada) and the language of counter styles (surrealism). And de Man, locating the term's birth in the late fifth century of Christian history, goes on to record its manifestations in various world literatures, especially in the eighteenth and nineteenth centuries, and particularly in the thought of Rousseau and Nietzsche. For Nietzsche, he notes, as for Rousseau, the term was most often the opposite of history and thus a synonym for "life," though elsewhere in Nietzsche it is associated with the decadence of contemporary Germany. De Man takes his evidence of this conflicting use of the Modern (negative when viewed as the exhaustion of the will, and thus a measure of the distance between the Greek and the contemporary; positive when set against the tyranny of history and tradition in the name of "life") from the *Umzeitgemasse Betrachtung II*, which favors the positive view. But *The Will to Power* affirms primarily the negative view, contra Rousseau, and poses the question of man caught between history and Modernism: "Where does our modern world belong—to exhaustion or ascent?—Its manifoldness and unrest conditioned by the attainment of the highest level of consciousness." [11] Apparently, Nietzsche never escaped from the counterforces of Dionysus and Apollo, the orgiastic and the visionary, intoxication and dream[12]—immediacy and distance. Modern remains a negative term for the artist, the opposite of the animal vigor and the "aphrodisiac bliss" [13] that lie at the genetic origins of all art. This allows Nietzsche to locate art in the will to power, the impulse of life, yet to justify its conventions. "Every mature art has a host of conventions as its basis—in so far as it is language," Nietzsche writes; language is

11. Friedrich Nietzsche, *The Will to Power*, trans. Walter Kaufmann and R. J. Hollingdale (New York: Vintage Books, 1968), 48.
12. *Ibid.*, 419–20.
13. *Ibid.*, 422, 424.

a transcription of the aesthetic state, its "source," and thus, "Convention is the condition of great art, not an obstacle—."[14] Modernism, on the other hand, is self-conscious and either imitative (decadent) or self-consuming: "It is to the honor of an artist if he is unable to be a critic—otherwise he is half and half, he is 'modern.' "[15] The artist, however, must move beyond history and act, not retreat into a Rousseauistic innocence in order to arrive at a new immediacy: "The artist who began to understand himself would misunderstand himself: he ought not to look back, he ought not to look at all, he ought to give."[16]

Nietzsche here comes full circle to place the artist at his privileged point, beyond history, and thus once again at the point of immediacy with life. It is this circle into which Williams thrusts himself in the ascents and descents of *Kora* and *Spring and All*, in the deliberate Modernism which attacks the decadent Modernism of "traditionalists." The circle of these "deconstructive" texts inevitably encounters the paradox of Nietzsche's "modern." Williams commits the new art to a kind of repetition—in this case, repetition of the "attack" of the avant garde—in order to escape repetition. "So, after this tedious diversion," to return to that apology for *Spring and All*, "—whatever of dull you find among my work, put it down to criticism, not to poetry. You will not be mistaken—Who am I but my own critic? Surely in isolation one becomes a god" (Imag., 111). The new art must first be half and half, and thus in Nietzsche's terms, Modern.

The attack of *Spring and All* is invariably an act to "separate," to become like Poe a "man of great separation" and thus forge a "close identity with life" (Imag., 111); to separate art from nature, and thus from the subordinate function of a

14. *Ibid.*, 428.
15. *Ibid.*, 429.
16. *Ibid.*

copy, or symbol, or simile; to separate words from things, thus to recover words as "things" (Imag., 120). The necessary "cleavage" of prose and poetry (Imag., 133, 140) leads to the discovery of "a separate origin for each" (Imag., 144). Williams thus engages in the avant garde act, the Modernist act of self-criticism, deconstructing the traditionalists' plagiarism: that repetition and reduplication which asserts the continuity between art and its origins, but which further asserts a distance or separation of the image from those origins. If traditional art is implicitly logocentric, and calls attention to itself as a copy of a copy, the violence of avant garde attack intends to separate us from the reflectiveness of history. It places us in the site of a destruction, in the presence of an illusion being dispersed, and therefore at a point of violence where we are witness to the paradox of violence.

"It may be that the ignorant man, alone," goes one of Stevens' poems, "Has any chance to mate his life with life." [17] Spoken from the perspective of self-consciousness, in the distancing language of metaphor, the lines reveal the dilemma of Modernism—for Modernism at once knows its historicity and desires to forget it. If life is the "sensual pearly spouse," as Stevens' poem continues, if it is the "fire eye in the clouds" which "survives the gods" as the "wheel survives its myths," language possesses it only in metaphor and accentuates the distance of life from life in the figure of a marriage that "may be." The history of recent Modernism is the history of metapoetics, of a self-reflexive poetry which puts itself constantly in question as the only way of resisting the problematic of language. But in this very self-conscious, self-critical act, it throws itself beyond Modernism, beyond the fiction of recovered innocence, and into the freedom of a truly deconstructive adventure. If the characteristic late poem of Stevens is

17. *The Collected Poems of Wallace Stevens* (New York: Alfred A. Knopf, 1954), 222.

"The Auroras of Autumn," a poem of shifting and flashing lights, of the interpenetrations of sound and silence, and of successive "Farewell[s] to an idea" (that is, of son replacing father and mother), it is a poem which recognizes its own problematic and its own openness:

> There may be always a time of innocence.
> There is never a place. Or if there is no time,
> If it is not a thing of time, nor of place,
>
> Existing in the idea of it, alone,
> In the sense against calamity, it is not
> Less real. For the oldest and coldest philosopher,
>
> There is or may be a time of innocence
> As pure principle.[18]

Like Williams' fecundative principle, like the liberating function of the imagination, this "pure principle" need not be a valorized presence, a "first idea." It is the principle of freeplay, of freedom or liberation itself, that supplants the logocenter and mates the poet in his act (his life) with life. But once more, this is to anticipate the conclusion of this chapter, where Derrida's thought-function of freeplay and of the game (he resists calling them concepts of the origin) will be used to test the language of Williams' poems, those destructions which invent by violently doubling the "illusion" of presence. A "time of innocence" that "is" or "may be" becomes the principle of the variable, of indeterminacy, that initial play of chance which necessitates the throw of the dice.

IV

Williams' world, his city, is repeatedly threatened with discontinuity: of words from things, selves from selves, man from his "sources." History, indeed, is that discontinuity. The deathliness of the Library's closed and closeted space is that it

18. *Ibid.,* 418.

makes history and language a tomb of some lost origin, the
dream of presence or the "beautiful illusion." The Library is
the fiction of the continuum of history, of its telic inherence in
language, a fiction of place belied in the rupture inherent in the
name of place, between *Pater* and *son*. The "silence" of the
Library may speak to its citizens the presence of the Word,
but for the poet (that is, Pater-son) "IT IS SILENT BY DEFECT OF
VIRTUE IN THAT IT/ CONTAINS NOTHING OF YOU" (P, 122). The
absence of virtue is absence itself. The space is therefore
airless, suffocating, stale, lacking the elemental. The elemental
forces which rise to open this space, then, are constituents of
the mind awaking from its reverie, the mind reacting to the
stagnant repetitions. Flame, wind, and flood (and later earthquake) are the counterforces of inertia, of closed history. They
open by violence, as writing demystifies the "dreams" of dead
men which are confined in the "walls," of both books and
libraries (P, 100).

Book Three of *Paterson* is the book of deconstruction: of
Library and city. It celebrates the opening of cold books to air,
a chaffing of the latent fire there; therefore, it celebrates the
doomed city, the city which mythologically is the re-founding
of lost origins and historically is the place that obscures the
origin, leaves it behind, or brings it into question. The
elemental forces, then, are the beginning of writing: of
writing, as we have seen, which is an attack (P, 113), a fire
that consumes with "cyclonic fury" (P, 114) and the air which
fans the flames. Book Three celebrates what Derrida calls,
speaking of a philosophical rupture which leads from the old
discourse to a discourse on discourse, the end of the book and
the beginning of writing.[19] Thus writing illuminates, opens,
exposes, discloses, and becomes a "defiance of authority" (P,
119), like Sappho's lost poems which by accident survived.

19. See "la fin du livre et le commencement de l'écriture," Chapter One of
Jacques Derrida, *De la grammatologie* (Paris: Minuit, 1967), 15–41.

"Only one answer:" Dr. Paterson reminds himself, "write carelessly so that nothing that is not green will survive" (P, 129). The remonstrance comes directly after the prosaic warning which begins the third part of Book Three: "It is dangerous to leave written that which is badly written." Writing allows us access to the dream of books, at once demystifying the received text and recovering and exposing the polyvalence of the dream. Writing destroys by returning language toward the elemental. And though Williams, characteristically, sees this sometimes as a return to speech and the oral tradition (in direct contrast to Derrida's argument against the historical tendency to substitute speech or *parole* for writing or *écriture* in the hopes of reclaiming immediacy) and thus to the immediacy of an "effort" where alone one can reclaim "virtue"—despite this tendency, the poem for him is not simply speech, not immediacy. It is, indeed, a form of writing, a destructive interpretation of the old texts which intends to release the elemental energy they conceal. This new beginning, said Williams of Poe, is truly a return to the "local in origin," giving "actual quality to *things* anti-metaphysical" (IAG, 222).

"Write carelessly"—that is, against the grain, against authority. It means some new, but unwritten, measure, some new syntax for things, without the old connections, without the silently assumed *logos*. Writing, therefore, becomes a kind of drunkenness or madness, a calculated vulgarity. It brings the old "virtue" or logocentrism into question, catching in its violent reversals the simultaneous destruction-creation or end-beginning that all dreams or myths at once express and conceal, that every text harbors like a secret or a stain.[20] The

---

20. In "La pharmacie de Platon," *La dissémination* (Paris: Seuil, 1972), 71, Jacques Derrida begins with a definition of text: "Un texte n'est un texte que s'il cache au premier regard, au premier venu, la loi de sa composition et la règle de son jeu. Un texte reste d'ailleurs toujours imperceptible. La loi et la règle ne s'abritent pas dans l'inaccessible d'un secret, simplement elles ne se livrent jamais, au *présent*, à rien qu'on puisse rigoureusement nommer une perception."

torque of the "destroying fire" consumes the walls of the
Library and its flames become a "waterfall" or "cataract
reversed" (P, 120). The fire becomes a metaphor which calls
metaphor into question, since all metaphor reaches toward the
elemental indifference. To the contrary, the violence of
deconstruction reveals "in all things an opposite/ that awakes/
the fury" (P, 98).

All the motifs of deconstruction are coalesced in Williams'
anecdote of the jar, of the bottle (no doubt a container for
whiskey) which is warped into a "new distinction, reclaiming
the/ undefined":

<blockquote>

The glass
splotched with concentric rainbows
of cold fire that the fire has bequeathed
there as it cools, its flame
defied—the flame that wrapped the glass
deflowered, reflowered there by
the flame: a second flame, surpassing
heat   .   (P, 118)
</blockquote>

The flame is "Recreant" (a deliberate pun) and "good." It
simultaneously deflowers (another pun) and reflowers; and as a
sexual figure implies, deflowering is a de-virgination that
breaks up the discontinuity of an isolated self, or isolated thing.
The "chastity of annihilation" (P, 117) is, like a reflowering, a
new creation and a disclosure of the simultaneity of destruction
and creation. As in "Burning the Christmas Greens" (CLP,
16), the "Recreant" fire *quick*ens the green to red and then
black in the reverse womb ("contracting/ tunnel") or vortex
of the "grate." "Burning the Christmas Greens," like the
above passage from *Paterson*, is a poem that turns upon the
instant of transformation or disclosure, the instant in which
death and birth are simultaneous: the "time" of the Incarnation; the reversal, as in Yeats's phases, of the cycle of history;
the gathering of elemental forces into the single light that is the

origin of the spectrum; the moment, in short, of all myths of beginning.

The passage from *Paterson* catches the moment of "bottle: unbottled" (P, 119), the silent moment, that is, of the colon, where an anticipation of change and change itself exist simultaneously. The flame, like the imagination, does not annihilate, for in the "chastity of annihilation" annihilation is "ameliorated" (P, 118). The bottle is unbottled into the warp of its own infrastructure. It is not remade. On the contrary, its being is disclosed. For the bottle was made of glass and the glass of "fire-blasted sand," a fusing of the elements, just as the language of the Library is made of words that were once the spontaneity of original writing, like that of the cave painters. The bottle is a manufactured shape of glass which conceals the elemental nature of glass. It was made to contain an intoxicant (fire-water) that can never merge with it, but which, itself a fire, releases blockage and frees words.[21] Similarly, the language of the Library is a language bottled in received texts, the metaphor of a total meaning that is divorced from the words and stands superior to them. The Library deprives language of its hermeneutic potential, its openness and thus its true historicity. Just as it was fire which fused the glass, so does fire deconstruct the bottle to glass, the "undefined." The analogy with the language of the poem, torqued by the imagination into a process that mauls its historical shape, is not a forced metaphor. The analogy is proved in the historical event of the Library's burning in Paterson (like the Library of Alexandria). The poem demystifies the official history of Paterson, brings its "virtue" into question and reveals the ambiguous violence of every city, of all composition. Like the tongues of fire in the

21. See Gaston Bachelard, *The Psychoanalysis of Fire*, trans. Alan C. M. Ross (Boston: Beacon Press, 1964). Fire, says Bachelard, is the "prime element of reverie" (p. 18), and alcohol is "The Water That Flames" (pp. 83 ff.). Alcohol is also a "creator of language," because it "enriches the vocabulary and frees the syntax" (p. 87). Fire is the "principle of all seed" (p. 50).

book of Acts, which symbolize the Pentecostal regathering of
the scattered language of Babel in the descent of the Dove, the
flames that open the Library effect a reduction to "one"
through multiplicity. The scattering of voices in Book Two of
Paterson, that characterizes a modern city, is redeemed by the
regenerate fires of deconstruction. In the concealed *mythos* of
Paterson's history, there is an ascent and a descent, a scattering
and a regathering, a destruction and a creation, a city become a
poem, a "one" that is many.

Thus the "Poet Beats Fire at Its Own Game" (P, 118) and
becomes a fire-bearer. He creates the game by freeing the
elements from historical syntax, the old meaning. By multiplication he decenters, unbottles. The fire is a chemistry of
reduction by metamorphosis, and the end of the game (as it is
the beginning of the next) is the recovery of the elemental.
Earth, air, fire, and water are successively fundamental matter
and fundamental sources of energy, out of which everything
complex has grown and to which it tends to return, whether
language or city. Language and city are made to bespeak their
origins in nature, and their difference and distance from that
origin. Sexuality and drunkenness are similarly paradoxical
forces of deconstruction. They serve to break up the isolated or
discontinuous self, and merge self and other in an elemental
relationship. They repudiate the dream of the simple, separate
self, the immutable soul. Each is evidence of the resistance to
an entropy that draws things to a fixed center.[22] The poet, like
Willie in the early manuscript version of Book One, is an
"agent of the word," and the language is like the "waterfall of
the/ flames, a cataract reversed, shooting/ upward" (P, 120).
The language speaks him as he speaks it:

> Rising, with a whirling motion, the person
> passed into the flame, becomes the flame—

22. *Ibid.*, chapters on "Sexualized Fire" and the "Spontaneous Combustions" of
alcoholic fired creation.

the flame taking over the person
. . . .
The person submerged
in wonder, the fire become the person   .
(P, 121, 122)

The burning of the Library, the deconstruction of books, is also a demystification of the subject, of the self as center. The history of Paterson is not the history of men, but of its language. It is not the history of a place, but the history of place, of the city as a locus or ground manifest in a language. The new measure, then, must break up the set rhythm of a recorded history, a particular history, whether of one place or several men, in order to invent the game of invention itself:

> My own chief difficulty is a fixed "personal" rhythm which I detect constantly enforcing itself upon one through every form I attempt.
> I realize by this that we must break ourselves if we are to invent. We must destroy our own personalities which are, by this, definitely "malignant."
> We must be artist, that is, constant destroyers of ourselves, that part which is a fixation—and thus *NOT* ourselves, outwill our purpose to invent.[23]

The "theme" of "all the 'moderns',", says Williams, is a search for an "objective" way to redefine the "elements" of language (SE, 286–87). A purgation of personality is necessary because personality is the fiction of the subject as privileged center, as author-ity. Like the lesson of "the Bomb" in "Asphodel" (PB, 165), the destructive element is an energy which through its catastrophic and paradoxical force produces a rupture in history. This breaking of the *self* means the

23. William Carlos Williams (MS in the Lockwood Library of the State University of New York at Buffalo), Env. 43; works in this collection will hereinafter be cited as Buffalo MS. These were notes for his University of Washington lectures, some of which, like those of his Notebook, were incorporated into the essay, "The Poem as a Field of Action" (SE, 280–91).

destruction of the *I* which takes a privileged position in the sentence of the schoolmen (P, 189): "The mind must tear rotten structures apart before the way can be made ready for physical contacts." [24] Breaking down, then, means to destroy the distancing of history. At the same time, the field of a new and, as yet, unplayed game is constituted. The new game is a "field of action," or "The Poem as a Field of Action" (SE, 280–94) to use the title of a Williams essay drawn from his several lectures at the University of Washington in 1948. The "field" is generated by the process of breaking down the old, sclerotic time structures,[25] which conceal and deny the presence of the elemental. The "one great thing about 'the bomb,'" says Williams in this same essay, "is the awakened sense it gives us that catastrophic . . . alterations are also possible in the human *mind*, in art, in the arts. . . ." (SE, 287).

But Williams' terms, as we noticed earlier, do pose a critical problem. If the "catastrophe" of destruction-creation does rout the old "illusion" or "dream" of poetry—that illusion of a center upon which traditional poetry turns, a center that is unaffected by the structure it centers—the new structure is, or

24. Williams, "The Future State," Buffalo MS, Env. 67.
25. Compare the following from Williams' "An Approach to the Poem," Buffalo MS, Env. 41:

> Argument: when the poem is done, the new form invented, or flowered it "begins at once to become sclerotic and has to be broken down once more *to the elements*—elements (as when English first differed from Latin and Greek; as when Italian grew from Latin and Dante adopted it—the language of the people—and used it for his masterpieces. The elements were new. . . ."

And this, from his "The Attack on Credit Monopoly" (Speech given at the Institute for Public Affairs at the University of Virginia on July 11, 1936), Buffalo MS, Env. 50:

> What I want to show is that the artist, an individual, a worker, the type of person who is creative, who has something to give to society must admit all classes of subject to his attention—even though he hang for it. This is his *work*. Nothing poetic in the feudal, aristocratic sense but a *breaking down*, rather, of those imposed tyrannies over his verse form.

The essay uses the analogy of poetry's breaking down old forms and the need for a social credit which would break the "credit monopoly."

at least seems to be, itself the radiance of some privileged center. The world of Newton is replaced by the world of Einstein, one constant for another. But the new constant (speed of light; musical time) replaces the illusion with the undiscovered and increases the problematic of the center by opening the game.[26] Williams' repeated reference to and use of the analogy of chemistry, and of the metaphor of the poet as one privileged "to seek to discover that *possible thing* which is disturbing the metrical table of values" (SE, 286—my italics), reveals a radical redefinition of the structurality of his structure. The "possible thing" is the elemental, the unknown, perhaps even an absence which allows for the concept of "periodicity of atomic weights and so leads to discovery." The poem becomes a field located within known things, like the periodic table of elements, which composes a space housing an unknown disturbance, a dissonance, an undiscovered element that indicates the dynamic of the field.

Radium becomes Williams' "theme" (SE, 286), and as his theme, the center of his new field. But radium itself is a problematic. Its thingness is its energy, the rapidity of its change, its own tendency to break down not only within itself but to break down the lawless accretions of cellular cancer on which it may be focused. Radium, therefore, becomes the problematic of the elemental, the undiscovered element that makes possible the game. In Williams' structure, as in Madame Curie's "retort," the undiscovered element exists like a kind of mana "quartered apart,/ unapproached by symbols" (P, 108), a "gist" which allows for a nearly infinite number of

26. As I will argue in the last section of this chapter, Einstein's relativity theory, as considered by Derrida, implies not so much the presence of presence (the absolute of "light") but the rule of the game, which allows for the concept of open structure or freeplay. Also, compare this, from Buffalo MS, Env. 52, Williams' notes for an essay on George Antheil: "Destroy: welcome destruction; welcome disturbance, revolution to decompose the scum of life that besets us. Clear why we want this: place, ecstasy or pleasure, release, play—life: dead now."

substitutions or supplements in the table of elements. Radium as theme, then, is evidence of the freedom of the game; and though it does suggest the presence of mana, which Lévi-Strauss has said is the equivalent in myth of the zero-phoneme in structural linguistics,[27] this presence in the field of *Paterson* signifies the ultimate openness of the field. This gist is neither a presence nor an absence, but the law of nonlaw. The "finite" and centerless field of language is not a chaos, a structure without a center. But the center is unlocatable. It can only be signified by an arbitrary sign, what Derrida calls, drawing upon a term that has long haunted French thinking about language, the *supplément*. The *supplément* is crucial to Derrida's thinking on the freeplay of language. Like *différance*, the *supplément* is not a concept but a function, the function of the sign that cannot be a name for presence but is the name of something "older than presence and the system of truth, older than history," and thus a function that cannot connote the idea of an authoritative, fixed "center which arrests and founds the freeplay of substitutions."[28] It is that in language, a lack, that

27. See Claude Lévi-Strauss, "Introduction à l'oeuvre de Marcel Mauss," in *Marcel Mauss, Sociologie et anthropologie* (Paris: Presses Universitaires de France, 1950), quoted in Derrida, "Structure, Sign, and Play," 261–62.

28. The first phrase comes from Jacques Derrida's *Speech and Phenomena: And Other Essays on Husserl's Theory of Signs*, ed. and trans. David B. Allison (Evanston, Ill.: Northwestern University Press, 1973), 103; the second from his "Structure, Sign, and Play," 260. As Derrida acknowledges in the first, in a concluding chapter called "The Supplement of Origin": "The structure of supplementation is quite complex. As a supplement, the signifier does not represent first and simply the absent signified. Rather, it is substituted for another signifier, for another type of signifier that maintains another relation with the deficient presence, one more highly valued by the play of difference." In this study of Husserl's theory of language, and throughout *De la grammatologie* (Paris: Minuit, 1967), where he explores this function of supplementation in Rousseau's theory of language, Derrida emphasizes that this augmentation of a lost presence finally supplants the originality of presence itself, affirming the primordiality of difference. Again, difference is not a concept but a function. This is why Derrida, when he writes of the "supplement" (of the "sign," of "writing," or of the "trace") as " 'older' than presence" or "older than 'history'," insists that the "older" be understood in an "Ahistorical" sense. He rejects, then, the substitution of the supplement as a sign for a lost presence. The supplement makes forever

calls forth new signs, the additive or supplementary signs, and makes necessary the infinite substitutions without which, one might say, a new language, or new beginning, a "new measure," would be impossible. This lack which demands the *supplément* produces the superabundance of meaning, the plurisignification, of which language is capable, just as it indicates that there is no primary sign or master word, no Word, to which any particular sign may refer and stand as the sign of. It is in this sense that we might understand Williams' "radiance"—as a supplement and not the center.

V

If Book Three is the poem of chemical discovery, or as Williams said, of the "search for the redeeming language," it expresses an act which can only remember by forgetting. The poetics of deconstruction, as we have seen, involves the violence of the valid juxtaposition as a way of reducing distance and the privileges implied in the old syntax, and thus as a way of computing the finite field of language in which alone one can engage in the freedom of infinite substitutions, of play. The "redeeming language" is that which keeps its structure open, because it does not remember the past but reclaims in its own immediate field the freedom of language, of past languages, to change. It attempts to recover the elemental in language, for the elemental always consists of the elemental "N" of all equations, an inaugural freeplay.

Book Four, which with the possible exception of Five has received the most consistent critical disapprobation, poses the further problem, then, of the clash between two senses of structurality and thus two structures of language. Its three parts, which have seemed to critics to be the most absurdly disrelated of the five poems, compose a dissonance that lies at

inaccessible the origin; it marks the dispersal of the center. The supplement can itself only be defined by a series of "nots."

the heart of the whole. For if one cannot properly argue that the three parts compose a dialectic (of banal nostalgia for a past language of dream, the "pastoral"; the poetry of deconstructing that "dream," the dissonance of "invention"; and the reopening of history, the blast that turns end into beginning), he can argue that their interrelation generates a "dissonance" which reveals the "genius" of art to be the initial freedom of the field of language or poetry.

Paterson, Book Four, which begins with the modern "pastoral," is thus at once discontinuous and simultaneous with Book Three, an exploration of the "dissonance" at the center of language. If Corydon's vulgar poems, in part one, turn the traditional pastoral inside out, disclosing in their juxtaposition the ironic conflict of an innocent and a historical language, the lecture on atomic fission at the Solarium, in part two, is in Williams' words the situation which reveals the innocent "genius" of discovery. All of the poem's themes come to a focus and are turned inside out by that "genius"—which like Madame Curie's is a curiosity that cures, an invention of the elemental that functions by refusing to name it by the old names. Radium as "theme" suggests that "genius will out." Part two of Book Four is an exemplary exercise in analysis by juxtaposition. Beginning with the lecture at the Solarium, it quotes Norman Douglas on the death owed the son by the father; remarks parenthetically on Flossie's irritation that the perverse sexual matter of part one did not achieve the "pure poetry" of the earlier three books; reflects on the difference between Madame Curie's innocent and youthful genius and the leaden "experience" of the elder doctors who come to see the movie of her discovery; recalls the time when Billy Sunday, ex-baseball player and evangelist, was brought to Paterson as a strike-breaker; quotes a long letter from Allen Ginsberg in which he nominates himself as the son of the Paterson poet; pursues a complex exploration of the "chemistry" of Madame Curie's discovery of radium; echoes Pound's "Mauberley" by relating Carry Nation to Artemis (in mythology, one recalls, the active part of the maiden goddess, Kore[29]) as the measure of our "life today"; offers a page of August Walters' *Advertisement* for social credit as an answer to the curse of usury; and ends by relating Tolson's ode on Liberia to Allen Tate's "Ode to the Confederate Dead" and then to the Spanish civil war, the historically different but interrelated, linguistically different but interrelated, events which are bound together by "Selah," the Hebrew significa- tion of a pause which measures the time of the musical phrase. The attempted assassination of Walter Reuther is placed beside the name of Ben Shahn, and the two contrasted with Phideas' taking money and "credit" for a statue he did not deliver to the state. The mayors of American cities during the Civil War, who were "the fathers of many a later novelist no worse than the rest" (P, 185), are incongruously recalled, perhaps, as part of the debris of history. And the section arrives at its most dissonant conclusion, echoing Pound's remedy for usury in the "LOCAL control of local purchasing/ power" (P, 185), as the example of a "credit which derives from the "effort,/ work" (P, 185–86). "Work" is that which creates "Difference" (P, 186). Credit, the money of effort, becomes the "radiant gist," the "value created" where none before existed. Work repeats the original existence, the becoming of a difference.

The dissonance of this kind of juxtaposition realizes the extreme of dislocation in both language and theme, on the one hand, and reveals the structural presence of silence in the poem, on the other. "Difference" is more than Pound's

29. See C. Kerényi, in C. G. Jung and Kerényi, *Essays on a Science of Mythology*, trans. R. F. C. Hull, Bollingen Series (New York: Harper Torchbooks, 1963), 108. Persephone, of course, is the passive complement to Artemis, and "Artemis and Persephone are like two sides of the same reality."

difference between "slums" and the "splendor of renaissance cities" (P, 186). Difference is the elemental constituent of musical time, marked by the *"Selah"* which recalls an original stability but also makes the possibility for an infinity of substitutions. Juxtaposition discloses both the dissonance of theme (difference) and the *genius loci* of language—just as Billy Sunday's hymn (Brighten/ . . the corner where you/ are!" [P. 173]) was coopted by the usurious "United Factory Owners' Ass'n," itself a derivative of Hamilton's SUM, which broke the Paterson strike. The hymn discloses an etymological truth unrelated to its theological and historical context—the truth of the "local" language. Its "sun" relates to Madame Curie's light, discovered to inhere in the pitch*blende*, an original dissonance. Billy *Sun*day is nominally an ev*angel*ist, the deliverer of the word, which he does; but it is a word delivered into a prescribed situation, an energy perverted by usury to a perverse use. Nevertheless, the poem reveals the genius of Billy Sunday, his energy which channeled into the vortex of speech creates a radical alteration, even though it is used to thwart an effort toward breaking out, to drive a further wedge between man and nature. Billy Sunday, ex-ballplayer, violates the openness of the game.

"Love, the sledge that smashes the atom? No, No! antagonistic/ cooperation is the key, says Levy" (P, 117)—not sameness but difference lies at the non-center, an original polytropism or originary en-tropy that is the structural non-law of all languages. In Paterson, the Falls is the geological and geographical point at which the rupture becomes meaningful. It is the locus of change, like the place of radium in the uranium sequence, a sequence that moves "leadward" (P, 217) toward stability. The city rises properly at the point of the Falls, a manifestation of the discontinuity which lay at the beginning of history, of the separation of nature and culture, the "fecundative principle." The city mocks the pastoral, that dream of an idyllic world somewhere between the origin and the fall, at the head of some purer time.

The "idyl" of Corydon, with its pathetic yearning for Anticosti and a Yeatsian Innis*free*, is another version of pastoral, a final disclosure that lost origins are unrecoverable. The pastoral is history's death-wish. The city rises in the midst of it. "Two silly women" (P, 149), the idyl begins. But "silly" is misconstrued. No longer the simplicity of autochthonous man, silliness is now the mark of an abnormality, of historical man's neurosis: "Semantics, my dear" (P, 149). Corydon's poems exemplify the disappearance of "genius." Her language is an imitation of an imitation of the fall, circling like the helicopter of her poem over "vortices of despair" (P, 161), the absence marked by death. "Come with me to Anticosti, where the salmon/ lie spawning in the sun in the shallow water" (P, 167), she reads to Phyllis. It is her poem of desire, to escape the "unsexed" minds of the city where, "At the/ sanitary lunch hour packed woman to/ woman" (P, 166), the great beast denies all identity and in its "violent motion" dissolves all relations. The modern genius of Yeats and Eliot, their nostalgic genius, dominates and dwarfs her own. She has no language, and like the corpse sought by the helicopter over "Hellgate current," she has lost her "identity and [her] sex" (P, 161). Her poem accentuates the pathetic yearning for the undifferentiated inherent in all pastoral, or in a language which conceals its desire to return to the silence which preceded it. Her vulgar poem demystifies the eloquent nostalgia of Eliot's, the lament of the living dead.

The genius of Madame Curie, on the contrary, is the genius of curiosity, an innocence repudiating nostalgia for a lost truth. She evokes for Dr. Paterson the image of

> a nurse-girl
>   an unhatched sun corroding
> her mind, eating away a rind

```
                              of impermanences, through books
        remorseless   .
        Curie (the movie queen) upon
                        the stage at the Sorbonne   .
        a half mile across! walking solitary
                        as tho' in a forest, the silence
        of a great forest (of ideas)                        (P, 172)
```

Pregnant with discovery, she is literally spoken by the silence. Her discovery is not a design imposed upon nature, but the result of her capacity for imitating nature: by bringing forth, or disclosing. Her desire is like a womb "waiting to be filled" (P, 176). Like the virgin, she is possessed by the "silence" and made to deliver the son-sun.

In both senses of the word, her discovery lies in her "retort," for from the recesses of her silence she turns nature and language inside out. In the beginning was the "stain," of which "knowledge," the adherence to the known as signs of an absolute law, must be a "contaminant" (P, 178). The "radiance" she brings forth after "months of labor" has been known only as "a stain at the bottom of the retort/ without weight, a failure, a/ nothing" (P, 178). Like the zero phoneme, its function is discovered only when bombarded by contaminants, those supplements that are known elements. The precision of Williams' analogy is remarkable. As previously noted, he carefully explores the homologous structures of the Mendelief table of elements and language. Madame Curie discovers the presence of an absence predicted in the Mendelief structure: just as the Virgin brought forth the silent Word predicted in the prophecy of the angels. The undiscovered element was "nothing," evident only as a "stain." And even the discovered element, radium, is seen only when it is bombarded by the contaminants of oxygen and hydrogen. Just as the Word remained unheard until He was violated and withdrawn, until the tomb was opened and the Dove descended, heralded by tongues of fire. Language, like radium, expanded under the pressure of speech, tends to break down toward its elemental form. Like the uranium sequence, its energy is released by its relative instability: "the complex atom, breaking/ down, a city in itself" (P, 178). The hermeneutic of language is a process of simplifying itself— moving leadward.

Like the uranium sequence, however, language bears within itself its own conservative element, the lack that allows transferences between matter and energy. As lead is the most effective barrier against the destructive element of the x-ray, so it is the essential difference from that energy, the end product of the sequence of disclosure. The city, like a complex atom of uranium, is a "dissonance," a structure that is alive only in the process of breaking down, toward nature, just as it developed through the building up of towers. Its conglomerate of languages (towers of Babel) contains the fullest potential of disclosure. The modern city is the result of history, of the original dispersal of language. The poet, then, must break down this accumulated complexity to recover the elemental power diffused in it.

The poet, "playing the words/ following a table which is the synthesis/ of thought, a symbol that is to him,/ sun up!" (P, 179), is at once the *genius* and *genius loci*, the father and the son. He makes possible the play of supplementation. His measure acts within the given language to deconstruct it, to de-center it. He uncovers the radium, the "stain" or trace of the "nothing." The poet is a son of the sun, the language of his place. Like Thoth, he bears (and bares) the word of Ra. He is the genius of the freeplay of language, an enemy of stability:

> But there may issue, a contaminant,
> some other metal radioactive
> a dissonance, unless the table lie,
> may cure the cancer . must

lie in that ash . Helium plus, plus
what?   (P, 179)

Like the gamma rays of the radioactive emission, the poet's
speech is both destructive and purifying. Williams pursues the
analogy to its conclusion. Radioactive breakdown produces not
only x-rays but a "plus," the alpha particles of the helium
nuclei. "Helium plus" is a by-product of radiation, one of its
disclosures. Helium is the monatomic element, chemically
inert, of zero-valence—thus never known in its pure form.
Interestingly, it is the element most characteristic of the
"zero-point energy" that lies at the heart of quantum theory
and the uncertainty principle. Helium has never been reduced
to crystallization; localization of its atoms is impossible because
their kinetic energy defies the relatively static structure of
crystalline force. "Helium plus" is the kinetic or dynamic gas,
inert yet dynamic. In liquid form it has superfluidity. It is
nominally the sun-gas.

Helium plus recalls the "ignorant sun/ rising in the slot of/
hollow suns risen" (P, 4)—at the heart of the "dissonance"
that lies in the "valence of Uranium" (P, 176) is the dynamic
origin itself, the zero-energy of things which when released in
and through its contaminant may lift that which contains it.
The poem, Williams argued, lifts an "environment to expression" in this very sense: the dissonance in the valence of
language leads to discovery, to the release of an energy
("hydrogen/ the flame, helium the/ pregnant ash," P, 176)
that is a cauldron at the center. Poetry takes the closed
language of history and opens it. Poetry is the chemistry, and
the game, of language.

The Madame Curie section of *Paterson* is at once the
thematic and the chemistry of creation: "Chemistry gives us a
fruitful analogy—break down the form from the molecule, to
the atom and the atom to its electrons, protons or whatever else

may be found—for power to reshape the material." [30] The nature of language is atomic, its structure analogous to the structure of nature which resists the sclerotic. Breaking down "to the elements" is the natural direction of language, and the poetry of deconstruction takes the elemental direction of language. Poetic speech moves against the "vague irrelevances/ and the destructive silences/ inertia" (P, 180). The heart of any poem is its counterthrust against the meaning of the language of which it is made. In this sense speech discloses the zero-point of language, and in its freeplay of substitutions emits a light upon the image of a fixed or created world. Speech and writing are not different. Language marks the difference that repudiates all essence, all origins. It is the mark of primordial departure.

Writing is the counterthrust to the written, to the Book or the Library. Like the ratio of "money" to the "joke," the valence of true speech is always relative to a zero-valence (P, 182). But that zero is neither a presence nor an absence. It is

30. Williams, Buffalo MS, Env. 41. This is a cancelled passage once intended for the essay "An Approach to the Poem." Also the following passages, from the Notebook, Buffalo MS, which were notes for Book Four of *Paterson*: "The lecture on uranium (Curie) the splitting of the atom (first time explained to *me*) has a literary meaning—"; "in the splitting of the foot (sprung meter of Hopkins?) and consequently is connected theoretically to human life or life." In the same note he has the "Love is the sledge" line and the mention of Chaucer's Sir Thopas who broke the set rhyme. Yet, he can also write: "The analogy with radium is inadequate. So is the analogy with essences" (Imag., 294). The radiant gist is not unity, not a metaphor for God.

In an interesting letter to the editor of the *Transatlantic Review*, II (October, 1924), 305–309, Mina Loy begins with a poem on "Curie/ of the laboratory/ of vocabulary" who "congealed to phrases" the "tonnage" of the mind in order to "extract/ a radium of the word." The poem is quoted by Mike Weaver, *William Carlos Williams: The American Background* (Cambridge, England: Cambridge University Press, 1971), 214. Later in the letter Miss Loy speaks of Gertrude Stein's "process of disintegration and reintegration, this intercepted cinema of suggestion" which forces the reader toward "clarity of aspect": "Truly with this method of Gertrude Steins [sic] a goodly mount of incoherent debris gets littered around the radium that she crushes out of a phrased consciousness" (p. 309). See Walter Scott Peterson, *An Approach to* Paterson (New Haven, Conn.: Yale University Press, 1967), 195–99, for a discussion of Williams' chemistry.

that which permits and demands the supplement and substitution, the game. The "joke" marks the game of economics, the necessary dynamics of money. Like the structured freeplay of atoms breaking down from uranium toward lead, a finite language emerges and returns upon itself. Thus the theme of credit in the Madame Curie sequence: the "radium's the credit" (P, 182) in the same sense that money must be that which moves and discloses, and not that which when hoarded accumulates itself to itself. Money, like gamma rays and like language, must be an emission that cures the "cancer" of "usury." Its credit must be "related directly to the effort,/ work" (P, 186). If the letter of Williams' economics comes from Pound, its spirit moves in a somewhat different direction.[31]

The chemistry of values resides in deconstruction. Man's yearning for the zero-valence, the origin of all valences, reveals that his curiosity is his freedom. Thus Dr. Paterson notes the difference between the young boy and those "who surpassed him/ only in experience, that drug" (P, 172). The son's innocence, like the "nurse-girl" Curie's, is a "silence" at the center of "ideas." Innocence is an "unhatched sun" (read son or *logos*), an energy which works from inside out to eat away the "rind/ of impermanences" (P, 172). Discovery and birth, the advent in either case of the sun's son, expose the impermanence of the apparently permanent. Knowledge is the contaminant of innocence, which bombards and exposes the "radiant gist" of innocence itself. Knowledge is the "pig" father that conceals its own issue in language, in the son. The creative source is the "unhatched sun," deep in its silence, an

31. See Weaver, *William Carlos Williams*, 103–14, for the best account of Williams' interest in the American Social Credit Movement. Also see footnote 24 to the Introduction herein for an account of H. Levy's theory of economics and language which helped shape Williams' socialist inclinations. Compare Hugh Kenner, *The Pound Era* (Berkeley: University of California Press, 1972), 301–17, on Pound's version of Social Credit.

energy which can only be released by the contaminant of knowledge which splits the atom. Yet, as there is no pure energy, there is no pure innocence. Innocence is known only in the field of the contaminant knowledge, in the "stain at the bottom of the retort" (P, 178).

The Madame Curie section is dedicated to Williams' son because, presumably, all education is the education of sons. Experience is the antithesis of education. The passing from experience to innocence is a form of breaking down, or breaking up, of authority. It shatters both the inviolate dream of pure innocence and the tyranny of experience. War, the bomb, murder—they are integral to the creative energy of *Paterson*, like the paradoxical "urge to unity" in Nietzsche's Dionysian "will to annihilation."[32] It is a dissonance which saves us from the "destructive silences," splitting the atom of zero-valence. Creation lies at the point where destruction torques into disclosure, the point of openness. Which is to say, it lies at the point where the father, the genius of temporality (history, tradition, the received language), is succeeded by the son, the genius of place. The son's new speech is a supplement inaugurating a new game.

Paterson, therefore, is necessarily a pre-text; just as the books of the Library are the pretexts of *Paterson*. The chemistry of language brings the poem not to an end (leadward), but to a consummation, to use Dewey's distinction, in a "blast" that somersaults back into itself. The hanging produces a dissemination (a "dispersal" that is a "metamorphosis"). The poem ends in a reversal which breaks up a discontinuity (a particular history of place) and opens the poem to continuation by other sons. The poem is the energy of helium lifting hell to expression—for hell is absence, the inarticulate (literally, the concealed) and helium is the light and lightness of the sun, the

32. Nietzsche, *The Will to Power*, 543.

force which lifts out, unconceals. Phonemically, the two stand
as perfect opposites, of reciprocal difference, light and dark—
like the "obverse, reverse; the drunk, the sober; the illustrious/
the gross," the "knowledge" and "ignorance," of the Preface
(P, 4). Their interpenetration, "both ways," is the structural
necessity of Paterson, because their opposition can never be
resolved or dialectically synthesized. Therefore, they do not
recall any original unity.

Art is not the incarnation of a new Word, but a repetition of
old words violently broken free from their "text," the old
dream of presence. The rupture of the old language destroys
the teleology of the traditional poem. But the old language,
with its familiar concepts, remains in the new field like
contaminants. Old meanings are deflected against one another
as the only means at hand for releasing the elemental energy of
language. But that energy is not necessarily a continuing
presence, that idea of creative force that all literature seems to
celebrate. It is the freeplay of the game, the instability at the
center of all life. The advance of art, as I suggested in the
previous chapter, is not dialectical or teleological for Williams,
but spiral. The poem is like a "cyclotron," conservative when
it is most dynamic and destructive. This perhaps explains the
apparent contradictions in Williams' argument that only a
poem of the local, made of immediate speech, can serve the
tradition of poetry. Only this kind of poem can recover the
"cry" of the "pitiful dead," the utterance of the "white-hot
man" whose speech, the speech of old books, echoes like the
"emptiness of/ a cavern resounding" (P, 123).

VI

It is strategically necessary, in conclusion, to return briefly
to the thinking of Derrida with which this chapter began.
Williams' poetics deliberately proceeds to break up the
traditional discourse of history and bring into question the

New Critical idea of art as autotelic or as the incarnation of either the Word or consciousness. His "radiance" is not another metaphor for presence but the name of a function. It defers the a priori Truth and substitutes the "effort," invention. Like Derrida's *supplément*, radiance is the undetermined overabundance, the dissonance, of its field, which at once makes interpretation possible and suggests that "there is always more." [33] The gaps in the Mendelief table signify for him not simply a number of other undiscovered presences, but the elemental possibility of a total realignment of the relative values within the table; for the norm of that table, the element whose valence all other elements are measured against, is arbitrary from the beginning. It, too, is a supplement. But, one view of the Mendelief—not necessarily Williams'—is that it predicates presences, that it totalizes by accounting for the undiscovered in the gaps of the discovered. In this sense, it suggests that while all the elements are not uncovered, they someday may be—they are "predicted before found," like the radium of Madame Curie's retort. On the other hand, the "play" of such a table may suggest a potential infinity of elements within the finite structure, and even radical shifts of relative valence. In other words, the table makes possible two kinds of interpretation. And it is those two kinds of interpretation Derrida speaks of as the result of the "event" of having to think the "structurality of structure." Having got beyond, though one is never beyond, the metaphysics of presence, Derrida conceives of two strategies of interpretation: one he associates with the structuralist interpretation of Claude Lévi-Strauss; the other with the post-modern deconstructive analytic of Nietzsche. While both reject the tradition of metaphysics, its logocentricity, the two interpret the freeplay of structure, and thus the supplement in language, in two

33. Derrida, "Structure, Sign, and Play," 260.

diametrically opposed ways. In the following chapter, I am going to suggest that this description of two kinds of interpretation may correspond respectively to Modern and post-Modern poetry, or to Eliot and Williams. But I will defer that argument for the time in order to rehearse Derrida's, and to recapitulate what is at stake in Williams', view of language as a game, or the poem as an interpretation, an "attack."

As Derrida reads him, Lévi-Strauss's structural analysis brings history into question and places itself in tension with the very idea of presence. There remains, however, in Lévi-Strauss's concept of structure (of mythic repetition and reduplication) "a sort of ethic of presence, an ethic of nostalgia for origins, an ethic of archaic and natural innocence, of a purity of presence and self-presence in speech." [34] That is, Straussian interpretation, which disallows us the possibility of recovering the absolute origin of the structure we are exploring, proceeds as if that origin were nevertheless available, though endlessly deferred, beyond analysis or outside the very language in which it must be sought. It is almost as if one were reading a commentary upon one of the directions of Modern poetry rather than on the thought of a modern anthropologist. For Williams' reaction to history, to the written word, to temporal nostalgia, may indeed suggest a "nostalgia for origins" and a desire to grasp once again the innocence and immediacy of speech as self-presence. But this is manifest, rather, in the role of the "dream" of *Paterson*, a dream of the "whole poem" (or what in anthropology might be called the impossible dream of totalization), which is denied as soon as it is embraced.

Despite its rupture with the traditional thinking of presence, Straussian interpretation manifests only one of the possible interpretations of interpretation, Derrida continues. If in Lévi-Strauss we have the recurrence of the "Rousseauistic

34. *Ibid.*, 264.

facet of the thinking of freeplay," in which we turn with a sense of modern guilt toward the lost or absent origin and suffer the sadness or melancholy of a broken immediateness, there is yet an affirmative response, which Derrida identifies with Nietzschean joy. This interpretation embraces the freedom of a world without truth, without center or origin.[35] This is a world of open active interpretation, a world in which the question of the interplay of presence and absence, including the question of whether presence is recoverable, is preceded by the function of freeplay (*differance*) itself. In the beginning was the game, not a lost origin but the freeplay of interpretation. Interpretation becomes the immediate ground, because there is no ground. *"This affirmation,"* says Derrida, *". . . determines the non-center otherwise than as loss of the center. And it plays the game without security. For there is sure freeplay: that which is limited to the substitution of given and existing, present, pieces. In absolute chance, affirmation also surrenders itself to genetic indetermination, to the seminal adventure of the trace."* [36]

The necessity of a poem of the local lies in this play of interpretation. This poem commits itself to a *"seminal adven-*

35. *Ibid.* As Derrida well knows, Lévi-Strauss's concern for "archaic societies," his tendency to view them as "exemplary," never finally deceives him into thinking that his nostalgia for a lost origin can ever lead to its full recovery. The substance of a "travelogue" like *Triste Tropiques* makes this amply evident, in its expressions of the sadness with which the interpreter recognizes his historical exclusion from an ever-receding closed world. For the Straussian interpreter must recognize that the origins of his remote societies are sustained by a function that the interpreter can only recognize as a game, since he is excluded from it by the very privilege which allows him to study it.

Lévi-Strauss, as one would expect, rejects Derrida's interpretation of him, just as the critic Paul de Man rejects, in part at least, Derrida's interpretation of Rousseau's nostalgia and the kind of critique it implies. See Paul de Man, "The Rhetoric of Blindness: Jacques Derrida's Reading of Rousseau," in his *Blindness and Insight*, 102–41.

36. Derrida, "Structure, Sign, and Play," 264. This concept of "l'aventure *séminale* de la trace" is central to Derrida's argument. His consistent emphasis on *écriture* as prior to *parole*, writing being the mark of *differance* and the evidence of freeplay which repeatedly brings the dream of speech's unbroken immediacy into question and keeps the game open. The "seminal adventure" of language, as with life,

ture" in which the end is a "blast" or dissemination of the
seed-words that insure the continuation of the game. Dissemination, Derrida has written, is that which does not return to
the father, or to the origin, and hence is not logocentric.
Williams' insistence on the simultaneity of destruction and
creation, then, discards the "security" of nostalgia for the
"whole," a game played in the hopes that some origin is
recoverable or a truth retrievable, as in fact is assumed in the
"field" or context of an autotelic poem. Neither does Williams
hold that the poem's invention can generate a new presence or
lift out some hidden essence (some immutable "gist") from the
history that has concealed it. Destruction is for him a breaking
back not to the lost origin or center but to the "open tomb," to
an absence that is not, like Christ's tomb, the emblem of the
transcendent yet incarnate Word. It takes us back to the
beginning as openness, as flowering itself. "Destruction," he
once wrote, "according to the Babylonia order of creation,
comes before creation. . . . We must be destructive first to
free ourselves from forms accreting to themselves forms we
despise. Where does the past lodge in the older forms? Tear it
out." [37] "To destroy the past," he said, "is precisely a service to
tradition" (SE, 284).

The destruction of historical forms, of the tyrannous designs
(the "Texts") of history, opens up rather than closes the

---

involves dissemination, the breaking up of structure and even the concept of
structurality (elsewhere, the concept of the Book) and a recommitment to an
adventure which allows for the unutterable and unimaginable mutations of some new
birth. Yeats's image of the unnameable "beast" of "The Second Coming" might be a
literary instance, did not the figure of the beast and its implied antithesis with the
figure of man which it is replacing suggest something too determined, like a return to
an early bestial phase, the "savage god." Then there is Stevens "giant" on the
"horizon" of "A Primitive Like an Orb," and his "major man," both of which cling
very close to a new humanist adventure. See the title essay of Derrida's *La
dissémination* (Paris: Seuil, 1972). Dissemination denies the eternal return, the return
to the origin or to the father.

37. Williams, "Letter to an Australian Editor," *Briarcliff Quarterly*, III (October,
1946), 208.

possibility of signification and mandates the freedom that must be like the beginning. The "satyric dance" of *Paterson*, Book Five, and the "blast" of *Paterson*, Book Four, are ends that commit poet and poem to the "*seminal* adventure of the trace," to a new beginning that, like Yeats's shapeless and nameless beast, is the shape of the as yet unnamed. Derrida says that to embrace the affirmative interpretation, the Nietzschean joy, is to commit ourselves to look into a future where the "formless, mute, infant, and terrifying form of monstrosity," the "unnameable," takes its gestation. It is the freedom Williams finds in his ideal figure of the artist, the monster Lautrec. It is the "wonder" he finds in the local as against the "wonder" of those Puritans who domesticated their monsters and distorted themselves. It is the freedom of the "innocent" Curie and the "innocent" artist, standing on the threshold of a "new" dimension; of the figures in the "satyric dance" or the artist like Hieronymus Bosch or Brueghel, who conceived the monstrosity of the human mutation as the privileged view of the artist. This original artist is condemned to witness, to participate in, the seminal adventure of the coming to birth of what Derrida calls "the species of the non-species." The "new measure" Williams commits himself to seek is nothing other than the "measure" of the "non-measure," something to be discovered in the name of its difference from the known. Thus it is with joy that Williams resigns himself to existence, to the freeplay of a world without truth or origin, to the freedom of interpretation of which the poem *Paterson* is at once the "effort" and the deferred "virtue." The poem and the city are both a "nine months' wonder" which is "rolling up out of chaos" (P, 3), to end in a blast or dissemination (P, 204). Like the end game of chess, the poem dissolves itself into another game (P, 236). There is no return to the father, to authority, to the old leaden texts. There is only the cutting edge of language, of writing as a "rout" (P, 222).

5

At times there is no other way to assert
the truth than by stating our failure to
achieve it.   (SL, 304)

Poets are defeated but in an essential and
total defeat at any time, that time is
stamped in character upon their work, they
give shape to a formless age as by a
curious die. . . .   (IAG, 186)

The Poetics of
Failure

I

"Modernism," says Roland Barthes, "begins with the search for a Literature which is no longer possible." [1] It attempts to establish Literature as an object in itself, the sphere of a "dream language" with its total meaning. Modernism, he continues, desires to transcend, or destroy, historical duration and realize a new duration of Literature. It is, therefore, a kind of violence, a form of "murder." Modernism emerges from the destruction or perversion of an old convention to appear as a sort of "miraculous stasis, on the threshold of Literature," [2] a shape poised on the verge of becoming an "order" which in turn must be destroyed. "Modern poetry," as Barthes defines it, "since it must be distinguished from classical poetry and from any type of prose, destroys the spontaneously functional nature of language, and leaves standing only its lexical base"—that is, it destroys the mathematic (and this is Barthes' metaphor) which inheres in the relational economy of classical language and "retains only the outward shape of relationships, their music, but not their reality." [3] Barthes defines classical language as a language based on usage, not on invention—or in

1. Roland Barthes, *Writing Degree Zero*, trans. Annette Lavers and Colin Smith (New York: Hill and Wang, 1968), 38.
2. *Ibid.*, 39.
3. *Ibid.*, 46.

other words, a language based on the semantics of an
established system—and Modernism is the language invented
by the *Symbolistes:*

> The Word shines forth above a line of relationships emptied of
> their content, grammar is bereft of its purpose, it becomes prosody
> and is no longer anything but an inflexion which lasts only to
> present the Word. Connections are not properly speaking
> abolished, they are merely reserved areas, a parody of themselves,
> and this void is necessary for the density of the Word to rise out
> of a magic vacuum, like a sound and a sign devoid of background,
> like 'fury and mystery'.[4]

It is possible to measure the degree of Williams' "advance"
beyond Modernism in the light of Barthes' definitions. For as
we saw in the previous chapter, if creation and destruction are
simultaneous, there is an "advance" in art as it undergoes the
murderous act that releases it into its own "plane." Williams'
poetry, set against the tradition and its received conventions, is
a poetry intent on destroying the tyranny of the old mathematic and its language of usage. Therefore, it is intent on
becoming itself a poetry of invention. Invention, however,
implies disclosure and thus the recovery of a lost radiance. The
Modernism described by Barthes (which ranges from Mallarmé's cult of the Word to Eliot's autotelic poem) is nostalgic
for lost origins and deeply involved in the transgressions of the
very language that has distanced the Word. Or as Barthes
says, this kind of interpretation (search for presence) accentuates the "void" in which the "density of the Word" may rise
"out of a magic vacuum." Williams' poetry, on the contrary,
abandons the "density of the Word."

By setting himself the task of destroying a "symbolist"
poetry which, as Barthes says, has only a "vertical project,"
Williams aligns himself at the same time with and against the
Modernist project. He aspires to free language from the old

4. *Ibid.*, 46–47.

usage in order to invert, and in this sense discover, the enduring usage, the primordial relations. He wishes to return to the classical if by classical one means that which endures— but endures in man's perpetual articulation of his desire, not as abstracts of universal ideas. What endures for Williams is man's search for value, the recurrent effort to create value. But the search is conducted in the recognition that there is no ultimate value, that the hunt itself excludes the purity of capture.

Williams recognizes the dehumanization of Modernism, and hopes that by excavating language back to its origins he can disclose the epic of human beginnings as the becoming of relations. He wants to strike through the Modernist decon-struction of the classical with another effort of deconstruction. Or to use Derrida's terms, he wishes to destroy the Book, and with it the view of Literature as a Text or Word with a total meaning, in order to make writing possible once more.[5] For this he must abandon Literature, Barthes' "Hunger of the word."[6] "Waken from a dream," Dr. Paterson reminds himself near the end of Book Four, "this dream of/ the whole poem . sea-bound" (P, 200). His silences are parodies of the Symbolist silence, periods that thrust him forward toward a renewed invention. He forfeits the dream of the Word and embraces the failure to which this commits him: "I cannot tell it all" (P, 236). To make new is not to repeat an original unity. Invention is a murder. Violence is the original act of poetry, of language, that allows Williams to view the history of art synchronically, as the recurring pursuit of the dream which only succeeds by demythologizing the dream of the "whole": "The dream/ is in pursuit" (P, 222). Art survives as the articulation of "desire" which, as we have seen, is precisely what Williams thought to be the enduring life of the great

5. See Jacques Derrida, *De la grammatologie* (Paris: Minuit, 1967), 15–41.
6. Barthes, *Writing Degree Zero*, 48.

classics, the "virtue" lying beneath their sclerotic "sayings and elucidations." [7]

To return to a theme treated earlier, desire is lack which leads to pursuit, a circle that is closed only by death (and the imagination). The dream of totalization, or of the whole poem, is the dream the post-Modern poem necessarily forfeits. For it is precisely this dream the poem demystifies in order to disclose what is involved in the Modernist nostalgia for the pure origin, for the Word. The "sea," *Paterson*, Book Four, declares, is not "our home"—neither that totality of knowledge "whither all rivers/ (wither) run" (P, 201), nor even the symbol of truth captured in the ideal "form" of individual poems fully achieved (made whole). The sea, indeed, is that repository that gives back the flotsam of "weeds, bearing seeds," those "words" (P, 200) which float ashore and take root in new ground where a new beginning must germinate. The end is to repeat the original dissemination; it is the "blast," not unity. The totality exists only in the innocence of origins, and is embraced only as the desire to "begin again." And to begin again is to turn the "inside out." Thus the poet must reject the "nostalgic sea," the "Thalassa" which calls us "home" to unity, that indifferent "sea of blood": "The ocean of savage lusts in which the wounded shark smashes at its own tail is not our home. On the contrary, it is the seed that floats to shore, one word, one tiny, even microscopic word, is that which can alone save us"; "it is precisely then that to write is most imperative" (SL, 292). A poem must fail, then, in order to be; it must end at its beginning, where seed-words are dispersed into a new flood, the site of some original (venereal) birth.

> You will come to it, the blood dark sea
> of praise. You will come to it. Seed

7. William Carlos Williams, "The Embodiment of Knowledge" (MS in the Beinecke Library of Yale University, New Haven, Conn.), 89; works in this collection will hereinafter be cited as Yale MS.

> of Venus, you will return . to
> a girl standing upon a tilted shell . . .
> (P, 202)

The post-Modern poem declares itself to be "pre-art"; it renounces the "total poem" for its own imperfect "city, a marriage" (P, 106), a "place" tentatively named and made. Its task is first to generate what Barthes calls a "free language," a language not only free of received usage but one freed of the verticality of Literature. Writing, says Barthes, is "therefore a blind alley, and it is because society is a blind alley. The writers of today feel this; for them the search for a non-style or oral style, for a zero-level or a spoken level of writing is . . . the anticipation of a homogeneous social state; most of them understand that there can be no universal language outside a concrete, and no longer a mystical or merely nominal, universality of society." [8] The economics of *Paterson*, directed against the verticality of knowledge (the University and the Church) and against the divorce of the usurious capitalist state, is tied to the discovery of a language that manifests and is manifested in what Barthes calls the "concrete . . . universality" of a local language. The "homogeneous social state" promises a zero-level of writing, but it also commits the poet to the limitation of his poem, to the universality of the local. The poet must, as Dr. Paterson discovers,

> bring himself in,
> hold together wives in one wife and
> at the same time scatter it,
> to one in all of them .
> Weakness,
> weakness dogs him, fulfillment only
> a dream or in a dream. No one mind
> can do it all, runs smooth
> in the effort: *toute dans l'effort*
> (P, 191)

8. Barthes, *Writing Degree Zero*, 87.

"La Vertue/ est toute dans l'effort," and its achievement
"takes connivance,/ takes convoluted forms, takes/ time!" (P,
189). Presence (virtue) is denied; effort (freeplay) confirms
writing, in contrast to the written, as the truth of poetry. The
"mystery" of the lost Word is replaced by the violence of
"time," of a "pursuit" or "effort" which because it has no
beginning or end must repeatedly involve itself in a violation of
the object it desires—the inevitable whoring of the virgin. The
violent death which marks the end of *Paterson*, Books One–
Four, the hanged man's blast of seed, marks the ultimate
rupture of the dream and thus of the language of usage (of
history) out of which the poem is composed. It is the murder of
a murderer, the end of the dream of the whole poem and even
the possibility of a Book. This death opens the language to new
possibilities and frees the imagination from its death in the "sea
of blood." The recurring violence of Book Four evidences the
role of desire in the creative act. Desire is at the center of
history and language. Book Four's concluding violence begins
again by disseminating the seed of a "seminal adventure" and
dispersing the fiction of the Word.[9]

"Death/ is not the end of [life]," says the poet of
"Asphodel"; "There is a hierarchy/ which can be attained,/ I
think,/ in its service" (PB, 157). And that hierarchy (the
plane of "love") is achieved only in incomplete or open-ended
books, in poems which, like the *Iliad*, are the beginnings of
books or original poems, all having their origin in the desire
caused by "Helen's public fault" (PB, 158). Eros is understood
to begin in loss, in divorce or ravishment, without which it
could not be. It begins in desire and is fulfilled in a kind of
death, either the sacrifice of the self to the other or the
devouring of the other that also destroys the self as desire.
Thus "love" would be, if achieved, an ideal marriage, but in

9. Cf. Derrida themes of the "seminal adventure" and "dissemination," previously mentioned, Chapter 4, footnote 36, and elsewhere.

reality it involves a reciprocal desire. Helen's public fault is natural, and like Persephone's rape, a prelude and pretext. It marks the beginning of desire, and of history as "pursuit." But it also forewarns that the original "fault" can never be repaired—except in the redeeming wholeness or fictiveness of the myth which transcends the "epic." As the dominant theme of *Paterson*, Book Five, explores the paradox, art has "SUR-VIVED" (P, 244) as a "place" where death and love join in a continuum, where the "museum becomes real" and history whole. And Book Five is at once the deconstruction of Books One–Four and the removal of it to another "plane," into a theater or museum where wholeness or totalization is credible. There it exists both as fictive and as real (like a "reel house") as a "museum" of endlessly mirrored images. When art asserts its fictiveness, its apartness from nature, its non-representational totality, it asserts itself as the Word, but a Word already demystified. Reflecting itself, the post-Modern poem brings itself into question.

Paterson, Book Five, is born out of the murder of the "dream" of Book Four, which destroys the idea of Literature as self-sufficient. And yet it is a renewal of the dream—this time not the dream of the "whole poem" but of the continuum within poetry's discontinuities, of its repeated "dance." Every poem is like the allegory of the tapestries, a transgression of the idea of the Word and thus a failed effort to capture the living Word in the sphere of its "fiction." Every poem is like the "pre-tragic" dance of the satyrs, the ritual of a departure into history, the inauguration of "pursuit." Thus no poem can truly totalize: "I cannot tell it all" (P, 236). That, ironically, is the truth it has to tell. Each poem recalls its departure from the origin and its involvement in the transgression of "inaugural naming." In *Paterson*, and throughout Williams, the thematic of marriage is a form of that transgression, a ritual violation of the virgin, an acting out of the "public fault" that launches the ships of wanderers and generates poems of earth.

II

The Modernism of which Barthes speaks finds its literary model in the poetry of the French Symbolists, a literature which manifests the same rupture in the poetics of presence as does Nietzschean thinking in the history of philosophy. In American poetry, the rupture takes place somewhere between Transcendentalism and Imagism. It is marked not by a singular aesthetic or historical event so much as by sudden, repeated, and anguished attempts to reconcile the New World sense of beginning with the teleological faith in history. Each attempt is characterized by a bringing into question of the idea of presence or of the central (*e.g.*, Emerson's central man) which was the ground of Transcendentalism. Paradoxically, it seems to be the abruptness of the rupture which allows us to talk of the "continuity" of American poetry, of Adamic and Emersonian traces in our Modernism, and to pursue a line of historical and cultural developments in the new poetics of an insular literature, an American literature, written in the inherited or adopted English language. For there is no questioning this continuity, and the limbs, especially the two dominant ones, of its genealogy.[10]

10. I am thinking here particularly of Roy Harvey Pearce's very important book, *The Continuity of American Poetry* (Princeton, N.J.: Princeton University Press, 1961), which distinguishes between the Adamic, or Antinomian, strain in American poetry, moving from the Antinomianism of the early Puritans through Emerson and Whitman to such Moderns as Stevens and Williams, and the reactionary or traditional strain which denies the priority of the Adamic (and latterly, the Romantic) self and takes as its model poets in the classical and English (*logos*) formalist tradition. This last includes the Puritan orthodoxy, the Fireside Poets of the nineteenth century, and Moderns like Eliot and the Southern Agrarians. Pearce's book gives priority to the Adamic tradition, but he is careful to distinguish between Adamism of an idealist kind (Transcendentalism) and the early secular and Romantic humanism of a poet like Stevens, whose attempt to recover the idea of the central man can only bring it into question and throw him beyond even humanism.

But the historical dependence of our Moderns on their predecessors (of Frost on Emerson, say, or Cummings on the Unitarian vision, or Hart Crane on Whitman and Poe, or Williams and Stevens on Whitman and Emerson)—this line of influence is not in question. In our Modernism—whether Eliot, Pound, or Frost, whether Williams or Stevens or Olson, whether Robinson or Robert Bly—there is a rupture with the tradition which by its very violence tends to disguise itself as a continuity, and often as a visionary leaping of the gap laid open by the Nietzschean question. The line and the break leading from Emerson's central man to Stevens' fictive central man is only the most obvious case in point, allowing us to write the history of our poetics as either a sameness or a difference, either a continuity or a discontinuity. Between Emerson and Stevens, of course, lay the metaphorical "death of God," but not necessarily the disappearance of the central man. In Stevens an idealist humanism becomes a secular humanism, and Stevens is read as a historical end of Emerson, if not as Emerson turned on his head. Likewise, the line from Whitman to Williams—and more strangely, the difference that Pound notes in his "Pact" with Walt Whitman, and that Eliot confesses in his overly rhetorical divestations of his American roots, which only highlight his nostalgia. Likewise, the desire which ties Hart Crane's vision simultaneously to both Whitman's cosmic optimism and Poe's cosmic despair, that desire for a bridge which would allow the return of the Word into words or would reaffirm what Whitman once had and modern

More characteristic of the view of American poetry as deriving from an individualist tradition is Hyatt Waggoner's *American Poets: From the Puritans to the Present* (Boston: Houghton Mifflin, 1968), which sees the tradition from the exclusive perspective of Emersonism and seems to reject the problem that the Moderns' loss of anything like a transcendental unity of Self constitutes a rupture with the Emersonian central man. The distinction between Modern and post-Modern I am making here is made at the level of the ontological problem posed in the language of our "Adamic" poets.

man had lost, the capacity to engulf multitudes and to reach, in moments of enthusiasm, beyond desire.

The gap which separates American Modernism from its immediate ancestors, then, does nothing to obliterate, or even blur, the lines of historical influence and confluence. The common metaphors, indeed, are more the evidence of the gap than a denial of it. For the rupture is manifest, as in Derrida's view of the philosophical rupture, in the necessity, nowhere identifiable as a specific historical time or incident, of poetry's beginning to think the "structurality of structure." Modernism had to begin to think its own center and thus become a discourse on discourse. If one were to supply his "names" for this event, to complement Derrida's philosophers (Nietzsche, Freud, Heidegger), he might offer Melville, Dickinson, and even Poe. The "event," however, is ahistorical and the "names" are not really important, nor could they be confirmed without a longer argument than is possible here. But one need only point to the Symbolist strain that Charles Feidelson discovered in American literature, especially in Melville, to see the roots of this discourse in Transcendentalism itself, and to recognize it in the metafiction of Melville, especially *Pierre* and *The Confidence Man*. Emerson's thought ultimately led toward a skepticism that threatened to question the presence of a transcendental center, and thus to a thought which could only escape itself by a leap of thought, a leap of faith, that rejoined ex-centric man to central self. Melville pursued the shock of recognition into silence, a paralysis of questionings of the center. And Poe—while substituting a center of absence (God as nonmaterial unity) for a center of presence (the creation as extension)—carried his discourse into an aestheticism which brought itself into such severe question and subjected itself to such acute guilt that only an utterly idealistic aestheticism could reconstitute the world with a center. It was this Poe whom the *Symbolistes* discovered, an implicit Poe who most crucially realized the Modernist rupture in an art which accentuated the center as the presence of an absence, the music of nothingness.

But such a condensed rendering of nineteenth-century metaphors hardly suffices as more than another rhetorical gambit, an assertion which I hope to pursue in a later study. For now, the statements must stand as the beginning of a more significant rhetorical assertion: that the Modernism we associate with Eliot and the New Criticism must be seen in the light of this rupture, and not, as commonly interpreted, in terms of its attempt (reactionary) to recover the traditional sense and order of history as presence. Or to put it another and perhaps more accurate way, though Eliot desired to recover the lost Word of history, his poetry and the criticism to which it gives birth cannot escape the "universal problematic" of "language" into which Modernism was thrown. The "world" of the New Criticism is characterized by the inescapable Modernist dilemma of being unable to think the center apart from or outside the structure. This is to say, aestheticism and Modernism go hand in hand in their rejection of the Transcendental origin, and yet are joined in the guilt for what has been lost and the eternal hope for its recovery. Eliot could not will himself, or his art, into a time that preceded this rupture, and thus could not escape making his own poetry a part of the Modernist discourse on discourse, a poetry about poetry. At best, Eliot's ideal of the autotelic poem could only symbolically utter the inherence of the Word.

Despite Eliot's professed historicism, and his concern with the tradition, the thing which characterizes the rhetoric of his criticism (and his poetry as well) is the absence of presence. To put it another way, history and art can only be an imperfect sign of the divine, an immanence available not to the will but only to an ascetic ecstasy. History and knowledge bear marks of guilt, as in "Gerontian," and only in the silence and innocence of the unspoken Word is the Word known in the world. As in the borrowing from the sermon of Lancelot Andrewes, the "sign" signifies an absence in itself in order to signify the "wonder" that it stands for—"The word within a word, unable to speak a word." [11] The timeless monuments of history, of his early essay, "Tradition and the Individual Talent," are signs in time which signify an order that originates outside time and therefore seems to speak for the traditional idea of presence. But such signs in Eliot repeatedly become comments on themselves, and point to the silence of their own center. The sign is not of the center, but a mediation, a supplement. Eliot's symbolism is Episcopal, not Catholic, and thus a sign of history's lack, of language as a part of the universal problematic. Signs, and poems, become aesthetic objects (John Crowe Ransom would later call works of art "precious objects"), each of which affirms its own center, its own silence, and not a creative origin outside itself. They are "symbols" of a lost significance. But by their own objective presence, their supplementation, they signify the Incarnation, itself a supplement that signifies the closure of history. These works, then, are evidence of man's desire to recover lost presence, and to redeem his original fault.

The enigmatic thing about Eliot's poetics, and the entire poetics of the New Criticism that derived from him, is the urgency with which it detached art from life into its own self-contained system, thus affirming the artifice of the center as the fiction of presence. The impersonality of art which Eliot asserts in "Tradition and the Individual Talent" cannot affirm a center or source outside the system of the work, except in some mysterious, lost origin. And those interpretations of Eliot's work which ascribe to him the faith in something like a Jungian universal unconscious, or which accept the fundamen-

11. T. S. Eliot, *The Complete Poems and Plays, 1909–1950* (New York: Harcourt, Brace, 1950), 21.

tal structure of the Christian *logos* as an explanation of his ideal of the "autonomous" poem, do not honor the discourse of his method. For the Eliot who traveled to Spain or Southern France to stand in the presence of the prehistoric cave paintings, before he wrote "Tradition and the Individual Talent," and the one who derived his aesthetic from both the *Symboliste* and the Metaphysical poets, is a poet fully involved in the Modernist problematic.

What Eliot "interpreted" as the associated sensibility of the Metaphysical poets was the structure of the "self" as an aesthetic whole, a cosmos of centered elements in tension; or in other words, something different from the modern Bradleyan self, which is composed of those fragments of perception of which it is conscious. He aestheticized Renaissance philosophy, but in doing so, he brought into question the center which, because it is both within and without the "great chain of being" (both beginning and end), could hold otherwise irreconcilable opposites in tension. Eliot's metaphysical "conceit" becomes wholly an aesthetic trope; his ideal of a reassociated self is the mark of contemporary dissociation. Poetry separates itself from life by feigning wholeness, by declaring itself a *sign* of wholeness. It is nostalgic for the old order. Eliot's interpretation, that is, reconstructs the "structure" of an historical *epistèmè* in terms of an aesthetic, of an Image that is, in his term, autotelic, but which by its very formal wholeness acknowledges itself as art, or ritual. This "form" is the symbol of an otherwise imperfectly known perfection, and thus a shadow representation of desire.

Eliot's poetry self-consciously separates itself from the world of sense experience, from life, from history, by the very acknowledgment of its centeredness and its artifice. Only by indulging the metaphors of religion as analogous to the metaphors of art can he bridge the distance between life and art. The metaphor of the Incarnation becomes his bridge, and

selflessness (the state of innocence or will-lessness) his definition of recovered wholeness. But behind it all lies the
problematic, what he called in the *Four Quartets* the "primitive
terror" that confronts anyone looking backward "behind the
assurance/ Of recorded history" [12] toward the lost origin.
What he evidently saw in the depths of the prehistoric caves
was the silence and darkness of the center, at once the terror it
inspired and the potentiality for signification it admitted. What
he saw in his poetry was the sadness of the absence of
presence, and the guilt which animated every effort toward its
recovery. For him the poem becomes the supplement of an
ideal of wholeness which is itself a sign of history's lack.

That Eliot chose, willfully, to substitute the metaphor of
God for the "Something that is probably quite ineffable"
which lay at the origin should not tempt one to define his
poetics in terms of his professed orthodoxy. It is not historical
cunning, or the "contrived corridors" of a history made up of
multiple spars of Knowledge, that motivates Eliot's passiveness
and impersonality or his orthodoxy. On the contrary, the
admixture of innocence and intellectualism, emotion and
knowledge, that bewilders his critics, discloses the kind of
interpretation in which his poetry is involved. From beginning
to end, from the dissociations of "Prufrock" to the "complete
consort" of "Little Gidding," his effort is to reconstitute a lost
whole, to recover a lost origin. His theme is fragmentation and
guilt, the history of language and thus the history of history
itself. His desire is to recover, if only in the game of art (so like
the ritual of religion), the sign of the lost origin: the ineffable
"still-point," the "silence" so fundamental to the structure of
words and music.

The ideal of the "right" sentence in "Little Gidding,"
"where every word is at home,/ Taking its place to support

12. *Ibid.*, 133.

the others," tying end to beginning, is the ideal of "Every poem an epitaph." [13] "Little Gidding," the last of the *Quartets*, those ritualized poems which attempt to evoke a figurative (still, silent) center within the brilliant articulations of their sounds, confesses to the endlessness of the search: "We shall not cease from exploration . . ." in search of a "condition of complete simplicity." [14] That condition is of course the condition of unity, of the "fire and the rose" as "one." But it is only realizable in art, in the poem, in ritual, in those "signs" or "monuments" which are in history yet hint of the center which is outside it and known only by the slanted names. "History may be servitude,/ History may be freedom" [15] —thus a line in the third section of "Little Gidding," the section which introduces the metaphor of the hanged man (here, Christ) and leads to the figure of the Dove descending in section four. It is the figure of the "symbol perfected in death," and the perfect symbol of the problematic of language in Eliot. It links his poetry with Gnosticism in its attempt to transcend the paradox. Into the darkness at the center of the prehistoric caves, or into the silence at the center of words ("Words, after speech, reach/ Into the silence" [16]), the Word descends "With flame of incandescent terror/ Of which the tongues declare,/ The one discharge from sin and error." [17] "Little Gidding" ends the *Quartets* by summing up the Eliot poetics. If history is either "servitude" or "freedom," history is the problematic; and therefore language is the universal problematic. The gesture of poetry's "exploration" is a gesture toward the recovery of what is lost. In Derrida's words, it "dreams of deciphering a truth or an origin which is free from freeplay," and thus free from the condition of the very medium, homeless words, to which it is condemned.

13. *Ibid.*, 144.
14. *Ibid.*, 145.
15. *Ibid.*, 142.
16. *Ibid.*, 121.
17. *Ibid.*, 143.

What I have been arguing, in a necessarily elliptical way, is that Eliot's poetry, and the poetics that stem from it, is analogous to the kind of interpretation Derrida associated with Lévi-Strauss. For while Lévi-Strauss's interpretation of myth discards the idea of history or presence, and acknowledges the freeplay of its structure, his pursuit of a key for myth displays a "sad, *negative*, nostalgic, guilty, Rousseauist facet of the thinking of freeplay" which holds to the faith that its origins might possibly be recovered. At the same time, however, it admits that there is no end to his project in time or language. Straussian interpretation, says Derrida, "lives like an exile the necessity of interpretation." This is not, of course, to associate Eliot with the familiar primitivist view of Rousseau, nor certainly with the modern nostalgic anthropologists. But it does cast some light on the endless "exploration" and the desire for "stillness" which will quiet the restlessness of desire that stands at the thematic center of Eliot's meditations. Desire is his theme, desire which "itself is movement/ Not in itself desirable." [18] In the end, the most problematic thing in Eliot's poetry is the presence of the Word which it repeatedly evokes, the presence of presence which has become the familiar point of departure for discussing him. For that presence is the very thing that distinguishes the wholeness of the poem and sets it apart as a thing of value. That silent Word is his ultimate object of desire, and it proves only to be a supplement.

The rhetoric of the New Criticism, especially the insistence on the autonomy of the poem or its autotelic structure, only supports the Eliot problematic. The act which separates out the poem as artifact from the booming, buzzing confusion of empirical experience implies a ritualization of language which restores to it a distanced origin: "prayer is more/ Than an order of words," [19] and so is the poem. In the "context" of the

18. *Ibid.*, 122.
19. *Ibid.*, 139.

poem, the tensions that hold to-gether the many reveal the symbolic presence of the One. But the recovery of the center, in the art object, acknowledges the fictiveness of the interpretation. Poem is Symbol. Even the psychological dualism of I. A. Richards held up the model of the artistic field as a gestalt of unity. In other words, whether one follows the basically theological (and by extension, cultural) metaphors of Ransom and Tate or the basically psychological metaphors of Richards,[20] the interpretation leads to conclusions similar to Eliot's. The New Criticism is involved in a profound nostalgia for origins. This is true, I think, not only of the recognizable "new critical" poets, but of poets as different stylistically and ideologically as Frost and Hart Crane.

What in another context I have called the "poetics of failure" applies here, for it is precisely a poetics of failure which characterizes this game of Modernism. Not "failure" in the aesthetic sense, however; for it is precisely in that moment when the ideal of an autotelic, autonomous poem realizes (if it could) its perfection that it calls attention to its separateness from life. It reveals the presence, the new Word it would capture, as no more than the ritual prize of the game: whether the achievement of stillness, or the illumination of a desired value. It is not artistic failure, indeed, that characterizes the dramatic "failure" of a Crane lyric, which aspires to achieve "*as a whole* an orbit or predetermined direction of its own" and thus the condition of an "absolute" poetry:

> Its evocation will not be toward decoration or amusement, but toward a state of consciousness, an "innocence" (Blake) or

20. I think here particularly of I. A. Richards' hope that poetry can "save us" by conditioning the efficiency of our neural responses and thereby making communication more pure. But perhaps a better example even than Eliot's defence of ritual would be John Crowe Ransom's metaphor for the game of love as analogous to the aesthetic capture of the poem, so that the poem's form is like the conventions of courtship into which one enters because it enhances (as opposed to ravishing) the value of the object which is ultimately captured. See Ransom's essay, "Forms and Citizens," in his *The World's Body* (New York: Scribner's, 1938. Reprinted, Baton Rouge: Louisiana State University Press, 1968).

absolute beauty. In this condition there may be discoverable under new forms certain spiritual illuminations, shining with a morality essentialized from experience directly, and not from previous precepts or preconceptions. It is as though a poem gave the reader as he left it a single, new *word,* never before spoken and impossible to actually enumerate, but self-evident as an active principle in the reader's consciousness henceforward.[21]

That "new *word*" is the poetic self's desire, and his lack. Crane defines the poem as voyage or quest, which must end by capturing the reader in a moment of unbroken immediacy; it is a bridge that is a recovered presence, a Verb. Thus poet captures reader and possesses him in that moment of desire. Just as Eliot's poems cannot "cease from exploration" and yet foresee an "end of all exploring" in our return to the point of departure which we will "know" for the "first time," Crane's launch themselves from the real toward an unknown which if reached will fold end back upon the beginning. The quest or voyage is an agony of self-sacrifice, of lacerating guilt, of nostalgia. For what Crane's poems realize is that to possess the object of desire is to annihilate it, and thus annihilate oneself. Crane's ecstasy is self-sacrificial, a frenetic violence of language. But his dream is like Eliot's, a dream of recovering the pure origin, without again violating it.[22] The poems of both "fail" because they must *defer* such an ideal end, perhaps out of their deference for (and love of) words.

The failure expressed by Williams, and, I believe, the later Stevens, is of a different order. Again, this has nothing to do

21. See Brom Weber (ed.), *The Complete Poems and Selected Letters and Prose of Hart Crane* (New York: Anchor books, 1966), 220–21.
22. Thus the thematic of the Dionysiac rhythm, the rhythm of fragmentation (individuation) and ecstatic reunion, in such condensed poems as "Lachrymae Christi" and "Wine Menagerie," and the self-lacerating failures of vision that haunt the poet who walks in the world (like the Satan of *Job*) in *The Bridge.* Certainly one can take the recurring figure of the poet as "exile" in Crane's work to be evidence of the kind of interpretation Derrida describes, whether rightly or wrongly, in relation to Lévi-Strauss and Rousseau. Crane's poet "lives like an exile the necessity of interpretation."

with aesthetic failure; nor is it related to the thematic of the recoverable center, the nostalgia for origins. Williams' "failure," on the contrary, is the irony of the "capture" which must violate its object. This is the dream of the "whole poem" or the nostalgia for an original marriage which repeatedly reminds itself that all acts of possessing the virgin are like original transgressions. There is no end, only new beginnings. Like the joyous affirmation of Stevens' "never-ending meditation," which asserts the principle of freedom to precede the principle of presence, Williams discovers the "survival" of art to lie in its freedom from the "necessity of interpretation." It is precisely his discovery of a world "without truth, without origin" (to use Derrida's words) that defines the principle of Williams' imagination, and the nature of that early "resignation" to reality. It is precisely the ex-centricity of history and language which makes the search for a "new measure" both necessary and free.[23] It is the hermeneutical game, figured as a "satyric dance," which is celebrated at the very end of *Paterson*, Book Five, the "game of chess" which is "all we know." It is a game

23. The poetics of "Imagism" apparently allows for both interpretations. On the one hand, Imagism led directly to the formalist concept of the autotelic, autonomous poem. The idea of an "intellectual and emotional 'complex' in an instant of time" yields to a formalist, spatialist interpretation, with the idea of the poem-image as gestalt. On the other hand, the presentational emphasis of Imagism (see note 20, Chapter 2, herein), with its rhetorical opposition to representation or mimesis, seems to imply the poem as a hermeneutic, as a bringing to light of a totally new "complex." Pound's own figure of the poem as universal, and thus as something like the equation of analytical geometry (see Ezra Pound, *Gaudier-Brzeska, A Memoir* [New York: New Directions, 1970], 90–91) in opposition to the symbolic or allegorical assimilation of set values in a simple mathematical equation, also allows both interpretations. But Williams' argument against Imagism, that it was not structural, offers Objectivism as a structural alternative which would generate the poem as an open field. The poem as Object became a field of interchangeable parts, not a totalization but a structure which defined itself precisely because it lacked a stable center and therefore demanded the "supplement" which gave it a continuing and changing life. When Pound moved from Image to Vortex, he moved toward a figure for a dynamic structure which incorporated the idea of the non-center that implied the initial openness of the beginning. But he nevertheless at times evidences a nostalgia for the lost and recoverable presence or *virtù*.

characterized by the demythologization of a whole series of myths of presence: theological, historical, and aesthetic. For *Paterson*, Book Five, is the poem of interpretation par excellence, which, in removing from the field of history, art, and myth the privilege of presence or center, participates in its own game of infinite substitutions simply for the joy of it. In this sense, it completes the "seminal adventure" advanced at the end of *Paterson*, Book Four, that necessary deconstruction of the myth of history which has violated the American "effort" of beginning "again." It is a "game of chess" Eliot wanted to refuse.

III

Paterson, Book Five, is a poem-about-poetry not in the sense of setting poetry apart from life, but in the sense of a poem interpreting its own hermeneutic power. It becomes the discourse of a method, the method of *Paterson*, Books One–Four. Book Five is a poem about the originating power of language, and about the inevitable failure of the poet to give ontological status to his poem. It is about the impossibility of capturing the Unicorn, the Word, without murdering it, or of revealing the essence of language without disclosing its fictive status. "The dream/ is in pursuit" (P, 222), the poem asserts—the pursuit of the missing center or Unicorn, the very process of which discloses the lack at a center and gives whatever serves in its place an extraordinary and supplemental significance. In art alone are "male and female" married, and irreducible differences held in tensions. In art alone does the supplement of the center reveal at once freeplay and order, form and the superabundance of signification. In art alone can we contemplate the contradictions and polarities and paradoxes of our desire for the whole.

The dominant theme of *Paterson*, Book Five, resides in the legend depicted by the medieval tapestries now housed in the

Cloisters and displayed under the auspices of the New York Metropolitan Museum of Art. Peter Brueghel the elder's "Nativity" (*The Adoration of the Kings*), like the many other works of art named in the poem, offers a similar "scene" (P, 226).[24] If each work appears to derive from a teleological or eschatological view of history, a history redeemed by the Incarnation of the Word, Williams turns its meaning inside out to reveal the fiction at the center. And thus he decenters the myth each exists to illuminate. He discloses them, that is, as present "interpretations" of a still more original myth. By interpreting the interpretation, he uncovers the freedom of art that transcends the determinism and received value of the historical structure. But he also discloses that there is no still-more-original myth or ur-myth, that the repeated "scene," like those Brueghel "witnessed frequently/ among the poor" (P, 226), were designs repeated on any local ground. The artist sees the fictions man lives "from the two sides" (P, 228).

Book Five demythologizes the Christian legend, disclosing its aesthetic, and thereby substituting the priority of freeplay for the priority of *logos*. Art is a "rout" of the received grammar of history. Gertrude Stein's experiments or Paul Klee's elemental reductions; Dürer's *Melancholy* or da Vinci's melancholic smile in *La Giaconda*; Bosch's monsters or Freud's —they are all examples of the art of demystification which

24. The *Adoration* to which Williams' poem alludes hangs in the National Gallery, London. Another, in the Musées Royaux des Beaux Arts, Brussels, uses many of the elements of the first, but there is no greybeard at the center. Indeed, it is the rustic Virgin who is the center of both pictures, and therefore the child, as Jerome Mazzaro has pointed out, *William Carlos Williams: The Later Poetry* (Ithaca, N.Y.: Cornell University Press, 1973), 166–67. And it is surprising that Williams, who uses the virgin-whore motif throughout *Paterson*, Book Five, does not make this point. In the London painting, however, the greybeard takes an imposing place. It is possible to explain Williams' interpretation as a lapse of memory, but more likely he wanted to emphasize the de-centeredness of the painting and to demythologize the centrality of the Virgin and the Word. That is, he emphasizes the social profusion rather than the logo-center. In any event, this reading is more consistent with the total context of *Paterson*, Book Five.

exposes (or discloses) the true mystery of origins, and man's ultimate freedom from them. Each of these works is for Williams an original, and therefore like (including the difference implied by "like") the "satyric play," or pre-art. Each reveals art to be a fictional play within language. They are art at its most "devout" because they are a "ridicule" of Art, parodic deconstructions of their tradition. In these works "deformities take wing" (P, 221), since deformities are the creations of the tyranny of traditional form, history's monsters. And one recalls that *Paterson*, in its first four books, has been itself such a "satyric play," filled with monsters and grotesques, those figures of "wonder" which have dotted the history of Paterson and allowed its citizens to define their own normality in relation to outrageous difference. But the poem reveals the necessity of these monsters to Paterson's history, for its myth has given the monstrous a centrality by making the monster a sign of wonder, supernatural. Williams instead discloses the monster as the ex-centricity of nature, its superabundance. All original art, then, must incorporate the monstrous dissymmetry, yet make "deformities take wing" and become "Centaurs" (P, 221). It takes us into the presence of original difference. The monster is a genetic expression of the unnameable new, emerging shape, truly a shape of "wonder." He is the freeplay of nature. Thus he stands for the original decentering. Like Toulouse-Lautrec, he is therefore a figure of the artist, halfway between nature and culture. He is in-between, and divided or incomplete. He is the embodiment of desire, and the emblem of man's need of wholeness.

The tapestries of the Cloisters, which Williams says he visited often, detail the myth of the hunt for the Unicorn as an allegory of the Incarnation. But the tapestries themselves, and even one dimension of the multiple allegory they depict, have a distinct historical origin and role. At least some of the seven panels, as previously noted, were done to celebrate the marriage of Anne of Brittany to Louis XII and thus function in their way to augment the redemption of history (the king's own continuing family reign) desired in that marriage. The miracle of the tapestries' survival is itself a counterpart of the myth of renewal they celebrate: like Sappho's manuscripts, they are historical examples of art's endurance. During the French Revolution they were condemned to destruction along with any other surviving evidence of the royalist tradition. The happy chance of their dislocation and survival offered Williams a concrete example of the historical discontinuities which art bridged, revealing therein a timelessness which in itself is a measure of history. The tapestries were instances of an art implanted into a new and alien ground, but not of an imported tradition. They were the language of place (both in the sense of precisely detailed texture and of the historical events they allegorized), but a place lifted out of history and made real in its complete space. That place is the "museum" made "real," the ruins of an old order rearranged on a new ground. The tapestries manifested a "total culture" and disclosed in that totality the infrastructure of culture—any culture, since "Anywhere is everywhere"—including its interpenetrations with nature. In their allegorical detail they achieved the necessary abstraction of art, yet revealed the concrete, timeless reality of a primordial event.

That event is the "hunt" and its implied transgression. Williams' reference in "Asphodel" to the "rituals of the hunt" depicted in the prehistoric cave paintings is one of the common themes of the two poems, and suggests, since "Asphodel" was originally intended to be *Paterson*, Book Five, that these rituals were from the beginning Williams' key to any extension of *Paterson*, Books One–Four. What they indicate, clearly enough, is Williams' desire to relate his "epic" to an original art, to disclose the simultaneity and synchrony of culture in the original and originating patterns of its imagination. His repeated insistence on the universality of the particular expresses likewise the problematic of the universal, since, like the rituals of the hunt, the universal patterns which art reveals to inhere in the particulars of history turn out to be patterns of human desire. Art discloses man in his original nature to be the wanderer and therefore the hunter. He is both the pursuer of the Unicorn and its destroyer. He lives a pattern of desire that must violate its object.

The myth of the Unicorn derives from Eastern folklore, but in the Middle Ages it became associated with the tradition of courtly love. It therefore became assimilated to the myth of the Incarnation, and the Gnostic doctrine of the Word. The tapestries, then, appear to reconcile two apparently antithetical world views, Christian and pagan, as well as the metaphysical opposites the two embody. Moreover, its allegory attempts to reconcile the irreconcilable differences within the Christian system: love and violence, life and death, the sacred and the profane, order and freedom, the Word and words. The "hunt" for the Unicorn, indeed, implies at once the creation and the pursuit of that presence which reconciles differences. But the "capture" of the Unicorn, like the Incarnation it evokes, implies his ultimate death and transcendence. The meaning of history rests eventually on the god's historical absence and symbolic presence. The Unicorn, then, is what we might call the superabundance of signification in both myth and poem—a superabundance which is there precisely because the Unicorn has not been or cannot be possessed without destroying it, and cannot be allowed to disappear without destroying the field of which it is the mysterious center.

The capture or enclosure of the Unicorn involves a transgression, a murder, which fulfills the sacrificial theme of the creation. As Christian allegory, its theme is *felix culpa*. But the rituals of the hunt, whether those depicted in the caves of

Altamira or Lascaux or those of the tapestries, indicate the problematic of any one particular "meaning" for the murder. Indeed, if the tapestries repeat on another plane the thematization of the hunt which is man's earliest known art, the poem interprets in its process, its "hunt," the tapestries. It therefore interprets the interpretation of an interpretation. What we have is a sequence of decenterings of the myth, an uncovering of the rituals and a bringing into question of the Word. The capture of the Unicorn, the enclosure of it in the garden of artistic space, is revealed as a dream upon which the meaning of Christian history has revolved. This dream is at once mythopoeically true and historically a fiction. The myth of the enclosed garden becomes an ultimate ambiguity, the fiction of fiction which must be concealed. The mystery of the center must be protected. Otherwise, this myth of language puts itself in question.

The deep resonances of the Unicorn myth could not escape Williams. Post-Freudian psychoanalysis had argued, of course, that the Unicorn was a "purely phallic conception." [25] Its pre-Christian meaning could easily be transported into the Christian context, so that the phallic nature of the Unicorn might become, in Ernest Jones's interpretation, symbolic of God's breath which was blown into the Virgin's lap. But as Odell Shepard has shown, the range of its application, from profane to sacred literature, is astonishingly varied and in large part contradictory. [26] In Richard de Fournival's *Bestiaire de l'amour*, [27] for example, the Unicorn is identified profanely with the poet. In Carl Jung's table of symbols, it is variously but

25. Ernest Jones, "The Madonna's Conception Through the Ear," *Essays in Applied Psychoanalysis* (London: Hogarth Press, 1923), 33.
26. Odell Shepard, *The Lore of the Unicorn* (New York: Barnes and Noble, 1967).
27. See Adolph Zeckle, "The Totemistic Significance of the Unicorn," in George B. Wilbur and Warner Muensterberger (eds.), *Psychoanalysis and Culture: Essays in Honor of Geza Roheim* (New York: International Universities Press, 1951).

systematically identified as one of the alchemical symbols of
Mercurius or the anima,[28] which of course has its counterpart
in Christian symbolism: the Virgin represents Mercurius'
"passive, feminine aspect, while the unicorn or the lion
illustrates the wild, rampant, masculine penetrating force of the
spiritus mercurialis." [29] But among the more significant of
Jung's many and varied interpretations is the following: "It is
to be noted in the ecclesiastical quotations that the unicorn also
contains the element of evil. . . . Originally a monstrous and
fabulous beast, it harbours in itself an inner contradiction, a
coniunction oppositorum, which makes it a singularly appropriate symbol for the *monstrum hermaphroditum* of alchemy." [30]

Strip away the occultism and one discovers that the Unicorn
manifests, in whatever context it appears, the inner contradiction of any excessive signification. Its identifying characteristic, that which distinguishes it from a recognizable animal, is its
singular horn. Whether phallus or symbol of unity, it is a
logical de-formity, a kind of stain which allows it to be
interpreted as either good or evil: good because the horn is an
emblem of unity or *logos,* bad because it is monstrous,
abnormal. Williams seems to recognize this in *Paterson,* Book
Five. In the more orthodox Christian allegory, the Unicorn is
Christ, and in the allegory of the tapestries His capture in the
lap of the Virgin, the enclosed garden, is presaged by the lure
of the fountain. Odell Shepard has indicated how central to the
legend of the Unicorn is the ritual of "water-conning." [31] In
the chivalric tradition the Unicorn, whose magic horn purifies
poisoned water, was considered to embody the ideal of
exceptional power and exceptional responsibility. In another
version, he does not purify impure water but discovers the

28. See C. G. Jung, *Psychology and Alchemy,* Vol. 12 of *The Collected Works of C.
G. Jung* trans. R. F. C. Hull (New York: Pantheon, 1953), 414–15.
29. *Ibid.,* 419.
30. *Ibid.,* 426.
31. Shepard, *The Lore of the Unicorn,* 73–74.

underground flow or the source of the pure and makes it available to others.[32] And the Unicorn of Gnosticism is related specifically to water, the element of life, and through it with the One from whom came the original division of the four elements and all subsequent being. (So is the burden of the *Paterson* poet: to sound impure water, to recover the source.) The Unicorn's capture by the Virgin, in the Christian allegory, is a kind of water-conning, and in its way a double transgression of the Virgin, in that it is a return to the source that recalls the ambiguity of that source. The Incarnation renders the Word mortal, and the Unicorn, in *Paterson*, Book Five, calls "for its own murder" (P, 208), while the Virgin is deflowered unless the "legend" sustains the paradox of virgin giving birth.

But in the basic Christian allegory, like the one which inspired the tapestries, each detail bears its own unambiguous meaning. Here is Shepard's interpretation: "its one horn is said to signify the unity of Christ and the Father; its fierceness and defiance of the hunter are to remind us that neither Principalities nor Powers nor Thrones were able to control the Messiah against His will; its small stature is a symbol of Christ's humility and its likeness to a kid of His association with sinful men. The virgin is held to represent the Virgin Mary and the huntsman is the Holy Spirit acting through the Angel Gabriel." [33] The huntsman, to return to the tapestries, is the king; but in the legend he is the Holy Spirit who acts through the Angel Gabriel. He is the divine poet. And the poet's, or surrogate father's role, is to sacrifice, hence murder, the Unicorn, wherein his meaning is fully disclosed. For his meaning does not lie in the Annunciation, which is Gabriel's word to the Virgin, or in the birth, the Incarnation, but in the Crucifixion and Ascension which are implicit in both. The

32. *Ibid.*, 152–53.
33. *Ibid.*, 48.

descent of the Dove, the Holy Ghost, comes only with the
Ascension, the return of the *logos* to its origins. With the
withdrawal of incarnate presence, the spirit of its meaning
pervades history, is everywhere and nowhere. The tapestries,
if they may be said to correspond at all to Shepard's recounting
of the allegory, place the huntsman in an ambiguous role.
Gabriel's announcement is simultaneous with the decentering,
and the decentering is the moment at which the true meaning
of the Incarnation is revealed. The Holy Ghost, one notes
from a verse of the Gospels which Williams includes in the
poem, is the Father who begets the Child upon the Virgin,
whom Williams calls "Miriam" (P, 228). The poet is the
surrogate father of the Word, the speaking subject who in his
descent breaks up the unity of the Word, begets a son, and
whores the source:

> The Unicorn roams the forest of all true
> lovers' minds. They hunt it down. Bow wow! sing hey the
> green holly!

> —every married man carries in his head
>   the beloved and sacred image
>   of a virgin
>   whom he has whored .
>   but the living fiction
>   a tapestry
> silk and wool shot with silver threads
>   a milk-white one-horned beast
>   I, Paterson, the King-self
> saw the lady
>   through the rough woods
>   outside the palace walls
> among the stench of sweating horses
>   and gored hounds
>   yelping with pain
> the heavy breathing pack
>   to see the dead beast
>   brought in at last

across the saddlebow
among the oak trees.
(P, 234–35)

Previous to this passage, the poet has spoken of the "demon" mind which drives us to the hunt of the "Unicorn and/ the god of love/ of virgin birth" that can be seen but must not be touched or realized (P, 233–34). The demon is desire, which projects the ideal as an emblem of its lack and violates that idea in its insistent hunt to possess it. The lover-king-poet is the Pater-son, creator and destroyer, sacrificer and sacrificial victim, dreamer and realist, the author of the Text and the one who must bring into question his own text. He is Williams' answer to the Fisher King of Frazer, and, of course, of Eliot.[34] And Williams has written his own poem demythologizing Frazer's text, just as, in the passage quoted above, he demythologizes the legend of the tapestries. The poet imagines himself within the legend of the tapestries, in order to touch rather than simply see the "lady." And by so doing, he whores the lady; just as the tapestries, by identifying the Virgin and Anne of Brittany, brought into question the allegorical relevance of the Incarnation rather than, as was intended, mythologizing the lady Anne as the Virgin come again. The poet, entering the world of the tapestries, cuts through its Christian symbolism to the pagan (that is, natural) world "outside the palace walls." The capture of the Unicorn by the maiden is, thus, a return of the poet to the source, a legend that all original art has secretly (and often silently) tried to tell.

Love is desire which leads to the hunt, and the pursuit leads to the death of the hunted. Georges Bataille has called the ritual of the hunt, as made evident both in primitive art and

34. One might contrast here Williams' use of the myth of the Incarnation and the subsequent descent of the Dove, with T. S. Eliot's use of the Paraclete in "Little Gidding," parts three and four, in *The Complete Poems and Plays*, 142–44, and Ezra Pound's in Canto 74, *The Cantos* (New York: New Directions, 1970), 429, where it stands for the pervasive "light" of *"virtù"* which informs some old cultures but to which the present world is blind.

civilized sexual pursuits, a ceremonial transgression of a
fundamental taboo: "the taboo [against murder or sexuality]
cannot suppress pursuits necessary to life, but it can give them
the significance of a religious violation"; thus the "act of killing
invested the killer, hunter or warrior, with a sacramental
character." [35] And Bataille further speculates that the prehistoric representations of the hunt in Lascaux were expiatory
offerings for the transgression of the hunt, the murder, and that
therefore they "must have been intended to depict that instant
when the animal appeared and killing, at once inevitable and
reprehensible, laid bare life's mysterious ambiguity." [36] Life is
necessarily a transgression of taboo; its hero is, therefore, a
"sacramental character." Sexuality is linked with sacrifice,
transgressional violence redeemed in ritual. The tapestries of
the Cloisters have lifted the primitive or elementary structure
of the hunt into the sophisticated rituals of the court, and
rendered it as courtly love, in an attempt, so necessary to
historical man, to conceal the nature of "life's mysterious
ambiguity." For this ambiguity is at least partly ameliorated if
one can conceive of a continuity between man the transgressor
and the privileged center of God, rather than the shock of
recognition of the difference between man and animal.

The myth of the Incarnation is the myth of this continuity,
sealed by a love that contains and transcends the violence of
the sacrifice it entails. The medieval vision, Williams' poem
suggests, is like the Catholic vision of Père Sebastian Rasles—it
keeps the two worlds, the sacred and the profane, in "touch,"
continuous. But the history of religion violates this mythic
continuity. The Puritan vision which Williams detests so
eloquently divorces the human and the sacred, and thereby

35. Georges Bataille, *Death and Sensuality: A Study of Eroticism and the Taboo*
(New York: Ballentine Books, 1969), 68.
36. *Ibid.*, 68–69. See also Georges Bataille, *Lascaux ou la naissance de l'art* (Paris:
Skira, 1955).

enforces the discontinuity between selves. It leads to self-anni-
hilating violence, a contrast to the engendering violence of
love. Or in other words, the Puritan vision separates love and
sex (violence); life becomes evil, as do those pursuits necessary
to it. Sexuality, which once had the character of a mysterious
and sacred transgression, is divested of its ambiguity and
justified exclusively on the grounds of God's will to prolong
the race. Sex no longer serves as a force mediating love and
violence, a force that links the self with its mysterious origins
and sanctifies them. Williams' demythologizing of the tapestries returns to them and to his own poem the mysterious
ambiguity of the hunt.

The tapestries become a metaphor for the entire poem: the
"pursuit" which violates the "dream" and in turn becomes
the "dream"; the poet's own water-conning, his search for the
source through the purification of the filthy Passaic and the
fouled language; the ritualizing of the violence of "pursuit";
the discovery of the elemental ground of language in an
originating murder; and finally, the weaving of the story, the
fiction, which closes the hermeneutical circle of history.
Paterson, Book Five, however, features the tapestries as a
plethora of detail, a "picture" moving "from frame to frame
without perspective" (P, 236). Any one of the multiple
details—a flower, for example—exists first and for itself; it is
not subsumed by the whole. It is "like a knight in chess" (P,
236), its identity precisely and relationally defined in the
perspectiveless "canvas" where its subordinate function and
value is nevertheless characterized by a latitude of freeplay.
For what Williams stresses in the tapestries is not the Unicorn
(which invites its own murder) as center, but the necessary
ambiguity of the "hunt" which captures the Unicorn and
realizes in that capture the creative act of man the transgressor,
the namer and thus murderer of the transcendental Word.

The tapestries presumed to discover the allegory of the

Incarnation to be doubled in the marriage of Louis and Anne, and thus ritualized the transgression of that marriage. For that marriage, in fact, did take liberties with Church law in that Louis had had a childless marriage of twenty-two years annulled and Anne's first husband had been dead barely nine months. The legend is made to serve the dignity of man, not to say the continuity of history in the "divine right" of kings— but at the expense of necessary sacrifice. Just as marriage, according to Bataille, is a ceremonial violation of the taboo against sexuality, and thus but another example of religion as the ritualized violation of sacred laws, so are the tapestries disclosures of marriage as a transgression. The transgression is necessary, however, if the line of the king is to continue, for he must have heirs. The capture of the Unicorn is also his death, in the same sense, as Bataille shows, that the marriage ceremony is ritualistically the initial sexual act, the violation of the virgin.[37] In both instances, a death takes place which makes continuity possible. It is in this sense that one can speak of the tapestries as analogues of the poem itself, for there must be a sacrifice of the Word if language is to have its life, if it is to renew itself, since language is the difference and thus the negation of the idea of the Word.

The very nature of a tapestry, the "story" it tells aside, bears within itself the idea of functional art. Like myths, tapestries are anonymous, the product of the cultural order and not a single subject. They are, to say the least, a "weave" of interpretations, a tale told upon a central conception that becomes, in the telling, more rather than less ambiguous. The level of detail always preempts the level of allegory, the cultural intention, just as the interpretation stands forth from the thing interpreted. But the specificity of the detail betrays the simplicity of the meaning. Tapestries, especially those

37. Bataille, *Death and Sensuality*, 104–107.

which allegorize, are mythically inseparable from the problematic of language and from the legend of original transgressions. There is, of course, Helen's weaving of the story of her violation, the legend of history and war, and Penelope's delaying act of weaving and unweaving, keeping the suitors at a distance and preserving her original binary role. But the legend which lurks behind the ritual of the hunt told by the tapestries of the Cloisters, and more particularly behind Book Five of *Paterson*'s demythologization of those tapestries, is the legend of the original violation which gave birth to the metaphor for poetic language: the rape of Philomela which, as Sophocles revealed, provoked the indelible expression of the "voice of the shuttle." Geoffrey Hartman has offered us the provocative and indispensable notion that this metaphor, linking "craft (cunning) and craft (art)," is the crucial figure for literary language.[38] Bataille, more directly, concludes that "language does not exist independently of the play of transgression and taboo."[39] *Paterson*, Book Five, about tapestries and ritual hunts, about violence and transgression, about the taboo of form which all original art routs, is a poem of language about language.

Dr. Paterson's endless search for a satisfactory marriage; his repeated frustration which is suffered commonly by the townspeople; the failed affair of Corydon and Phyllis; the letters from "C" complaining of that "blockage" that afflicts her life and Paterson's; the whoring of the virgin—these are only a few of the transgressions in *Paterson* which make the "hunt" both necessary and problematic. They are forms of divorce or discontinuity that only the most rigorous ritual might cure. Thus the poem is a hunt which assumes the

---

38. Geoffrey Hartman, "The Voice of the Shuttle: Language from the Point of View of Literature," *Beyond Formalism: Literary Essays, 1958–1970* (New Haven: Yale University Press, 1970), 337–39.
39. Bataille, *Death and Sensuality*, 272.

problematic of the hunt—as both a transgression and a cure. For as it murders the idea of the Word, it brings together in a single field the difference of words, the multiplicity of flowers which are the true evidence of the origination or flowering principle. *Paterson* must turn the history of Paterson inside out, and in doing so transgress the laws of teleological history in order to offer its own new fabric. The sacrifice of the Unicorn in *Paterson*, Book Five, incarnates this inversion (this "blast") which is repeatedly taking place in the process of the whole poem: just as the poet-father sacrifices himself when he gives to be sacrificed his poet-son. The given language of Paterson, the English language, is turned inside out and thus disclosed to be not the fixed language of history but the elemental language of poetry.

IV

In a poetic note added to the manuscript of *Paterson*, Book Five, Williams articulated the relevance of the flower passages both to the tapestries and to his poem:

> (the whole flower episode
>   is an image of 'my wife')—as an image,
> a beloved image, a secret image
>   of an inviolate virgin
> —whom I whored   .   .   (as all men do) to their wives.

>   (Yale MS)

It is clear throughout *Paterson* that the woman is the poem the poet makes, and the idea of the perfect or "whole" poem he violates in his making. In Williams' play, *A Dream of Love*, the poet-doctor, now dead, returns to speak to his wife Myra: a man, he says, "must create a woman of some sort out of his imagination to prove himself. Oh, it doesn't have to be a woman, but she's the generic type. It's a woman—even if it's a mathematical formula of relativity. Even more so in that case—but a woman. A woman out of his imagination to match the best. All right, a poem"; for just as a "woman must produce out of her female belly to complete herself—a son—so a man must reproduce a woman, in full beauty out of the shell of his imagination and possess her, to complete himself also" (ML, 200). Myra calls this "the rape of the imagination." Woman, Williams has said, is the "completer," the mother, the earth: "Our ancestors with their myths concerned with the earth, the season of rebirth, fruitfulness, had faith in the flower, the ripening grass and animals which consumed it. They had reason to believe in woman as the great completer. Without her, nothing. So it might be, as it has always been, a faith in Proserpine." [40]

The myth of Kore which runs throughout Williams' poetry is a myth of continuity (the eternal return) which depends on the violence of a discontinuity. It is another version of the whoring of the virgin. If man must create a woman (or poem) to complete himself, he must complete himself by creating a difference. The myth of Kore is a myth of disclosure which necessarily involves taboo and transgression: the loss and retrieval of the virgin. It is the image of poetic language, which oscillates between a yearning for the unmediated disclosure of

40. Williams, "Faith and Prayer," Yale MS. One might compare this very early observation, "Correspondence: the Great Sex Spiral," *Egoist*, IV (August, 1917), 110: "the male pursuit leads only to further pursuit, that is, not toward the earth, but away from it—not to concreteness, but to further hunting, to star-gazing, to idleness." And he goes on to identify man as a drunk, dominated either by women or by the "drunkenness there is in it. *Soyez ivre.*" "Female psychology," on the other hand, "is characterized by a trend not away from, but toward the earth, toward concreteness, since by her experience the reality of fact is firmly established." Man, he claimed, is the "vague generalizer" and woman the "concrete thinker." The poet must combine both qualities.

C. G. Jung's remarks, in *Psychology and Religion, West and East*, Vol. 11 of *The Collected Works of C. G. Jung*, trans. R. F. C. Hull (New York: Pantheon, 1958), 395, bear comparison: "*Perfection* is a masculine desideratum, while woman inclines by nature to completeness. . . . If a woman strives for perfection she forgets the complementary role of completeness, which, though imperfect by itself, forms the necessary counterpart to perfection. For, just as completeness is always imperfect, so perfection is always incomplete, and therefore represents a final state which is hopelessly sterile."

its sources and the revelation of difference (multiplicity).
"What do I look for in a woman?" Williams wrote in his
Autobiography: "Death, I suppose, since it's all I see anyhow in
those various perfections" (A, 222). Women mediate sacred
and profane: they "keep some proportion, remain sound even
in debauchery, relate the parts to a whole, act, that is with the
body, the related parts, together, not a part of it, as to be sure,
they must to survive" (A, 224). And he goes on to reflect on
the fortunate "deformity" of Toulouse-Lautrec (to whom
Paterson, Book Five, is dedicated), which led him to live in the
"warmth" and "comfort" of a brothel. Not having to "possess"
the girls, he could see their completeness, their "proportion,"
in their apparently unbeautiful parts. He could rise above
desire, not having to possess and therefore annihilate the
Other. For Toulouse-Lautrec, the deformed artist, saw what
Dr. Paterson discovers: that the deformed are completed by
deformity, by a dance of contradictory parts. The deformed
manifest man's continuity with nature, yet his difference from
nature's wholeness. Woman the completer becomes the
essential difference that makes one imagine harmony:

> . . . all
> desired women have had each
> in the end
> a busted nose
> and live afterward marked up
> Beautiful Thing
> for memory's sake
> to be credible in their deeds
> (P, 127)

Only in the poem, the poem which discloses its own
transgression, do "all the deformities take wing" (P, 221). The
whore and the virgin prove to be an "identity:/ —through its
disguises" (P, 210), through the sameness of their difference.
The woman with the broken nose is a violation of the ideal of

beauty as the poem with a broken measure is a violation of the ideal of poetic form. But the broken measure reveals the true meaning of the "identity." The Unicorn, the Beautiful Thing, the virgin—they are all ideals (ideas of wholeness) which are absent or are violated. They are centers which are decentered, producing the difference which alone discloses the true nature of Beauty. "It is the woman in us/ That makes us write" (CEP, 34)—for the woman is the impulse to complete, the figure of man's lack and the object of his desire.[41] In the tapestries the Unicorn is captured by the Virgin; the earth possesses the Word and incarnates it there. And the Word is only released in the marriage which violates the Virgin, in the man's whoring of the virgin. The fiction of the Word is shattered, and difference emerges. Marriage involves the identity of a difference. It always involves two, desire and the other's desire. It is, therefore, the metaphor of all human "interpenetration." It is, as we have seen, the ground of a "city."

Brueghel's art and Mezz Mezzrow's jazz present this same creative violation. Brueghel paints his "Nativity" with a "potbellied/ greybeard (center)" (P, 226), and with the "Baby" on his mother's knee, born there "among the words," amid the "bustle of the scene" of the poor. Though in fact, as

41. In a very early letter to Viola Baxter Jordan (December 5, 1911) which Mike Weaver quotes in *William Carlos Williams: The American Background* (Cambridge, England: Cambridge University Press, 1971), 24, Williams indicated his early thoughts on virginity: "To be alive means you are committed against virginity either by yielding to passion or by holding passion off. It begins at about the age of three and every blush proves there is no virginity. A few know their lack and good it is for all of us. Others mistake simple natural economy for the true principle which, as all abstract truths are, is a myth to us." In *The Great American Novel*, he spoke of marriage as "of the church because it is the intersection of *loci* by which alone there is place for a church to stand. Beauty is an arrow" (Imag., 216). And in his *Autobiography*, speaking of Charles Sheeler's art and life, he remarks: "The poem (in Charles's case the painting) is the construction in understandable limits of his life. That is Sheeler; that, lucky for him, partial or possible, is also music. It is called also a marriage. All these terms have to be redefined, a marriage has to be seen as a thing. The poem is made of things—on a field" (A, 333). See also Introduction, footnote 19.

noted earlier, neither "greybeard" nor "Baby" but the Virgin
herself centers the Brueghel canvas. It is a scene which honors
"an old man, or a woman" (P, 227), a birth that marks the
death of an old order and effects a strange, magical continuity
with the new. Mezz Mezzrow's remarks on the blues, which
Williams quotes (P, 221), insist that a white man can learn the
music, that the blues is a way through the discontinuity of
separate or ethnic selves to a harmony, a simultaneity of
suffering and joy, in which difference is held in relation. Art
survives, then, because it fails of wholeness, of totalization;
because instead of delivering to us the Word it breaks up the
Word and leaves us in the opening of a new beginning like the
"Baby" of Brueghel's painting, which is not centered but
whose meaning is dispersed throughout the painting.

Bataille claims that the transgression depicted by the
prehistoric cave painters is the transgression of the sacred
world of animals to which man originally belonged. Man,
emerging from his natural state, discovers himself as a
murderer of the animals, of the sacred. He thus discovers his
own discontinuity with both the sacred and nature:

> As soon as human beings give reign to animal nature in some way
> we enter the world of transgression forming the synthesis
> between animal nature and humanity through the persistence of
> the taboo; we enter a sacred world, a world of holy things. . . .
> The spirit of transgression is the animal god dying, the god whose
> death sets violence in motion, who remains untouched by the
> taboos restraining humanity. Taboos do not in fact concern either
> the real animal sphere or the field of animal myth; they do
> concern all-powerful men whose human nature is concealed
> beneath an animal's mask. The spirit of the early world is
> impossible to grasp at first; it is the natural world mingled with the
> divine; yet . . . it is the human world, shaped by a denial of
> animality or nature, denying itself, and reaching beyond itself in
> this second denial, though not returning to what it had rejected in
> the first place.[42]

42. Bataille, *Death and Sensuality*, 80.

I have quoted at such length not simply because Bataille offers an illuminating gloss on the anthropology of the tapestries, but because he offers us an analogy for the poem, the language of the tapestries. The thematics of *Paterson*, Book Five, present art as an embodiment of this paradox, as a repetition of the "dream" which lies in the "pursuit." Art therefore depicts the moment of a radical denial of the old order. Art survives as a transgression of itself, of its own sacredness. It is original because its true moment is the moment of originality, of its original violence. It marks man's departure from nature both as a loss and a gain, a "mysterious ambiguity." It launches man toward "death," yet it celebrates his "escape" through this "hole" that is the "imagination" (P, 212). The imagination throws him into desire and toward death, but it allows him to dream the dream of wholeness. It allows him to know himself as free, to experience that "which cannot be fathomed"; in "art alone" is the true marriage of "male and female" (P, 212). It allows him to make, to complete, to place—to generate the *ouroboros* of language:

> a secret world,
> a sphere, a snake with its tail in
> its mouth
>   rolls backward into the past
>   (P, 214)[43]

Art becomes a "reel house, a real house" (P, 214). The Cloisters asserts itself as artistic rather than religious space, and thus reaffirms the fictiveness of the art it houses. It is, nevertheless, a timeless (synchronic) space housing the panels of an art which tells the story of Time with Death at the

43. This is, of course, the figure (*ouroboros*) which Jung (*Psychology and Religion*, 236–37) calls the "creative pneuma," and the alchemical symbol of the *logos*. It is "unity, a root of the whole," the figure of the hermaphrodite. But in Williams the "sphere" functions more like a helix, or an inverted bell, and becomes the symbol for language and for the "poem," a "secret" world into which the imagination "escapes" and the initial play begins again.

center. Art survives as the myth of the violated center, from which its life, its "motion" or freeplay, comes. Art is the living transgression, the ritual of the "hunt" for wholeness, the pursuit which discovers the necessary violence of the creative act. Like Gilbert Sorrentino's pun (P, 214) on the whore house as a *"Casa real"* that is also a "reel" house (a Dionysian theater?), the museum contains this myth of marriage.

The proportion which Williams attributes to women, the proportion of related but asymmetrical parts, is reflected in the figure of the dance which concludes *Paterson*, Book Five. The dance is another figure for the poem itself, the poetic image. The dance is "satyric" (P, 221, 239), a "pre-tragic" dance, and not like the Yeatsian image, a dance of transcendence or purification. For Yeats, at the end of Romanticism, the ideal of proportion is the woman in motion, the singularity of the dancer in the solitude of her perfect Unity—the image of art, as Frank Kermode says, caught for Yeats in the idea of a "dancing girl in the midst of the sea." [44] It is a "unity of being," Kermode adds, ". . . so complete as to be unobtainable"—leading in the Yeatsian antithesis to disaster, of Venus defiled or Helen stolen, and finally to the restoration of Crazy Jane. But Kermode does not note that it is a question. The Yeatsian question, that is to say, reopens the problematic of the Image—it is a question to which there is no answer.

Williams accepts the given of the whored virgin, the desired woman with the busted nose, and the dance of the centaurs. It is a dance of beginnings, a Dionysian rout, a breaking up of the sacred unity into an original difference, a first measure. And just as it celebrates the original breaking out, the original difference, it celebrates the original regathering, the pleonasm

44. Frank Kermode, *The Romantic Image* (New York: Macmillan, 1952), 58. Compare Friedrich Nietzsche, *The Will to Power*, trans. Walter Kaufmann and R. J. Hollingdale (New York: Vintage Books, 1968): "Perhaps light feet are even an integral part of the concept 'god' " (p. 534); or as he quotes from his own Zarathustra, "I would believe only in a God who could dance" (p. 535).

of primordial language. The dance is sexual, and thus a ritualized transgression. Celebrating the continuity between nature and culture, it celebrates the necessary breaking of the circle, the ecstasy of beginnings.

There is a remarkable passage in *Spring and All* that illuminates the figure of the dance (the poetic image) like no other in Williams' canon. It begins by describing the imagination as a "radioactive" force which liberates fixed forms and inaugurates a motion and thus a shifting of relations in a field of force. Imagination, therefore, violates the descriptive or imagistic function of words, setting them "free"; it is the deconstructive force discussed in the previous chapter, deconstructive and disseminating. But in the passage Williams uses the example of John of Gaunt's speech in *Richard II*, and argues that the "imagination is wrongly understood when it is supposed to be a removal from reality," when it means "to imagine possession of that which is lost":

> It is rightly understood when John of Gaunt's words are related not to their sense as objects adherent to his son's welfare or otherwise but as a dance over the body of his condition accurately accompanying it. By this means of the understanding, the play written to be understood as a play, the author and reader are liberated to pirouette with the words which have sprung from the old facts of history, reunited in present passion.
>
> To understand the words as so liberated is to understand poetry. That they move independently when set free is the mark of their value
>
> Imagination is not to avoid reality, nor is it description nor an evocation of objects or situations, it is to say that poetry does not tamper with the world but moves it—It affirms reality most powerfully and therefore, since reality needs no personal support but exists free from human action, as proven by science in the indestructibility of matter and of force, it creates a new object, a play, a dance which is not a mirror up to nature but—
>
> As birds' wings beat the solid air without which none could fly so words freed by the imagination affirm reality by their flight

Writing is likened to music. The object would be it seems to
make poetry a pure art, like music. Painting too. Writing, as with
certain of the modern Russians whose work I have seen, would
use unoriented sounds in place of conventional words. The poem
then would be completely liberated when there is identity of
sound with something—perhaps the emotion.
I do not believe that writing is music. I do not believe writing
would gain in quality or force by seeking to attain to the
conditions of music.
I think the conditions of music are objects for the action of the
writer's imagination just as a table or—
According to my present theme the writer of imagination
would attain closest to the conditions of music not when his words
are disassociated from natural objects and specific meanings but
when they are liberated from the usual quality of that meaning by
a transposition into another medium, the imagination.

(Imag., 149–50)

Williams' poetics is encapsulated in this lengthy circumlocu-
tion which moves *Spring and All* to the threshold of its open
ending. Gaunt's speech to his son, Bolingbroke (later Henry
IV), is more than conventional advice.[45] It is made in the space
of Bolingbroke's silence, his inability to respond to being exiled
and dispossessed. Gaunt literally gives words to one he had
given life, just as his words of anguish had given Henry "time"
(Richard reduced the exile from ten to six years) though a time
that can never be filled up (since Gaunt will die and Henry
will never see his father again). Gaunt's advice is that an exile
can escape his poverty by imagining reality, by making a
"virtue" of "necessity." His are the words of historical man,
man exiled from Eden, from presence, from the Word. More
important, the speech is soon repeated in Gaunt's famous
patriotic evocation of England as "demi-paradise." [46] This last,
passionate utterance is his own final imagining of plenitude—
truly, as Williams writes, a "dance over the body of his

45. William Shakespeare, *King Richard II*, Act I, Scene iii, ll. 268–93.
46. *Ibid.*, Act II, Scene i, ll. 31–68.

condition." For immediately after, Gaunt speaks his dying words to nephew Richard, a final utterance on finality which doubles the earlier one on imagined reality. Gaunt's condition is his gauntness, as he puns to Richard, a condition embodied in "grave" words. "Can sick men play so nicely with their names?" asks Richard,[47] who barely waits for an answer. Williams recognizes the play on words as the virtue of a necessity compelled by an absence, a loss of the center, which has issued in a chaos of familial relations, the breakup of the orderly continuity between fathers and sons, the violent removal of the proper King or law. The name of the center becomes Death, that which makes the play of words both possible and necessary. Death is not only the sign of the violence that defines history, the sickness not only of Gaunt but of the state; it is that which makes imagining possible. Death clears Gaunt's throat for "grave" prophecy, just as it allows him to fill in absence with the fiction of presence, the *Logos* of an ancient Eden doubly lost in England's present history.

The music of this passage, says Williams, comes from the play of words within the play, which also involves the breaking away of words from history's facticity. Kings and dukes may or may not have punned, but an imagining of history, an imaginative interpretation of history, is made possible in one very crucial sense by the decentering of the King-Word. Shakespeare deconstructs history. He removes it to the plane of imagination by simply depriving it of its sustaining center. He takes us into the timeless play of its myth, where every word reveals its potential double, where the "pirouette" of words broken free from the "impositions of art" (that is, from the burden of mirroring history or reality) reveals the imaginative play that is and always has been at the center of

47. *Ibid.,* Act II, Scene i, 1. 84.

history. Words sustain the dream of an orderly and meaningful history, the dream of original unity, rather than words being sustained by the Word. The necessity of poetry, its virtue, is that only the imaginative play of words can free man from the tyranny of its order, its dream of non-difference. Only poetry involves us in the "dance" of language that restores us to a present freedom—the freedom to interpret.

The "dance" is a precise figure, then, for a "free" relationship, an original relationship. In the beginning, at the point of emerging being, there are necessarily two, opposites in reciprocal tension, interpenetrating. And it is from this primordial relationship that man derives the "one," a vision of an original unity. But this primal unity is only the "dream" of historical man. The act of writing, bringing words to the dance and creating a "play," rediscovers this original moment as an original violation, as difference. The dynamic of language reveals the necessity of the whored virgin: "The word is not liberated, therefore able to communicate release from the fixities which destroy it until it is accurately tuned to the fact which giving it reality, by its own reality establishes its own freedom from the necessity of a word, thus freeing it and dynamizing it at the same time" (Imag., 150). The dance which ends *Paterson*, Book Five, announces the liberation of the word, just as the previous passage in its dance of pronouns liberates the pronouns, separates "it" from "it," word from the fixity of meaning which "destroys" it, and sets it once again beside the difference which gives it reality. Like the blast at the end of *Paterson*, Book Four, the dance of the "Satyrs," which is "pre-tragic" (P, 221), brings us not to the end of a poem, and thus to a text, but to the openness of history. Thus, it leads to the "tragic foot" (P, 239). Like the legend of the Unicorn, the dance reveals that all this has happened before and must continually happen. There is no liberation without a capture, no freedom without the violence of an originative act. Only the dance can free the word from its text and return it to its place at the beginning, to the moment of its original difference. The poem is a "cloister," the place or field of the "dance," and thus a place of simultaneous taboo and transgression, where the sacred and the profane are held in vital, reciprocal tension.

Poetry cannot attain to purity, or become a copy of music. Yet music, like the dance, is an apt figure for the poem if we understand the analogy of words to things. The analogy holds so long as one recognizes the isomorphic structures of language and nature. The poetic "music" Williams rejects is the idea of a poetic language that is pure, an unbroken immediacy, a form that would dissolve the difference of words. He argues, to the contrary, that words can never be homogenous with nature, nor can they survive separated from a proximity to nature from which they were primordially separated at the origin, that is, in the act of naming. Art survives, then, only because it captures the incessant departure and return, the dynamic of *logos* as an original breaking out, as the naming of man's difference, which situates him, gives him place.

The poem must be the dynamic of man's "descent to the ground of his desire," the cycle not of his return to his origins but of his repeated participation in an original violence. In art is discovered not only the dynamic of the word but its difference from the being of nature, for what art discloses is the inevitable failure of art to give its language, its images, the ontological status of nature. The poem advances by turning the "inside out," by beginning again, by performing upon the local an act of original violence. It is not a copy of nature but the radical "obverse" of nature, the gathering that complements nature's multiplicity; it is the city (man) lying beside the park (one, two, three women, like flowers). Thus the poem is not a plagiarist of nature, for nature in its repetitions is a plagiarist of itself; it is the poem which gives to nature its ontological priority, by bringing all other priorities constantly into question. The poem is an imitation, not a copy, of nature, because it is the myth which reveals that being and becoming are the same thing and involve an initial and mysterious violation. That is, the poem is an imitation of the dynamic of nature, of its seminal adventure, its freeplay.

The satyric dance and the ritual of the hunt, secured in the cloister of artistic space, are the basic figures for the poem as act (writing) and the poem as open field. For the dance and the ritual incorporate violence in a harmony or measure, and reveal the paradox of a closure which is repeatedly reopened by an original violence. The Cloisters is for the poet of Paterson like the caves of prehistoric Spain, a space concealing the poem of origins which exist within every local space and must be opened (interpreted or demythologized). Both are spaces that housed the legend of original writing. *Paterson*, Book Five, "opens" the reality of the Cloisters in the same way the excavators opened the Magdalenian caves or, more appropriately, in the way subsequent interpreters attempt to disclose the hidden language of those caves, which was itself an enfolded writing. The opening is itself a recurrence of an original violence:

> Dreams possess me
> and the dance
> of my thoughts
> involving animals
> the blameless beasts
> (P, 224)

Like Gertrude Stein's "rout of the vocables" or the "abstraction/ of Arabic art" (P, 222), all original art is "satyric" and marries the dream of the sacred with the blast of an original violation and dissemination. All original art imitates the beginning of history as now, because it returns to the original event of language as man's departure from his natural state. The "blameless beasts" and all of the historical violence associated with sacrifice (and *Paterson*, Book Five, at one remarkable point, concentrates in the dream of one of Dr. Paterson's friends the vision of the martyred Jews as modern historical variants of the "blameless beasts," P, 223)—the idea of history as implicit in the violence of sacrifice and of art as the dream that makes this reality bearable is the subject of *Paterson*, Book Five. And it confesses the necessary failure of art to provide a fuller vision, to disclose itself whole.

On the contrary, the poet "cannot tell it all" (P, 236), if he is to be original, for the act of telling (or writing) marks the rupture of the origin. "We know nothing and can know nothing . / But/ the dance" (P, 239)—because to "know nothing" would be to know the primal unity. What we can know, by being held in the "space" of the poem, is the original violation, the paradox of the *logos*; for that paradox lies at the "point of white penetration" of the poem's intersecting lines. Writing can only comment on itself. This is the "luminous background" (Imag., 315) that shines through the "interstices" of the poem's measured dance, the difference of the converging lines. The poem reveals to us the first measure, and thus reveals to us that "to measure is all we know" (P, 239). Knowledge, that is, is our knowledge of transgression and of the ambiguous "light" that lies within the language into which we fell. It is the ultimate recognition of freeplay, that there is no Truth and that that truth has made us free: "to dance to a measure/ contrapuntally" (P, 239).

Representative American verse will be that
which will appear new to the French . . .
prose the same.

(*The Great American Novel*)

Americans have never recognized themselves. How could they? It is impossible until
someone invent the *ORIGINAL* terms. As
long as we are content to be called by some-
body else's terms, we are incapable of being
anything but our own dupes.

(*In the American Grain*)

Postscript '90

In a time when the very mention of "French thought" provokes what I like to call the envy of disdain, Williams' little dig at the hauteur of the continental avant garde in his parodic narrative, *The Great American Novel*, like his dismissal of the French appropriations of Poe (see *In the American Grain*), might remind us that the enabling conditions for "American" writing, which has always been charged with the responsibility to "make it new" or to "begin again," have in turn involved an act of renunciation, a performative repudiation of authority, of tradition. But also, paradoxically, a performative renunciation of the very modernity in which it found itself, what Harold Rosenberg characterized as the "tradition of the new." For the American, to reject Europe, ironically, compelled him or her to meditate the question of origin, to confront the problem not of the absence of origins or even the challenge of being *sui generis*, but of adjusting the "self" to the crisis of modernity, that its origin lies in the Hegelian moment of self-reflection or self-production and thus in a moment of a "self" irreducibly doubled and originally without identity. It likewise entailed another risk, the production of an idea of "self" so extreme in its isolation or unique in its signature that it will bear its country's name as a "representative" peculiarity; that is, the reflexive engendering of this "democratic" self, at once unique and representative, had produced at the same time what de Tocqueville saw as the anonymity and thus the undoing of "self" as individual or essence.

What Hegel described as the production of the "I" within the reflexive moment of "sense certainty," the French sociologist anticipated for the "American" experience of discovering its democratic status, that its freedom fated it to sameness and its literature to a normative ordinariness. Its literature would be some "pale fire" of the tradition it had renounced; its newness an appeal to what it might be, if only it could break free from what Emerson called, at the beginning of *Nature*, its "retrospective" impulse to produce criticism, biographies, and so on, instead of having an "original relation to," or creative participation in, "the universe." The anxiety of the American writer or "literatus," as Whitman names the poet to come and his poems which "will be" (it is almost always a prospective "being," or at least named as the future anterior, as what will have been), is more than an anxiety of influence, a combat of individual poets with intellectual precursors, since the very formation of an "American" self precludes almost any of the formulations of psychoanalytic description. A "simple separate person," in Whitman's phrase, would be at once the absorption (introjection) of all other selves and a representation of all its democratic peers; yet, different from itself, an "ephebe" and thus incomplete and open to its futurity. The "simple separate person" as "En-Masse" would therefore be a "person" without identity, a pure possibility whose being "will be" performed, acted out. If the "American self" and "American verse" are performative, then, they might appear most "new" when they repeat, even quote, the old, like the iteration of a speech act. Every representative "American" writer must write his or her own signature, at once an original and a counterfeit—the "American" signature of the "new."

Any American literary critic writing today in the "new" discourses called poststructural or even postmodern must be quite conscious that he or she shares the irony of Williams' American,

especially if the object of the critic's writing is "American verse."
Thought, Emerson has written somewhere, is of "no country,"
and neither is literature if it achieves the condition of universality
generally ascribed to it, that is, to literature as an institutional
form. And poststructural thought, or better, writing, especially
that which has gone by the name deconstruction, suspends and
puts in question the very nationalism, "French thought," by
which contending discourses have attempted to circumscribe it;
not simply because it has seemed to emanate from or to be translated through this country, but more significantly because it is a
certain "language." Jacques Derrida's contention that the very notion of a national language is unthinkable—"there are always two
languages in language"—not only works to disrupt the thinking
of a "history of ideas" or ideologies, but contaminates the politics
of nationalism and its institutional structures. Literary criticism,
at best a marginal discipline, cannot escape the limits he discerns
in such thinking, nor can literary history. Nor could the American writer, from Emerson to Williams and beyond, including
their critics. "Language," which is not a singularity or even a medium, is the crux of all thinking of the new and of tradition, thus
of history. The "American" writer has always had to begin, again,
in a borrowed language, and it has always haunted his or her
quest for a pure language, an "American idiom," which is precisely a language within language, a performative and perhaps
originary language, but never pure or virginal. If the American
writer has always had to think the possibility of a "new" and
"American" writing, that is, the need to invent a national identity
in "original" terms, he or she has had at the same time to think its
impossibility; and thus meditate the paradox that "American
literature" is deferred in the very moment of its writing. Does
not the same thing hold for the idea of an "American criticism,"
or for "American methods," say, pragmatism? When Williams
quotes George Barker, in *Paterson*, Book Four, to the effect that
"American poetry is a very easy subject to discuss for the very simple

reason that it does not exist" (P, 140), he situates not only the problem but the conditions for his poem. For by quoting the outsider and the negative, Williams does not accept his cognitive assertion; he performs upon it a new and yet-unrealized notion of "American poetry." It is performative, it "exists" as the "will be," and is only in the sense that what we read is in the future anterior, of what will have been. The quotation inaugurates the possibility of a *sui generis* writing/thinking, of "American poetry" as performative self-quotation, like Poe, for example, whose plagiarisms in turn have instigated, provoked, or otherwise teased "French thought" into a series of "quotations" that ramify throughout diverse fields of modern discourse. I am thinking, of course, not only of that "literature" Poe provoked, from Baudelaire to Surrealism and beyond, but of the play of his texts in the extra-poetic discourses of the "human sciences." Self-quotation, without beginning or end, is the originary condition of the modern, and Poe is one of the names for "American" originality.

American writers have always seemed to address this impasse, to have known it always already. It marks what Harold Bloom calls our belatedness, yet it is more than a sense of our being late, at the end of history, and anxious over the monumental past. It is not simply that we are young, yet old, as Charles Olson contends: "We are the last 'first' people"; or that we long for an even earlierness, a pristine newness, a primitive earliness, but that we seem nostalgic for the future, as the popular repartee has it. Modern writing, as quotation and self-quotation, is performative and idiomatic, imitative and deformatic, echoic and dissonant, familiar yet uncanny, or like Poe's writing, verse and per-verse. Americans, Williams seemed to understand, literally begin themselves, or write an idiogrammatology, a performance both new or unique and commonplace, exceptional and ordinary, monstrous and mimetic, "American" in that one cannot decide whether it is looking back or looking forward. The "American" condition, the idiomatic, is the condition of its language, and "Language is in its

January" (Imag., 280), is Janus-faced, as he writes in *A Novelette and Other Prose*, in the context of distinguishing the American writers' position from that of the French, even the Surrealists whom he praises for trying to achieve the "classical excellences of language," a writing not "adjunct" to ideas, like philosophical or scientific writing, but devoted simply to "words." But the Americans have no such purity, or simplicity, to aspire to in writing, no such notion of a pure (that is, literary) language; and so in repeating the Surrealist strategy of writing the American must reverse it or overwrite it.

By writing, by "wiping soiled words or cutting them clean out" (Imag., 317), as he claims for Marianne Moore, American writing effects a translation or transposition, produces a new context and new categories, a locus or "local" writing that alone deserves the name "American," the space of a writing to come: not "Bound without,/ Boundless within," or formally unified and reflective of the great generalities, like "soul"; "This is new! The quality is not new, but the freedom is new, the unbridled leap," and this "new" is what it will enact, not a mythic reflection (Imag., 320). It will be, this performance, like hanging a French painting, a Matisse nude, say, in a gallery in New York City, a performative quotation. For, Williams goes on, when Matisse painted the nude he painted her in the full context of a natural scene of which her body was a part, like a Diana or an Aphrodite; and the Americans in New York, if they have seen or painted a nude, have seen only the generalized naked body: "No woman in my country is naked except at night" (Imag., 321). The American context (and its language) is without poetry, or quite simply lacks the specificity of context that art provides in producing the real; it is words imported from elsewhere upon which and within which the American writer begins again, and thus not a context yet—only, perhaps, to come.

When I began to write a study of Williams as representative American writer, in the early 1970's, "deconstruction" and

"French thought" were names, often indiscriminately applied, for a rising tide of imported discourses just beginning to upset the balance of intellectual payments in the American academy and particularly in the putative and marginal discipline of literary criticism. To many American academics, they were metonyms for the posturing obscurantism and intellectual elitism—for the anti-humanism and even Anglophobia—that a hitherto relatively secure Anglophiliac discipline, nurtured by an uninterrogated faith in scholarly empiricism and critical commonsensism, and a strange amalgam of aesthetic formalism and historicist anti-intellectualism, quickly identified as a fundamental threat to what Wallace Stevens had satirized as the "Academy of Fine Ideas." As a number of younger critics began to hear this strange communication from abroad, and to respond in a manner recalling Stevens' "They will get it straight one day at the Sorbonne," their elders reacted by rereading the line to say, they "might" get it "straight" some day, but not in *these* words. Like Williams reacting to the American penchant for importing everything and imposing it on the American topography, academic criticism saw a foreign contaminant within its institutions. Americanists, already marginalized because their subject matter was such a thin and pale imitation (a pale fire) of the great tradition, as were their own methodologies, responded in kind, though pragmatically, to this faddism. It would certainly soon go away, since it was as un-American as the Poe the French kept sending back in the form of high modernist prophet. On the other hand, this discourse "arrived," as William James had written of radium (he meant its discovery as a volatile and unaccountable elemental force, demanding a new kind of understanding), as a kind of return of the repressed, like the French Poe, indeed, but inmixed with various other modes, methods, languages—philosophical nihilism, psychoanalysis, structuralism, phenomenology, semiotics, and so on—that demanded either repudiation or strategic co-optation.

Deconstruction, that is, arrived without passport, like a

Franco-Prussian agent, ventriloquized in an American idiom. There was no time to write the history of this mi-immi-gration, and perhaps it has no history, or clearly no identifiable originary voice, especially since its continental accents seemed distinctly American, without distinction or like one of those figures in a Nabokov novel—or like Poe. And we would eventually learn that in certain specific cases it would indeed be an inflected simulacrum of Poe's uninflected voice, the same Poe returned to us through Baudelaire and Mallarmé and Valery, through Freud via Marie Bonapart, and so on, returning to us like our thoughts coming back, in Emerson's phrase, "with a certain alienated majesty." But if they were Poe's, were they "ours," these orphans which could never know their father; if Poe's, were they not Dupin's, rather than the American Poe, that Poe which Williams had argued the French could never have understood precisely because he was so uniquely American, without history or paternity and thus without a voice of his own? What we heard returning from France, then, may have originated in "America," but that is to say, also, that "America" is a non-origin. It had no language, no context, no "place," as such, except what Poe had invented, a hollowed-out "interiority" that Williams claimed was the mark and void of "American" originality. The French discourse returning Poe to us once more, then, repeated for the young American critic the return of the repressed, a silenced word. I wanted to read "America" through Williams, who claimed Poe was the singular American, more so than Whitman, but found that Poe could only be read through France, or through what Williams insisted were the most revealing mis-readings. Deconstruction arrived as an "American" text of sorts, estranged, like a double reading. I had my entry.

But not a method. Not even an "American method," whatever that might be, especially if we recall Freud's demurrer in *Civilization and Its Discontents* that he did not "wish to use American methods." That is part of the problem. It is assumed that if the

critic approaches a text in a different language, even when that
language echoes or ventriloquizes the apparent language of the
poem, then the critic either is applying a system from another
genre or discipline (philosophy, visual arts, psychoanalysis, and
so on) with its own internally coherent language, or is employing a jargon, the language of the other, and not a language cog-
nate with the text—as the New Criticism assumed that a certain
formalist-aesthetic language could replicate the figural reflexivity
of the text, and that criticism should speak in the voice of poetry.
Deconstruction, in its many words, said only that it could never
write in any language but the text it was inhabiting, since that
text was always already two languages at least. Poe's idiom,
both French and American, was the "American idiom," both creative and destructive Williams had said repeatedly: "Creation and
destruction are simultaneous" (Imag., 311, 127). Was this not
the opening to one word, *deconstruction*, and thus to an
idio(gram)matic rather than Ideogrammic method? Could I assume that "America," that future scene not of "history," as Hegel
claimed, but of some other working out of "spirit," was always
already the writing space of deconstruction? I needed to do nothing such. There before me were the texts of Williams, and thus
Poe, and a certain "American" writing, and . . .

II

I do not want here to try to write a "history" of *The Inverted
Bell*, which is after all only another book of literary criticism that
appears to read a particular writer through the prism of certain
theoretical assumptions. But some explanation, not self-clarifica-
tion, is in order if I am to oversee its reissue and redirect its
"message," understanding the problematics of the message in in-
formation theory today. I thought, and still think, of *Bell* (not
quite a *Glas*, but a certain "tintinnabulation" nevertheless) as,
first, a reading of one American writer, a symptomatic but not
necessarily central writer, because that notion of centrality or ex-

emplarity implies a kind of homogeneity or categorical average that "American" literature refuses, thus making heterogeneity the only common (non-)quality that would define it as a history or a canon. That is, Williams became for me, even more so than Stevens—a very different poet who offers similar problems in reading—Williams is for me what he himself had glimpsed, a double of Poe, an idiomatic echo, similar yet different, and thus an eccentric signature. More so than Whitman, as Williams recognized, though Whitman often seems the mad Poe's idiot brother, Poe signs for the American (just as the chapter on Poe becomes Williams' signature of what is *In the American Grain*), in that he is forced to write upon a blank page reversely, like the white upon black inscriptions that mark his textual cosmos in *Eureka* or the ceaseless reversals of *Pym*. Poe, the most abstract and displaced of writers, is also the most specific and "local," says Williams; he is one who wrote literally at the level of character, of the letter inscribed on the page, without reference, like Shakespeare, as Williams will claim, who is "ignorant" yet thinks through his characters rather than through concepts or themes. Thus the perversity of Poe, and, one might say, his perfect plagiarism. Poe's originality derives from his absolute lack of it. Nothing he writes is not already written, and in overwriting it, he reveals it as a blank; the double negative of his derivative writing, like the echolalia of his most banal or ordinary poems, locates writing, American writing, in the very place of originality that has been denied by the paternalistic Anglo tradition. Poe refuses what Pound calls the "American habit of quotation," the slavish repetition of the great English tradition. He purloins everything in an echolalia that exposes the "pale fire" of the earlier, turning quotation into a performative scene that foregrounds the artifice and secondariness of the earlier text. His originality, as Williams would argue, lies in his gesture of exposing false origins; unlike those "Plagiarists of Traditionalism," as Williams calls Pound and Eliot in the opening section of *Spring and All*, who nostalgically hope to recuperate the power of some lost origin, Poe performs quotation into originary self-quotation, by the artful hoax. He plagiarizes plagiarism and reveals that like the "twins" in "The Fall of the House of Usher," an original literature will not produce "collateral issue" or natural children, but like the fictional story within the library of that same tale, it is centered upon the abyss of an interiority without substance (in the tale, the *mise en abime* of the coat of arms in the story doubles the non-center into which both the "house" of Usher and the story itself collapse). Poe's "originality" resides in his allegories of influence, Williams seems to say, and not his anxiety. He exposes the "American" non-identity in his drive to produce its "*ORIGINAL* terms."

My response to this charge need not be rehearsed here, though as noted it has had a certain life in some of the subsequent "histories" of recent literary criticism. But it occurs to me now that one of the responses I might have made, and did not, was that if indeed I had turned all discourse into univocality, or even sameness or noise, I was at that moment most American, most modern. What I did resist, however, was the accusation that I was trying to make the theory not only account for the poetry but indeed ventriloquize it, and thus in turn make the poetry echo a sameness that collapsed antithetical theories. Two points here, and they apply in general to the problematics I find haunting all the discourses of recent literary criticism: one, the assumption that one can identify a discrete theory or theories which in turn might direct a methodology that can be *applied* to reading a discrete discourse called literature, poetry or poem, or even (literally) a text, meaning a closed or self-reflexive entity—this is an illusory ideal long since dispatched from criticism, and by critical discourse itself; two, the assumption that because "theory" and "methodology" cannot be isolated as pure or determining discourses, any more than can a pure poetry or closed text (work, book), that one can validate practice "against theory." What Miller found in *Bell*, the apparent application of two discrete and contradictory critical positions, signified by Heidegger's theory of poetic language and Derrida's deconstruction of Heideggerian logocentrism, was a misreading and misapplication of the one "proper" theory, deconstruction. I was wrong, then, about Derrida and deconstruction, as a mode of reading, but also as a "theory."

This left out of account, I believe, the question of not only whether *my* "deconstruction" was a sufficient account of a "theory of language" that might determine a methodology of reading, but whether deconstruction presumes a "theory" at all; and further, whether Heidegger's *poesis* can itself claim such authority or be appropriated in critical praxis, particularly in terms of deconstruction's exposure of its residual logocentric groundwork. In short, Miller accused me of applying contradictory theories, of resorting to contradictory critical vocabularies, but not of *applying* a theory; for in mistakenly making different theories the same, I had made them univocal with the creative texts, the poetry which they accounted for or answered. This still assumes the posture of "critical" or analytical, even hermeneutical, reading, that there are theories more or less correct, right or wrong, true or pseudo, and thus philosophically mastering or totalizing re the literary. It maintains the philosophy/literature binarism that resides in the heart of what is called Western thought, and is everywhere evident in the debates between the priority of philosophy and literature, truth and representation, and so on, that not only remain unresolved in modernism, but are exacerbated by the despair over their irresolution. The crisis may be seen to reside in such a fundamental problem as how to read a single text, presuming its singularity or closure, and how not only to master or totalize the text, but to communicate its "sense"; and to avoid in this act of receiving and sending on some truth or meaning of the text, one's own distortive or blinded, subjectivized or politicized, ideological or dogmatic judgment. Even a pragmatics of interpretation does not discount its "method," the regulating authority that pleasure or satisfaction with a solution, a sufficient reading, implies.

These remain the commonplace assumptions of literary criticism; and so far as what I did in *Bell* is complicit with these largely uninterrogated assumptions, that I did or did not produce a right reading of Williams, did or did not derive the proper method from the many available, did or did not choose the correct one, the jury must remain in antechambers with the judge. For what I did and still do understand as the lesson of deconstruction is that theory and practice are never finally inextricable, nor finally reducible. It is, interestingly enough, an unresolvable issue which seems to be situated in the pre-origins of human "thought," or as Derrida would say, is earlier than Being and can only go by the non-proper name of "differance." It marks the crux I sensed when I first looked into a Williams poem, perhaps like some figural Cortez, a historical error on Keats's part, we know, first looking into "Chapman's Homer." And saw there Williams "first" looking into Poe . . . ; looking into his "American" origins for that which demanded his poetry—which is to say, language, or better, an "American idiom" which did not yet exist. I wanted, to paraphrase Williams, to write a critical reading, and discovered reading is wanting. The question everywhere in Williams' writing, poetry or prose, is language: "The language is the key," he scribbled on the cover pages of an early manuscript version of his introduction to *Paterson* (Lockwood Ms., Env. 36); "Haven't you forgot your virgin purpose,/ the language?" he writes at the very beginning of part III of *Paterson*, Book One, and then immediately asks again, "What language?"—this after a long section in which he has recounted a kind of allegory of language on the model of nature or the elemental, but a nature or element now understood in terms of that nature which appeared as "dynamics" in Henry Adams' *Education*, "radium" as a destructive/creative force and the sign of transformational rather than stable or conservative forms—"radium" which, as Adams said with Nietzsche, denied both God and grammar.

What he was suggesting was a different notion of language from that we understand in philology, or as either ordinary or natural language; and however unscientific his story, particularly as an account of natural language or, especially, poetic language, it clearly put in question our assumptions about language, about the sign and the image, that had governed our ways of reading and writing about literature, and our theorizing about the "nature" of poetry. At the same time, it became apparent that indeed all of what we call modern thought had located itself in the place and problem of language, of mediation. And the most provocative of modern discourses had confronted it not simply in terms of a new, revisionary, and scientific description, the alternative to philology, as in structuralism, but as a problematics. Heidegger's "theory" of poetic language, in short, is not linguistic, but a part of his meditations on the philosophy of being or, more precisely, his de-structuration of logocentrism. And Derrida's *De la grammatology* does not presume, in its deconstruction of structural linguistics and structuralism in general, to supplant the deconstructed "system" with a more true philosophy of language. Deconstruction, whatever else one may say about it, is a severe questioning of so-called scientific models and methodologies, and in particular, the model of language that Derrida sees as a reinscription of logocentrism in those "human sciences" (structural linguistics, semiotics, structural psychoanalysis, etc.) and postmetaphysical philosophies (Husserlian phenomenology, even Heidegger's thinking "beyond" metaphysics or thinking the "end" of philosophy) which have claimed to go "beyond" Western thought and to provide a new hermeneutics (say, in Gadamer and Ricoeur).

III

The Inverted Bell, whatever the contexts of its composition, remains a "reading" of an "American" scene of writing: of Williams, yes, but also, as previously noted, of Williams "reading" his predecessors, like Poe; and then of my reading certain "thinkers" who also seem to have been reading "Poe"; and so on, in a circle neither closed nor open and clearly not hermeneutical. It therefore circulates in the problematics that recent discourse calls the "turn toward language," and what Williams saw as the "revolution of the word," that which he associated with a certain notion of "writing," which may or may not have anything in common with Derridean *écriture*. But it clearly does relate to what in language studies today is called "performative," though a notion of performance generalized beyond the specifics of a "speech act" theory and all the assumptions it makes for this unique "use" of language. Would a refocusing upon Williams' notion of performative "writing," his "attack," make available a clearer understanding of what he contributes to "American" literature? Perhaps, but it would certainly make it clear that he did not provide a "new" theory of language.

What can one write, then, today of Williams' "idiom," of his exemplary "place" in what we literary historians call the "modern/postmodern" production of the "new"? I would be most deconstructive, I suppose, if I simply and enigmatically said, Williams writes—his name, his signature, Williams. He wills the new; he writes the veritable *I am* of an American *will* to be, to be America's Will and thus like England's W.S. Too clever, you say, to claim that he wants to sign for America, for its heterogeneity, for that which came through the Mediterranean, and Caribbean, and Latin America, a tradition so rich it could only appear in the signature, William Carlos Williams, a tradition of the "new" inscribing that much older even than Europe, and thus one which gives its "reply to Greek and Latin with the bare hands" (epigraph to *Paterson*). Williams asks, is there an American writing, and thus an "American" identity? Or rather, why isn't there, since all of what appears as its "*ORIGINAL* terms" seems to betray any claim of originality, especially the Adamic signature that so many scholars insist they have found in our metaphors. To the contrary, says Williams, it is in Poe's echolalia that we find that signature, the beginning of writing as the refusal of nonidentity:

Either the new world must be mine as I will have
it [he thinks of Poe as thinking], or it is a
worthless bog. His attack was *from the center out.*

. . . .

His concern, the apex of his immaculate attack,
was to detach a "method" from the smear of common
usage—it is the work of nine tenths of his criticism.
(IAG, 219–21)

Williams' positioning of Poe within the "American grain" is an allegory of positioning itself. Before Poe there is only "colonial imitation" of the great Anglo tradition, which he must clear away if he is to realize a "juvenescent *local* literature" or new beginning, a new world literature that is to be understood not on the model of representation or centering, but on a "new" idea of "originality," and thus a literature for which there is not yet any possible "model," including the model of language. It is in these meditations on Poe, who was, as we related in *Bell*, to have been the metonyic figure for a long section of *Paterson*, Book One, that Williams begins his reflections on the question of originality, place, and language, which he unites in the word *local*, distinguishing it at the same time, as he does in an essay on Marianne Moore's poetry (see Imag., 310 ff.), from any such literary category as "local color." In both essays, the "local" is related to the "mathematical," and thus to the "geometric principle of the intersection of loci" (Imag., 311) and by extension to the "imaginative" as a concept of energy field, that which is organized upon a center without substance or mass, as Williams would later extend the figure to the concepts of relativity and even quantum theory. Writing as "attack," beginning "from the center out," would therefore be a beginning as repetition, as reversal and resistance, an act not determined by an existing or a substantive "center," or subject, but an act that produced the center, as simulacrum. But it would not, could not produce just another center, a substitute center or new subject to replace an old one.

Poe, says Williams, could not achieve an American originality simply by reduplicating a European one, for this would condemn him to the "unoriginal" or "*FALSE* literature," whereas his gesture of writing against was a founding act: "On him is FOUNDED A LITERATURE" (IAG, 223). A founding act is originary, a "first" act, though logically it can only be a repetition, and not a grounded act: "He declares, maintains himself, presupposes himself and IS first rate. First!—madly, valiantly battling for the right to BE first—to hold up his ORIGINALITY" (IAG, 223). He "declares" by iteration, names himself into being, as Williams notes by citing Poe's autonymic production of himself as "seer" or "Orphicist"; yet this self-proclamation produces the "vast IDEA" which is himself out of the "people's ordinary tongue." He produces himself as "language," out of language. Through an iterative speech act, he becomes "first," a "locality": "The language of his essays is a remarkable HISTORY of the locality he springs from"; and that "locality" is inscribed in words "dissociated" from their referents or familiar uses, words without "aroma" but with "luminosity" (IAG, 223–24). Thus the pure logic of his criticism, his "'childlike,' simple deductive reasoning" or that order of words which only relate to themselves, a reflexivity revealing at once everything and nothing at its "locus." This "place" of "language" is the originary place of the subject: "Poe conceived the possibility, the sullen, volcanic inevitability of the *place*. He was willing to go down and wrestle with its conditions, using every tool France, England, Greece could give him,—but to use them to original purpose" (IAG, 225–26). By performing with the structural tools of language, by repeating their laws of iteration, he becomes "original," he invents the American language as repetitional "writing": "Americans have never recognized themselves. How can they? It is impossible until someone invent the *ORIGINAL* terms" (IAG, 226).

Therefore, it should come as no surprise that the new terms are the same as the old ones, the original terms later yet earlier, a "perfect plagiarism" as Williams would call nature's repetitions in *Spring and All*, in contrast to those of the "traditionalists," who have been and still are, in the figures of Eliot and Pound, plagiarizing the great English tradition. Thus Williams recounts his allegory of the origins of an American language/literature as another version of natural language, but with a difference. What sounds Rousseauistic, Emersonian, or even Whitmanesque— though in the latter two, at least, I find the conception problematical—in its argument for a prelinguistic origin of language, in nature, turns out to be not simply an inversion that finds nature to originate language, but finds the two to be always already inextricable, an original multiplicity, a heterogeneity or original remainder. Thus founding is grounding, so that Williams can say that "American literature is anchored, in him alone, on solid ground" (IAG, 226), that is, in his "method." The solid, elemental ground, his natural language which is his "method," is therefore a new sense of nature, the nature of modern physics, fire, or the new sense of the sun, radium, so that Williams must characterize Poe's poems as centered upon a "mystery" or unnameable that is "so shaken with desire, that it has come off as a flame, destroying the very vial that contained it," an "acid power," and so on (IAG, 232). As it would become in *Paterson*, this elemental force or "fire," at the same time a thing or element, with weight and properties that cannot be seen unless bombarded by contaminants, a force at once destructive and creative, at once "breaking down" or undergoing transformation and producing analytical effects (like x-rays) upon its others, can bear no proper name. The old name of language, however, remains. It is *silent*.

I have explored that thematic at length in Chapter 4 of *Bell*, but here I want to rehearse it in a different register. At the conclusion of his meditations on Poe's signature in *In the American Grain*, Williams turns to the question of "theory" and "method" in a poetry which, unlike the criticism, had virtually consumed itself, like that "flame" that destroys its form. This because its "acid power to break down truth" has been "*forced* upon love—" rather than, like the criticism, being addressed to the pseudo-logic of European thought and its American imitators. In the poetry, Williams argues, Poe had to turn his "attack" upon that which he needed but lacked, love, and so upon that which he could not give—that "mystery" of the pure; of that, love, which could exist only without contamination, as a unity, but was knowable only as separation, as desire. Poe's obsession with love, with his desire, which could focus only upon his absent wife, meant that he had also to turn toward "nothing": "In his despair he had nowhere to turn. It is the very apotheosis of the place and the time" (IAG, 232). Poe's experience becomes an allegory of "America," without "place." His writing/act changes from "heat" or anger addressed upon the unoriginal to a "light" focused into a void, "*forced* upon love": "I meant that though in this his 'method' has escaped him, yet his poems remain the single stuff of his great 'theory': to grasp the meaning, to understand, to reduce all things to method, to control, lifting himself to power—" (IAG, 232). "Theory" is "place" and "place" is "nothing" in America. His poetry, rather than approaching "the gods," Williams notes, leaves the poet "caught, instead, in his time"; and thus in this no-place that in turn negates him, so that rather than attacking, his writing is attacked: "the place itself attacked him" (IAG, 232).

Poe's ground, his theory, is an *abgrund*, in which nothing reflects nothing, thus emptying out the subject. The "interiority" which Williams has praised Poe for discovering is a different sense of place or position from any notion of self developed by the Transcendentalists, a new sense entirely of "theory." It is a "fire," a new sense of the "sun" as he would develop it in *Paterson*:

> Fire burns; that is the first law.
> When a wind fans it the flames

are carried abroad. Talk
fans the flames. They have

manoeuvered it so that to write
is a fire and not only of the blood.

The writing is nothing, the being
in a position to write (that's

where they get you) is nine tenths
of the difficulty . . .

　　　　　　　　　　　　　　(P, 113)

"Writing," that "destroying fire," is an "attack" that at once clears the old "ground" and produces a new sense of ground, and position, what Williams calls the "place" of the "sun," and also of the "son." In order to make possible the writing of *Paterson*, Williams had to think the new possibility of the writing position, as he said of Poe and of the American writer in general. This position or problematics is the question that all of his writing, prose and poetry, criticism and improvisations, meditates—the "theory" that will be the conditions for a "new" poetry, or "first writing," as he calls it in an epigraph he coined for *The Embodiment of Knowledge*, the first chapter of which bears the title "The Beginnings of an American Education," a kind of textual letter to his own sons from a father, as he will write in *Paterson*, who owes those sons a "death" so that they can "begin again."

IV

　　The Embodiment of Knowledge is a "book" Williams wrote in the late 1920's as a communication to his children on the deficiencies of their American education which, Williams thought, attacked its progeny in the same way America had attacked Poe. That is, it threatened to displace them with the European mind, in the same sense that the American had always been molded by European institutions and practices, that "body of knowledge" which over-whelmed the primary American characteristic, its independence and energy. (The text was not published until 1974, so that my references to it in *Bell* are to the manuscript in the Beinecke collection.) The American educational system, he argues, has become a mechanical repetition of its European models, delivering a received "knowledge" upon impressionable and yet unformed young minds and therefore repressing the energies that might allow those minds to develop their own "local" shapes, as opposed to the old logical authority. The gist of the problem lay in the teaching of literature, which American institutions seemed to define as a representational discourse in which one could see the dominant forms and understand the immutable values of the great Western tradition. In short, literature was taught thematically and thus as a set of representative "ideas"; it was a vehicle for philosophy. The case of Shakespeare is for Williams the most telling, particularly the kind of criticism that began with his "life" and then proceeded to his thoughts (his dramatic themes) as they reflect his culture. This tends to mute the real "life" of Shakespeare, Williams continues, which is a "life" of "deeds," of speech acts or the "deeds of speeches" (EK, 12), which like performances produced repeated new forms out of the old "words." That is, Shakespeare was a writer: "Shakespeare's work is all words"; "[T]he only real in writing is writing itself." Thus, writing does not represent thought but is a thinking that breaks up "thought" into the shapes of a provisionally new knowledge: "It is pure writing that can't get away from itself to be thought. Thought is not writing, to write betrays both writing and itself" (EK, 11–13— I will return to this statement later). In a subsequent chapter, Williams takes up the question of Shakespearean authorship and identity, and argues that Bacon could never have written Shakespearean plays because Bacon was interested only in ideas, logic, and inductive applications of the "tools of knowledge," while Shakespeare was an innocent who did not think, except as writing is thinking: "In Shakespeare the characters *are* his thoughts" (EK, 136), and thus his "deeds" or performances; and this is what defines his humanism against Bacon's "analytic" and "inhuman" thought. Shakespeare was an "ignorant man" in the sense that he was not shaped by classical "knowledge" and his writing was not derivative: "Thus the real revolution in literature as in all the arts is not formal in the derivative classical sense but a break with all that is taught and an emphasis on all that is *learned*" (EK, 137, 138).

Between these considerations of Shakespeare as one whose revolutionary "writing" is more original than even the Surrealists' "revolution of the word," Williams had turned to other of the arts for examples of the two notions of thinking and writing, especially to the Cubist painters and their relation to certain "American" experimenters, like Gertrude Stein, whose "representational" writing exceeds Joyce's in its deformations—a writing Williams calls "representational" because it does only what writing can do, it "represents words" (EK, 17–25). Only in this sense, he claims, can one think of an "objective" art, of that which takes its material as its method, in which "words" are the only "real," and not "symbols" or substitutive. By distorting that which they purportedly convey, emotion or object referent, surrealist writing re-marks "reality." This is a familiar argument, that writing writing penetrates the illusion of the other as object and signifies itself as act/thing. It doubly marks itself. Thus avant garde writing signifies not the self-consciousness or self-reflexivity of the sign but the undoing of self-reflexivity. It returns us to the "word" not as *logos*, but as "shape," and to writing as the production of a "local," a "place." Just as Klee had to produce the most sophisticated abstraction in order to simulate the primitive, in order to repeat the primitivism of the cave painters. And in achieving this childlike effect of the object which represents not nature but the mark itself, he reveals to us the hieroglyphical abstractness of the primitive. The primitive is not naïve, then, but always already mathematical, abstract, "local."

Writing, then, is like myth; it is prephilosophical. But strangely

enough it is the elemental ground of thinking. It is what Williams
calls "embodied" knowledge, or the "word" (shape/thing) on its
way to meaning. Writing, at once an attack on ideas (the word-
concept) and the condition of any "new" thought, is therefore
the "place" of knowledge, the placing or positioning of thought:
"Before any of the arguments begin they must be placed, for
from place, a place, begins everything—is in fact a place. Syn-
chronously occupied by everything and at the same time space
itself—nothing but. Before science, philosophy, religion, ethics—
before they can begin to function—is a region susceptible to
argument. It is not the past, whose sole property is place" (EK,
130). This "place" of knowledge, this "certain position of the
understanding anterior to all systems of thought, as well as of fact
or deed," takes a different name in various systems: "It is the
'night mind,' the chaos, the source of religion; the preconscious,
the savage, the animal, the plant, the inorganic—what you will"
(EK, 132–33). But as a precondition for all "knowledge" it is object, not subject; "Objectified, it is place itself—on which all arguments fall" (EK, 133). This "emplacement of thought," its
precondition for Williams, is language, but language in a very
special sense. It is the "poem." We might today call it performative. Williams' "theory," then, is not a theory of primordial language, but the contrary notion, that "theory" is speech act, the
precondition of "position" (positing). It is the "position" not of
consciousness, but of a certain pre-conscious, which Williams
calls "adolescence," and adolescence is that "pre-systematic period as the period of emplacement" (EK, 134).

   Thus Williams' letter to his sons is an address to "language,"
which will also be a meditation on Poe's "theory" that is the
precondition for a "juvenescent *local* literature" (IAG, 217).
"America," Williams notes, as the embodiment of the idea of
"democracy," that stage of political adolescence, is another name
for this "position," this "theory." "America" is adolescence, and
"adolescence is not a unique condition, an underdevelopment,

negative, the shadow of something else. But positive" (EK, 134, 135). As "a quality of being anterior to systematic knowledge," this position of adolescence, of democracy, of "America," is the position of the poet, of the "local." The poet attends the place of language as the physician attends his patient, a reader of symptoms, but also in the way a father attends the development of sons who will inevitably displace him. As in *Paterson*, the poet like the old men burdened by the "drug" of "experience" must supervise the displacement of that kind of (conceptual) "knowledge," and undergo the coming of a "new" knowledge, "knowledge, the contaminant" which like the impurities of oxygen and hydrogen bombarding radium produces a "luminosity" or a figuration preceding concept, like that "stain at the bottom" of Madame Curie's "retort" (P, 171, 172, 178).

We might conclude, then, by reflecting on the "position" Williams accords "language." It is not a theory of language he produces within his "poetics," but rather the language of "theory." As he defined Poe's American signature (against French *Poeisme*) in a passage noted earlier, his own poems "remain of the single stuff of his great 'theory'" (IAG, 232). But "theory" is not a formulable set of principles (not even Poe's "Poetic Principle" or "Philosophy of Composition") from which the poet might derive his practice or "method," except perhaps that of his criticism; but is, rather, a "space" of possibilities that he engenders in the place of origin. If Williams calls it Poe's "interiority," he does not identify it as subjectivity or consciousness. Williams names it "place," the place of "eccentric genius" which is unnatural, unlike the Emersonian or Transcendental "genius," and therefore a space in which a *"beginning* literature . . . must establish its own rules, own framework" (IAG, 229—Williams' italics). It is marked, this space, by a certain "madness" and is "peopled by shadows and silence, and despair—it is the compelling force of . . . isolation" (IAG, 231). This figural place (of shades, of silence) is the cryptic space of his "love of his wife," and like all crypts is composed of the language of desire. Therefore, as he says of "place" in another context, an essay entitled "The Importance of Place," it is the space of a "disorder," a chaos, and marked by signs of the senses rather than by word-concepts: "Judge by the eyes and ears, touch and taste—reject everything from no matter what source that is without a place there" (EK, 135). This would entail rejecting others' words, words tied by reference or concept to thought, for figurations of emotions that have not yet achieved a distinct form. Poe's "interiority," his place of "love," is a place of "adolescence," so it is no wonder that he was fixated upon the adolescent woman. This adolescent language of shadows and silence is either receding or appearing, "flowering," so that it can only be conceived as a "shape" and a "chaos." "Adolescence," as we will see, is some kind of medium place between the undifferentiated and the differentiated.

"Theory" is adolescence—it is preconceptual, prephilosophical, and yet a "locus" or field of energies. Williams calls it "imagination" and, as we have seen, associates it with the elemental language, with the "stain" of radiation, of radium being bombarded by contaminants in Madame Curie's "retort":

> I sat down in front of my elements, then, and looked at them rather blankly, I imagine until, to my surprise, they suddenly appeared to my imagination as arrangements of some one ground fiber which became known as electron. Thus, I say my imagination saw them but to my eyes became apparent another arrangement which was very tangible, for these few and so far indestructible elements began to take on a kind of rhythmic order according to weight and density which ascended in a broken scale through them all. A form began to emerge, a law as permanent as the elements themselves, a truth perhaps! Why, I had made a discovery! Here was something not an element yet as permanent as any element.
>
> (EK, 165)

The "complex arrangement of nature" is the "truth" of "language." This is not a theory of "natural language" but of nature as "electron" which operates according to the laws of dynamic relation or relativity. This language inscribes its economy in the field of the "poem," and is beheld there as the shadows and silence of word-shapes—say, in words like *Nevermore*, single words that are many, less and more. These words are earlier than meaning, oxymorons that signify original crossings of sense, chiasmatic figurations that defy philological or linguistic categories. Yet, they are loci, elements in the field of writing. "Writing" and "theory" occupy or define the same "place" in Williams.

In one of the notes appended to *The Embodiment of Knowledge*, the editor, Ron Loewinsohn, stands perplexed before Williams' cryptic remarks on "writing": "Thought is not writing, to write betrays both writing and itself"; and in a footnote he quotes the sentence in order to offer the following clarification: "*Sic*. The infinitive 'to write' lacks an object. 'Thought' seems the most likely possibility, i.e., '. . . to write [thought] betrays both writing and itself" (EK, 193). For Loewinsohn, "to write" cannot be an "intransitive verb," even problematically, as it is for Roland Barthes—and evidently for Williams—an act with transitive and transformative force but not productive of the old cognitions, "thought." "Thought," Williams tells us, is the congealed by-product of thinking, and always a repetition of a previous idea; writing breaks up thought and is yet the adolescence of thought, in the sense we have seen above, where Williams claims that Shakespeare's thinking takes place in his "characters" and "words," that is, in writing. Writing is performative, and it "betrays" phonetic writing or the mimetic inscriptions of "ideas." Just so, the "local" precedes locution: "from place, a place, everything begins—is in fact a place" (EK, 130). The place of writing, of the adolescent poem, is primordial and original only in the provisional sense that we no longer think of the primary and the origin and the beginning as a pre-language, that is, as a unity or univocality, but rather address its originary multiplicity. There is nothing, as it were, "avant la lettre," and the "lettre" never sin-

gular; but ever "No ideas but in things." Writing . . . Silence . . .
Theory . . . "They" are the originary "*ORIGINAL* terms" that
Americans must "invent" by way of knowing themselves. Which
is to say, they must write themselves. Unlike Hegel's moment of
self-reflexive certainty, of the composing of the self "When I say
I . . . ," Williams thinks the American must define himself at the
moment of his birth—that is, adolescence—like that figure or
shape he espies at the bridge between Juarez and El Paso in "The
Desert Music." That silent, shadowy figure, like Poe's, is the figure of self as "poem": "Why does one want to write a poem?" he
reflects in "The Desert Music," a poem; and continues, "Because
it's there to be written" (PB, 117). Where? There? "Nevermore"
and "before" the letter, and right before our I's.

Index